**EMBASSY
OF THE
UNITED STATES OF AMERICA
Bangkok, Thailand**

December 27, 1968

Right Rev. Flavian Burns
Abbey of Gethsemane
Trappist, Kentucky

Dear Father Burns:

Thank you for your letter of December 13, 1968 and for the court order appointing you as executor of the late Thomas Merton's estate.

Please accept my sincere sympathy on the untimely death of Father Merton. His passing leaves a void not only for those who benefitted from association with him and from his writings and wisdom, but for humanity.

May I in turn express our appreciation for your assistance during the period immediately following Father Merton's death. We are also grateful for the strength and guidance provided by Abbot Primate Weakland and the Apostolic Delegate to Thailand, Monseigneur Loftis. Abbot Weakland will be writing you in detail.

I am enclosing a copy of the inventory which you requested and would appreciate hearing what disposition you wish made of Father Merton's personal effects. There is also enclosed a copy of the Foreign Service Report of Death, Official Death Certificate and translation, as well as letters from members of the Catholic Congress who found or examined the body. An extra copy of the Death Report is enclosed should you wish to forward it to the next of kin. As soon as the Thai police report is available I shall forward a copy to you. Father Merton had left some film to be developed at a photography shop in Bangkok. We have included these in his effects and have paid for the development from funds you deposited with the Department of State. A final statement of account will be forwarded following receipt of your instructions as to disposition.

If there is any further way in which I may be of assistance please do not hesitate to let me know.

Sincerely,

John L. Hagan
American Consul General

Letter from American Consul General to Abbey at Gethsemani,
Mott Collection, Northwestern University

The Martyrdom of Thomas Merton

AN INVESTIGATION

Hugh Turley
David Martin

McCabe Publishing
Hyattsville, Maryland

Copyright © 2018 by Hugh Turley and David Martin.

All rights reserved. No part of this publication may be reproduced, distributed or transmitted in any form or by any means, including photocopying, recording, or other electronic or mechanical methods, without the prior written permission of the publisher, except in the case of brief quotations embodied in critical reviews and certain other noncommercial uses permitted by copyright law.

Authors Hugh Turley and David Martin/McCabe Publishing
http://themartyrdomofthomasmerton.com

Book Layout ©2017 BookDesignTemplates.com

The Martyrdom of Thomas Merton: An Investigation/ Hugh Turley and David Martin —1st ed.
ISBN 978-1548077389

Acknowledgements

This book could not have been written without the help of friends, university libraries and professional archivists.

First of all, we would offer our gratitude to Dr. Paul M. Pearson, Director of the Thomas Merton Center at Bellarmine University for his assistance. In addition, there are many helpful experts at various institutions that contributed to this project including Fr. John Martin Ruiz, O.P., librarian at the Dominican House of Studies, Tara C. Craig, Head of Public Services, Rare Book & Manuscript Library, Columbia University, Nick Munigan, library assistant, Charles Deering McCormick Library Special Collections, Northwestern University, Anne Causey and Penny White at the Albert and Shirley Small Special Collections Library at the University of Virginia, Cate Brennan, Textual Reference Branch, National Archives at College Park, Maryland, Brother Lawrence Morey, archivist at the Abbey of Gethsemani.

Our appreciation goes as well to Dom John Eudes Bamberger, O.C.S.O. for permission to quote, Brother Dunstan Robidoux, O.S.B. for his advice, and His Excellency, The Most Reverend Rembert George Weakland, O.S.B. for always being available to talk with us.

We thank Mr. William Francisco Say for permission to reprint letters and the Merton Center for permission to reprint photographs. By Arne Kislenko, from The Journal of Conflict Studies, The Gregg Centre for Study of War and Society, Summer 2004. By Permission of Gregg Centre, University of New Brunswick. By Alfred W. McCoy, from *The Politics of Heroin; CIA Complicity in the Global Drug Trade*, copyright ©2003, Lawrence Hill Books. Reprinted by permission Chicago Review Press. By George Weigel, from "JFK After 50 Years", November 20, 2013, in *First Things* Religion and Public Life, by permission of First Things. Excerpt from *Conjectures of a Guilty Bystander*, by

Thomas Merton, copyright © 1965, 1966 by The Abbey of Gethsemani. Used by permission of Doubleday, an imprint of Knopf Doubleday Publishing Group, a division of Penguin Random House LLC. All rights reserved.

We would also like to thank Patrick and Kathryn Knowlton, John H. Clarke, and Mike Campbell, who made helpful suggestions on the manuscript and Alison Weir for sharing her book-writing and publishing experience.

Contents

Foreword i
Introduction 1
Part 1. The Thai Conclusion: Heart Failure 6
Tragedy in Thailand 7
The Thai Police Report 21
What Happened? The Police Versus the Witnesses
.... 31
The False Document 49
A Sham Investigation 61
Police and Clerical Legerdemain 71
Things Not Seen and Things Imagined 81
François de Grunne 93
Part 2. The Authorized Conclusion: Accident
.... 105
The Myth around Merton's Death 107
Building on the Myth 117
The Catholic News Service's Straw Men 137

The Not-to-Be-Shown Photograph..........................147

Michael Mott's Authorized Story of the Death.163

In Michael Mott's Wake...187

Part 3. The Enemies of Truth 199

Murder by the Book...201

Merton Was a Force for Peace and Truth............209

The Press in Full Cover-up Mode............................221

Penn Jones: Covert Agent?...233

Pope Francis and Thomas Merton..........................243

The Logical Explanation..247

The Forbidden Photos and the Six Trappists Again 255

Conclusion...267

Appendix 1...277

Appendix 2...281

Index..305

Dedication

To the following Benedictines:

Father Celestine Say
Sister Edeltrud Weist
Father Egbert Donovan
Father Odo Haas,

whose voices can now finally be heard.

Foreword

From the first moment of the sudden, unexpected event almost a half-century ago, the death of the famous monk Thomas Merton has been enveloped in mystery. After doing the only serious investigation of the episode and its aftermath ever conducted, the authors have concluded that it would be more accurate to say that his death has been wrapped in falsehoods.

The story of the authors' dedication to the unraveling of the mystery of Merton's death began in the early 1990s. Hugh Turley and David Martin were both living and working in the Washington, DC, area when, on July 20, 1993, the body of Deputy White House Counsel Vincent W. Foster, Jr., was found in the back of the Civil War relic known as Fort Marcy Park, off the George Washington Parkway on the Virginia side of the Potomac River.

Martin had been an intramural basketball rival of Foster's, graduating two years before him from Davidson College in North Carolina. He was also a longtime student of the assassination of President John F. Kennedy, and he immediately noticed parallels in the extraordinarily incurious press coverage of the two deaths, how the press uniformly acted as virtual salesmen for the very difficult-to-believe official story rather than as proper watchdogs on the government. That led him to begin to conduct his own inquiry into Foster's death, in the process of which his path crossed Turley's.

Turley was no more than a casual follower of the news at the time whose profession of magician took him all over the greater Washington metropolitan area and beyond. One day, sometime after the Foster death, his return route from a performance took him by Fort Marcy Park and he decided on a whim to go in and look around and see where Foster's body had been found. It happened that Reed Irvine, the head of the conservative press-watchdog organization, Accuracy in Media, had also chosen that time to visit the park. Irvine had also viewed the media-abetted official story of the Foster death with great skepticism, and he proceeded to give Turley an earful. Turley's political course from that time on was set.

Irvine was also something of a midwife for Turley and Martin's collaboration. With their mutual interest in the Foster case, Irvine and Martin were already working together, sharing insights and information, and Martin was on a panel for a program in Washington, DC, that Irvine had organized. The panel included, among several other people, the Washington bureau chief for the *Sunday Telegraph* of London, Ambrose Evans-Pritchard, who would later write *The Secret Life of Bill Clinton*, which contains perhaps the most incisive analysis of the Foster case yet rendered in popular book form. Turley was in the audience, and he introduced himself to

Martin at the end of the program. He said that he had been particularly impressed by the following poem that Martin had written and recited:

Solicitude

> Don't you think that the family has suffered enough?
> Why must you stir up this mess?
> He wasn't constructed of very strong stuff.
> He couldn't put up with the press.
> He must not have been what he seemed to be.
> He could not have been very stable.
> That he might have been killed for his honesty
> Is just a romantic fable.
> We'll fight for his right to be off in the head.
> What do you mean we offend you?
> If you should turn up mysteriously dead,
> This is how we would defend you.

Martin, to date, has written 75 articles on the Foster case, many of them with ample research assistance by Turley. These articles appear on Martin's web site, DCDave.com, including the six-part book-length series, "America's Dreyfus Affair: The Case of the Death of Vincent Foster," which focuses particularly upon the distorted press coverage of the event.

Turley collaborated with the dissident witness in the case, Patrick Knowlton, and Knowlton's lawyer, John Clarke, on the 20-page submission to the U.S. Court of Appeals three-judge panel that had appointed Independent Counsel Kenneth Starr. The court ordered that submission—an analysis of the case that completely demolishes the government's conclusion of suicide—to be included in Starr's final report on Foster's death, over Starr's strenuous written objections. It was the only time that an independent counsel had been ordered to include evidence of a cover-up to his own report. To this day, America's press has completely blacked out the news of that part of Starr's report. Turley, Knowlton and Clarke then wrote an in-depth, 500-page critique of Independent Kenneth Starr's report on Foster's death, filed in various federal courts, and later published as the book, *Failure of the Public Trust*. These documents appear on their website with the descriptive web address, fbicover-up.com.

The catalyst for the writing of *The Martyrdom of Thomas Merton* was James W. Douglass's 2008 book, *JFK and the Unspeakable: Why He Died and Why It Matters*. Turley had begun to cultivate an interest in Merton only about five years before when he discovered a Merton book being read by one of the friars at the Dominican House of Studies in Washington, DC, where Turley regularly attends mass. The blurb across the top of the paperback version of Douglass's book lays out his principal thesis, "He chose peace. They marked him for death."

The authors were surprised to learn from that book—whose "unspeakable" subtitle was drawn from Merton—what a powerful force that Merton had been for peace, both before and during the Vietnam War. Would not the same people who marked President John F. Kennedy for death have marked Merton, as well?

A virtually countless number of books have been written that pick apart the official lone-nut explanation of JFK's murder. In 1968, there were two other assassinations of major public figures who also chose peace, the Reverend Martin Luther King, Jr. and Robert F. Kennedy. Only around a half dozen books have been published that take serious issue with the official verdict in RFK's murder and about half that number concerning MLK, Jr.'s assassination. To date, not one book or even a serious newspaper or magazine article has appeared that examines critically the bizarre story that Thomas Merton was killed during a conference near Bangkok, Thailand, by a faulty (Hitachi) electric fan.

One of the major ironies we were to discover in the Merton death case is that James W. Douglass, himself, has been a party to keeping the lid on things, perhaps inadvertently. At a keynote address to the International Thomas Merton Society in 1997, he reported that a noted journalistic skeptic in the JFK case had traveled to Bangkok to investigate, and that man had come back with assurances that no foul play had been involved.

Douglass, a theologian and former college professor, is clearly a very educated man, but his education has been very different from the real-life education that the authors have received in researching the Vincent Foster death case and other Deep State scandals. Douglass was perhaps not sufficiently wary of the very common phenomenon known as "fake opposition." We have learned that it is never a good idea to take the word of one person, no matter how good he might appear on the surface, especially when that person is an American journalist.

In *The Martyrdom of Thomas Merton* we identify four men who have been most instrumental in imprinting upon the public mind the wholly unsupported notion that Merton died from accidental electrocution—a conclusion that had not been reached by the investigating police in Thailand. Merton, with his trenchant observations about the propagandistic nature of the American press—observations that were far ahead of his time—would not have been at all surprised to learn that two of those men were professional journalists. We have identified a fifth man as a sort of "Hamlet" in the case, who privately counseled one of the four against writing things unsupported by the evidence, but he held his tongue publicly and withheld from his own public writing facts that did not agree with the accidental electrocution conclusion. That man was also a journalist, and what is worse, a journalist for Catholic publications who had covered the conference where Merton died.

Perhaps Merton would not even have been as surprised to learn, as the traditional Catholic authors were, that the other two men at the heart of the promotion of the accidental-electrocution story were members of his own Gethsemani Abbey in Kentucky.

Together, these men erected a virtual brick wall preventing the truth from getting out about what happened on that fateful afternoon in Thailand on December 10, 1968. With *The Martyrdom of Thomas Merton*, we have broken down that wall.

Participants at Bangkok conference with Merton as identified by Fr. Celestine Say, who took this photograph on the day of Merton's death. Left to right:
Very Rev. Maxime Thong, Prior, Cistercian Abbey of Phuoc-Son, Thu-Duc, South Vietnam
Rev. Jean Leclercq, Abbey of St. Maurice, Clairvaux, Luxembourg
Rev. Thomas Merton, Abbey of Gethsemani, Kentucky, United States
Rt. Rev. Abbot C.P. Tholens, AIM Secretariat, Slangenburg, Holland
Sister Marie de la Croix, Cistercian Abbey of Notre Dame de Lourdes, Seiboen, Jurenji, Japan
Rev. Paul Gordon, Secretariat, AIM, Beuron, Germany

Sister Beda Kim, Fatima Hospital, Taegu, South Korea
Rev. Mother Rosemarie Enriquez, Prioress, Immaculate Heart of Mary Abbey, Vigan, Ilocos Sur, Philippines

Two thousand years ago the death of a Christian martyr was a supreme affirmation not only of faith, but of liberty. The Christian proved by martyrdom that he had reached a degree of independence in which it no longer mattered to him whether he lived on earth and that it was not necessary for him to save his life by paying official religious homage to the emperor. He was beyond life and death. He had attained to a condition in which all things were "one" and equal to him. [1]
-Thomas Merton

Introduction

The Trappist monk Thomas Merton might well have been the most significant Roman Catholic thinker and writer of the 20th century. His 1948 autobiography, *The Seven Storey Mountain,* sold over 600,000 copies in its original hardcover edition and, in one version or another, has remained continuously in print. Its Kindle edition, as of this writing, has 644 customer reviews with an average customer rating of four and one half out of five stars. Amazon reports that the

---

[1] Thomas Merton, *Conjectures of a Guilty Bystander*, Doubleday & Co. 1966, p. 92.

book has been published in over twenty languages and has influenced a wide range of readers from Graham Greene to Eldridge Cleaver. The *National Review* also includes it in its list of the 100 best non-fiction books of the 20th century.

Altogether, Merton authored more than 70 books and almost as many books have been written about him. Wikipedia lists 28 biographies alone.

The International Thomas Merton Society (ITMS), formed in 1987, has 46 chapters in the United States and there are 19 chapters and affiliated societies in other countries. The ITMS has four-day conferences on a biennial basis at various sites. Two of the first 13 conferences were in Canada; the rest were in the United States.

Merton was in apparent good health and at the height of his productive powers when he died suddenly and mysteriously while attending a monastic conference, on December 10, 1968, near Bangkok, Thailand. He was 53 years old. Up to now, no one has examined the circumstances of his death systematically, critically, and what is most important, honestly. That is our purpose here.

Initial research

We began to research the details of Merton's death in 2012 by contacting Father John Eudes Bamberger, O.C.S.O. (Order of Cistercians of the Strict Observance, also known as Trappists), to ask for his help. Fr. Eudes's name and email address had been given to Hugh Turley as someone who knew Merton. Fr. Eudes had lived at Merton's home abbey, the Abbey of Gethsemani in Kentucky. Turley wrote in an email:

> I am interested in the details of the death of Thomas Merton. Can you advise me if your community has any official records of Thomas Merton's death? Is there a death certificate? A record of who first found his body? Who determined the cause of death? Is there a police report or investigative records from Thailand? Was an autopsy performed to determine the cause of death? If any official records exist within your community, could you advise me how to proceed?

Fr. Eudes replied,

> I am the one who examined Merton's body when it arrived back from Thailand. He had burns over the right side of his face from the fan that fell on him when he grabbed it. It was enough of a burn that the Abbot of Gethsemani who also viewed the body could not identify him. There was a Korean nun who is also a physician also at the meeting when Merton died. She examined him after his death and was convinced he died from the short-circuited fan. I read her report. The two monks who discovered Merton with the fan still running and lying where it fell on him found it was short-circuited when one tried to remove it and got a good shock. That pretty well covers the information I have. I wrote a short note after

seeing the body. I think it is preserved in Bellarmine University Library in the Merton collection.[2]

The only document that Fr. Eudes offered was the note that he had written on the tag that was attached to Merton's coffin when it arrived at Louisville, about 50 miles north of the abbey. The short note said only that he and Abbot Flavian Burns identified the bloated and swollen body of Fr. Louis.[3]

"Father Louis" is the name that Merton was given when he was ordained to the priesthood in 1949. Fr. Eudes did not actually answer any of our questions. We didn't realize it at the time, but he was no longer at the Abbey of Gethsemani. He might have directed us there, but as we shall see, that approach was not likely to have been very fruitful, either. Eventually we found the answers to our original questions, and along the way we discovered that some key things Fr. Eudes had told us turned out to be inconsistent with the evidence.

We were quite surprised to discover it, but there are actually three conclusions about the death of Thomas Merton, the official conclusion, the "authorized" conclusion, and the logical conclusion, and there is virtually no agreement among them. As we shall see and as the label we have given it implies, the third one is the only one that really makes any sense.

---

[2] John Eudes Bamberger, email to Hugh Turley, April 2, 2012.
[3] John Eudes Bamberger, note on Merton's coffin tag, Dec. 17, 1968, the Merton Center, Bellarmine University.

Our next step was to email the director of the Thomas Merton Center of Bellarmine University in Louisville, Dr. Paul M. Pearson, asking him for guidance. He informed us that the best published accounts of Merton's death were by Michael Mott in what Pearson described as the "official" biography, *The Seven Mountains of Thomas Merton*, and by John Moffitt in the book about the conference in Thailand where Merton died, *A New Charter for Monasticism*.

We were to discover that Pearson was correct about that, but we were also to find, to our surprise and dismay, that both authors concealed absolutely crucial information about Merton's death, of which they were fully aware, and that Mott, in furtherance of the story that Merton died from accidental electrocution, wrote what he had to have known was not true.

Part 1.
The Thai Conclusion: Heart Failure

Thomas Merton's Destiny

He lived to a higher standard,
So it should be no surprise
That his unexpected death
Was met by the standard lies.

David Martin

CHAPTER 1

Tragedy in Thailand

The monastic conference

Invitations for the Asian Monastic Meeting came from the Alliance for International Monasticism, Vanves, France.[4] The gathering was held December 8-15, 1968, at the town of Samutprakarn at a Red Cross conference center named Sawang Kaniwat.[5] The facility was originally built to be a convalescent home. The 100-acre property included

---

[4] Journalist editor John Moffitt, a meeting attendee, has a complete list of all of the participants at the conference in Appendix D of *A New Charter For Monasticism: Proceedings of the Meeting of the Monastic Superiors in the Far East, Bangkok, December 9 to 15, 1968*: John Moffitt, ed., Notre Dame, 1970 pp. 332-335.

[5] We have used the spelling as translated by the U.S. Embassy. This area south of Bangkok is also spelled as "Samut Prakan" and is considered part of the Bangkok metropolitan area.

beautiful gardens and small lakes and canals for canoeing and fishing. There were painted bridges with pagoda roofs, two swimming pools, an aquarium and two large conference rooms filled with earphones for simultaneous translations.[6] The setting was hardly as primitive as some people might have imagined when they heard that Merton had been killed in Thailand by a defective fan.

The facility had one primary building with comfortable rooms with private shower baths. On the ground floor there was a lounge area, recreation hall, and dining area. An elevator provided access to a rooftop garden. Eight cottages were set well apart from the main building, requiring from 10 to 15 minutes to reach by walking.[7] Merton would be found dead in one of those cottages that he shared with three other people, some two hours after having given a talk and having had lunch.

Fr. Celestine Say, O.S.B. (Order of Saint Benedict), from the Philippines, was on the first floor with Merton; Fr. François de Grunne, O.S.B., from Belgium, and Moffitt, the poetry editor for the Jesuit *America* magazine, were in the rooms on the second floor of the cottage.[8] Merton left the lunch area in

---

[6] *A New Charter For Monasticism: Proceedings of the Meeting of the Monastic Superiors in the Far East, Bangkok, December 9 to 15, 1968*, John Moffitt, ed., Notre Dame, 1970 pp. 1-2.

[7] Sr. Teresita D'Silva, O.S.B., "Bangkok Diary" - Dec. 1968, *The Merton Seasonal*, Winter 1998, pp. 3-4.

[8] John Moffitt, "Thomas Merton the Last Three Days," *The Catholic World*, July 1969, pp.160-163.

the company of de Grunne, walking some five minutes ahead of Say. The last time Say would see Merton alive was when he saw him with de Grunne well ahead of him, bound for the cottage.

The entrance door on the first floor of the cottage opened upon a parlor room, with some chairs, that separated the first floor's two rooms. Merton's room was on the right side and Say's on the left. Both rooms had louvered windows in the front and sides of the cottage with plants in front of the windows. Stairs at the end of the parlor on the left led to the second floor.

Each floor had bathrooms. Merton's room had a private half bath with a toilet and sink, but no tub or shower. Merton could enter his half bath from a door in his room. Another half bath was in the parlor adjacent to Merton's half bath. Say shared the half bath in the parlor with de Grunne, because his toilet on the second floor was clogged.[9] Another door next to Say's half bath was to a shower shared by Merton and Say. To enter the door to the shower Merton would have to exit his room into the parlor and pass by the door to Say's half bath.

Screens partitioned the rooms and bed sheets hung as curtains, affording little privacy.[10] From an acoustic standpoint, the two rooms on the first floor occupied by Merton and Say were essentially one room. Anything that

---

[9] Celestine Say, letter to John Howard Griffin, June 25, 1969, Columbia University.

[10] Celestine Say, letter to Flavian Burns, Mar. 18, 1969, the Merton Center.

went on in one room could easily be heard in the other, and if a person wanted to, he could see into another's room.[11]

This setting of the scene is essential for an understanding of the circumstances of Merton's death as related by the various witnesses in the case. (See Exhibit 1 for a drawing of the first floor Merton's cottage.)

The conference was presided over by the Most Reverend Dom Rembert Weakland, O.S.B. Weakland stayed in a cottage next to Merton's cottage. At the time of Thomas Merton's death, Weakland was the Abbot Primate of the Benedictine Confederation.[12] Fr. Jean Jadot, O.S.B., also present at the Bangkok conference, later consecrated Weakland as Archbishop of Milwaukee, Wisconsin.[13]

When Merton was found dead, Weakland was the person who administered the Last Rites of the Catholic Church at 4:10 p.m.[14] Weakland also arranged through the U.S. Embassy for Merton's body to be transported back to the United States by military aircraft.[15] The U.S. Army took

---

[11] Abraham C. Florendo, "The Final Ascent on the Seven Storey Mountain," *Mirror Magazine*, Jan. 18, 1969, p.11, the Merton Center.

[12] John Moffitt, "Thomas Merton the Last Three Days," *The Catholic World*, Jul. 1969, p. 160.

[13] *The Washington Post*, Nov. 11, 1977.

[14] *A New Charter For Monasticism: Proceedings of the Meeting of the Monastic Superiors in the Far East, Bangkok, December 9 to 15, 1968*, John Moffitt, ed., Notre Dame, 1970 p. 84.

[15] Hugh Turley telephone interview of Rembert Weakland, Oct. 3, 2012.

possession of Merton's body just nine and a half hours after he was found dead. Katherine E. Barry, a secretary at the U.S. Embassy, claimed Merton's possessions.

It was odd and out of the ordinary that the U.S. Army should take Merton's body. The body was embalmed and, after five days, flown back to the United States on a military plane along with casualties from the Vietnam War.[16] Merton had vigorously opposed the Vietnam War, like Robert F. Kennedy and the Reverend Martin Luther King, Jr., who also died violently in 1968.

The first news of Merton's death

On December 11, 1968, the Associated Press reported that Merton had been electrocuted when he touched a short in a cord while moving an electric fan, according to anonymous Catholic sources.[17] The initial news reports did not include any important details such as who found Merton, the names of any witnesses or officials at the scene, or who determined that it was an accident.

On December 19, 1968, in response to requests for more details about Merton's death, the Abbey of Gethsemani sent out a "Dear Friends" letter that included, along with information about the funeral, a letter dated December 11,

---

[16] Report of the Death of an American Citizen Thomas Merton, American Embassy Bangkok, Thailand, December 13, 1968, National Archives, College Park, MD.

[17] John T. Wheeler, "Thomas Merton Dies in Electrocution Accident," Associated Press, Dec. 11, 1968.

1968, from "six Trappist delegates" who had been at the conference with Merton.[18] It is unclear to whom the Abbey's letter was sent, but it seems not to have been reported by anyone in the press. The letter stated that it was difficult at that time to determine the cause of Merton's death and then speculated that Merton may have had a heart attack or may have suffered a fatal electric shock. The Trappists' letter apparently received its first public attention when it was included in a book in 1973, which we shall discuss later.

The official Thai documents

The Thai authorities produced three official documents on Merton's death that we have been able to see, a cause-of-death doctor's certificate, death certificate (with a hand written police note on the reverse side), and a summary police report. Thai officials concluded that *cardiac failure* was the primary cause of Merton's death.

Doctor's certificate

The doctor's certificate exists in three versions, the original Thai language and two different English translations. An affidavit from the State Department states that an embassy

---

[18] Letter from the Monks of Gethsemani to Dear Friends, December 19, 1968, the Merton Center; Letter from Six Trappists to Abbot Flavian Burns, December 11, 1968, the Merton Center.

Clerk, Chan Bhansattabutr, translated the doctor's certificate on December 16, 1968.[19]

Dr. Luksana Nakvachara, completed and signed the doctor's certificate (Exhibit 2) on the cause of death, dated December 10, 1968, the day of Merton's death. Dr. Nakvachara wrote in English on the Thai language document that the death had been caused as a result of "Fainting – due to acute cardiac failure and electric shock due to accidental falling against the fan to the floor."[20] The doctor's certificate did not comment on a bleeding head wound observed by witnesses, which we shall discuss later.

Near the bottom of the English translation of the document, a National Archives copy (Exhibit 3), it states:

> Remarks: The patient died outside Samutprakarn Hospital. The remains were brought to the Hospital for the purpose of a post mortem by medical doctors and investigation authority as prescribed by law.[21]

Below these remarks, at the bottom of the State Department translation copy of the doctor's certificate one

---

[19] Chan Bhansattabutr, Consular Clerk, sworn statement authenticating Doctor's Certificate translation, Dec. 16, 1968, from National Archives, College Park, MD.

[20] Luksana Nakvachara, Doctor's Certificate, (Cause of Death), Samutprakarn Hospital, Dec. 10, 1968, Thai language original, from National Archives.

[21] Luksana Nakvachara, Doctor's Certificate, (Cause of Death), Samutprakarn Hospital, Dec. 10, 1968, English language translation, from National Archives.

finds a comment from an anonymous American Embassy consular officer that *is not* part of the translation. It states:

> * (CONSULAR OFFICER'S NOTE – NOT PART OF TRANSLATION): As will be noted from the copy of the original form, the comments under remarks are pre-printed on the form. In this case the remarks are not applicable even though correction was not made. The remains of Father Merton were released to the consular officer following post-mortem examination by Thai medical and investigating authorities at the place of death.

The post-mortem at the hospital prescribed by law—that is to say, the autopsy—was "not applicable" in the death of Thomas Merton, according to the U.S. Department of State. The anonymous consular officer said, in effect, that what is written on the doctor's certificate is not true.

The consular officer did say that Merton's body had a "post mortem examination by Thai medical and investigating authorities at the place of death." Later in this book it will be clear that whatever was done at the place of death—and was done there only—did not satisfy the eyewitness observers. They were deeply puzzled by the death scene and fully expected that a meticulous autopsy would be done to determine the cause of death.

Archbishop Weakland also supplied another English translation of the doctor's certificate to us. (Exhibit 4) He had been given copies of official documents by the embassy. His copies bear a stamp and signature of authenticity from the U.S. Embassy. Weakland's copy of the doctor's certificate is almost identical to the State Department translation, with the exception of this note under the Remarks:

> The patient died outside Samutprakarn Hospital. The remains were brought to the Hospital for the purpose of an autopsy by medical doctors and investigation authority in accordance with law. [22]

Weakland's translation copy and the original Thai language document, it should be emphasized, do not include the consular officer's "correction" to the document, leaving the impression that a standard formal autopsy was performed at the hospital.

The truth is that Merton's body had not been taken to the hospital, and no autopsy was performed. The police report confirms that the body was not taken to the hospital for an autopsy by saying, "After the investigation of the appropriate witnesses had been completed the body was turned over to George S. [sic] Weakland for funeral rites." The consular officer's comment also contradicts the police report in that it says the remains "were released to the consular officer" and not to Weakland. Merton's body remained at the conference center where a vigil was kept until 1:30 a.m., whereupon the U.S. Army took the body to an army hospital. We know of no evidence that an autopsy was performed at the army hospital, either.

In his memoirs, Weakland wrote that an undertaker had taken Merton's body from the center, but later he admitted that he had been asleep at the time and had written this

---

[22] Luksana Nakvachara, Doctor's Certificate, (Cause of Death), Samutprakarn Hospital, Dec. 10, 1968, English language translation, from Rembert Weakland.

because he assumed that the body would have been taken by an undertaker to be embalmed for transport.[23]

It is quite clear that no autopsy was done in "accordance with law" by Thai authorities. Dr. Nakvachara signed the doctor's certificate that falsely stated Merton's body had been brought to the hospital for an autopsy. The doctor's certificate has the seal and signature of the American consulate as "a true copy of the signed original."

Proper official procedures were not followed in the case of Merton's death, even though paperwork made it appear that they were. They had not been followed because the United States government, in a manner that also appears to be inconsistent with its usual protocol, had taken possession of Merton's body with what looks like unseemly haste. One may speculate as to the reasons for this takeover and the false paper trail, but innocent explanations don't come readily to mind.

Death certificate

Tawil Chaiplab, Assistant Registrar, signed the official Thai government death certificate, No. 388/2511. The death

---

[23] Rembert G. Weakland, *A Pilgrim in a Pilgrim Church, Memoirs of a Catholic Archbishop*, Wm. B. Eerdman's Publishing, 2009, p. 166; Hugh Turley telephone interview of Rembert Weakland, Jun 10, 2017.

certificate (Exhibit 5), dated December 11, 1968, declared that the cause of death was "Sudden heart failure."[24]

There are two English version translations of the death certificate. The U.S. Embassy certified each as a true copy of the original. The version obtained from Weakland (Exhibit 6), as previously noted, does not include a translation of the police investigator's note on the reverse of the death certificate. The second version (Exhibit 7), which we discovered at the U.S. National Archives, does include a translation of the police investigator's note. It states:

> (Reverse Page): The remains may be removed through the area of Amphurmuang, Samutprakarn Province and they may be allowed to pass through other areas as a post-mortem examination has already been made in accordance with the law.
>
> (Signed) Pol Lt. Boonchob Cheongvichit
>
> Investigator
> December 11, 1968[25]

Police Lt. Boonchob Cheongvichit's handwritten note on the death certificate agrees with the boilerplate on the doctor's certificate that a post-mortem examination or autopsy had been performed in accordance with the law. This additional note by a police officer that a regular autopsy had, in fact, been done strongly suggests that something

---

[24] Tawil Chaiplab, Death Certificate No. 388/2511, Samut Prakern Municipality, Thailand, Thai language original, from National Archives, College Park, MD.

[25] Tawil Chaiplab, Death Certificate No. 388/2511.

beyond mere inadvertence is involved here. The body was not taken to a hospital because the body never left the conference center before the U.S. military removed it, and the police, of all people, had to know that. The Thai police, in fact, demonstrated no interest in determining what really caused Merton's death, much less in why the U.S. government was so quick to take possession of the body. As we shall see, this curious lack of interest was shared by a number of other people whom one would expect to be most interested, but, fortunately, not everyone was so lacking in interest.

An affidavit from the U.S. State Department showed that the embassy clerk, Chan Bhansattabutr, translated the death certificate on December 16, 1968.[26]

The U.S. Embassy Report

The only U.S. government document regarding Merton's death is the Report on the Death of an American Citizen (Exhibit 8) by the U.S. Embassy in Bangkok, Thailand and, in apparent contradiction to what the Associated Press announced to the English-speaking world, it repeats the official Thai death certificate conclusion that "Sudden heart failure" was the cause of death.[27]

---

[26] Chan Bhansattabutr, Consular Clerk, sworn statement authenticating the Death Certificate translation, Dec. 16, 1968, from National Archives, College Park, MD.

[27] Report of the Death of an American Citizen Thomas Merton, American Embassy Bangkok, Thailand, December 13, 1968, National Archives, College Park, MD. The "letters from participants"

The document also has a couple of other curiosities. Alone among the initial reports released, it gives a time of death, that is, approximately "1500 hrs" (3:00 p.m.). That is a time of death that would persist, though tenuously, throughout the "authorized" narrative, right up to the present day. That time is also strongly suggested in the Thai police report released later, based on information provided by the episode's least reliable witness and by a witness statement that appears to have been manufactured.

The time of death is crucial, and it is indeed odd that the U.S. Embassy took the lead and has produced the *only* official document that states a time of death. We shall return to the subject of the time of Merton's death throughout the book.

The document, for what it is worth, also states near the bottom that it was sent to Abbot Flavian Burns of the Gethsemane [sic] Abbey on December 17, although the document, itself, is dated December 13. Maybe they meant that that was when they intended to send it, or perhaps they backdated their document after taking the required time to come up with a time of death.

On December 27, 1968, the U.S. Embassy in Bangkok sent Abbot Flavian a letter stating that, "Abbot Weakland will be writing you in detail." The embassy enclosed a copy of the doctor's certificate, death certificate with a translation, letters from participants at the conference who found or

---

referenced here may well be the witness statements that original Merton biographer, John Howard Griffin, said were part of the police report.

examined Merton's body, and its own Report on the Death of an American Citizen. [28] The embassy promised (see Frontispiece) to forward the police report to the abbot when it was available. This was the first mention of any existence of a police report.

---

[28] Letter from John L. Hagan, American Consul General, U.S. Embassy in Bangkok, to Abbot Flavian Burns, December 27, 1968, Mott Collection, McCormick Library, Northwestern University.

CHAPTER 2

The Thai Police Report

The police report

The police report promised by the embassy in December of 1968 had apparently not been forthcoming, because on June 30, 1969, John Howard Griffin, the celebrated author of the 1961 memoir, *Black Like Me*, who would at some point be chosen by Gethsemani Abbey's Merton Legacy Trust to write Merton's "authorized biography," wrote to Brother Patrick Hart and Abbot Flavian Burns of the abbey and suggested that they obtain documents from the Thai police and any photos or other records they may have. Griffin thought that these records should be part of the monastic archives at Gethsemani and that it would be best if the request for these documents came from the abbey.[29] We shall have a good deal more to say about Griffin later.

The U.S. Embassy in Bangkok delivered a "summary police report" to the Gethsemani Abbey. We were able to obtain a copy (Exhibit 10) from the Merton Center of Bellarmine University in Louisville. This report (in English) had been sent from Joseph C. Snyder III, vice consul of the embassy to Reverend Flavian Burns with a cover letter (Exhibit 9) dated July 30, 1969. The letter stated:

> Transmitted herewith is a translation of the concluding report of the Police Investigation into the circumstances surrounding the death of Father Thomas Merton. The translation was made by a local employee on the embassy staff. If you have any further questions, do not hesitate to write.[30]

No Thai language copy of the police report was included. The translator of the report was anonymous, which was not the case with the other Thai documents that the embassy had translated, a fact that might be significant.

In contrast to John Howard Griffin a half year after Merton's death, apparently no one in the press showed any interest in seeing the original Thai police report. Relying on these would-be eyes and ears of the public, we would not even know that such a report existed.

---

[29] John Howard Griffin, letter to Brother Patrick and Abbott Flavian, June 30, 1969, Moffitt papers, University of Virginia.

[30] Joseph C. Snyder, American Vice Consul, US Embassy Bangkok, Thailand, cover letter with police summary report, Jul. 30, 1969, the Merton Center.

The press is not the only unexpectedly poor source of information on this matter. When we first spoke to Rembert Weakland in 2012, he said that there was no police report. Weakland did send us copies of the Thai death certificate and the Thai doctor's certificate. But he apparently did not even know that there was a police report. Recall that in 2012 when we asked Fr. Eudes if there was a police report, he did not answer our question.

Moffitt wrote about Merton's death in his book about the monastic conference in 1970. Moffitt stated that what he had written was based on the accounts of the first four witnesses at the scene. At that point, Moffitt, Griffin and the monastery had the police report in their possession, but they were keeping it secret. When Moffitt corresponded with John Howard Griffin, he mentioned the contradictions between two witnesses, but he ignored the police report conflict with eyewitness accounts.

Abbot Flavian wrote a letter to Moffitt in December of 1969 giving him advice by sharing his own thoughts about Merton's "accident." He told Moffitt that his guess was based on his reading and studying of the handwritten reports of the first witnesses to reach Merton's body. Abbot Flavian did not mention the police report. It had arrived on August 7, 1969, from the U.S. Embassy while Griffin was staying in the hermitage at the abbey preparing Merton's biography.[31] Abbot Flavian, Moffitt, and Griffin certainly recognized the

---

[31] John Howard Griffin, *The Hermitage Journals*, Image Books, 1983 p.7.

conflict between the police report and witness statements, but they never said anything about it.

It appears that the first public announcement of the existence of the police report was from Brother Patrick Hart in 1973 with the publication of *The Asian Journal of Thomas Merton*, a record of Merton's final trip to Asia that Brother Partick co-edited with John Laughlin and Naomi Burton Stone. Brother Patrick, who had been appointed as Merton's secretary in the summer of 1968, and who later became the custodian of Merton's papers, revealed in that book that he had read the official Thai medical and police reports. We shall have more to say about this later.

The two-and-a-half page police report, released seven months after Merton's death, has no title, no author, and no date. The anonymity of the report, alone, strongly suggests that something very much resembling a cover-up is taking place. The police report does not have any official embassy stamp to authenticate it as a true translation of the original, whereas there is a clearly visible embassy stamp and authentication on both the doctor's certificate and the death certificate.

According to Griffin, the police report forwarded by the U.S. Embassy also included statements by the witnesses, Sister/Dr. Edeltrud Weist (Exhibit 11), Fr. Odo Haas, and Fr. François de Grunne.[32] The statements of both Dr. Weist and

---

[32] John Howard Griffin, letter to John Moffitt, August 18, 1969, Moffitt papers. The police report proper mentions no attachments.

Fr. Haas are available at the University of Virginia, Northwestern University, and Bellarmine University. Abbot Flavian and Brother Patrick withheld Fr. de Grunne's statement. There is also no report from either Fr. Egbert Donovan or Fr. Celestine Say, who were among the first witnesses to reach Merton's body. We learned from his correspondence that the police had interviewed Say, an absolutely key witness, as we shall see. [33] Say signed a statement, but that statement was not included in the police report supplied by the embassy.

Also missing from the police report are photographs, laboratory reports, and investigators' memos. An autopsy would be the cornerstone of a death investigation, but there was no autopsy, so there is no autopsy report. The failure to conduct an autopsy might very well be the greatest evidence of all of a cover-up.

Important facts from eyewitnesses were misrepresented and ignored in the police report. The names of the key eyewitnesses were misspelled:

Fr. François de Grunne was simply "De Grunne" with his first name omitted. Officially, he was the last person to see Merton alive and the first to find the body. He was upstairs in the cottage and, as we shall see later, his accounts of events

---

Therefore Griffin is the only known source that any statements were attached.

[33] Celestine Say, letter to Flavian Burns, Mar. 18, 1969, the Merton Center.

are inconsistent with those of other witnesses and are at times self-contradictory.

Fr. Celestine Say was misspelled as "Selistonese." Say was a very important witness who entered the cottage a few minutes after Merton. Out of respect for Merton's privacy, he tried not to look into Merton's room, but he was best positioned to hear everything in their partition-separated rooms over the next two hours, before Merton's body was discovered. Say's observations that we know of come from three key letters (Exhibits 12, 13, 14) that he wrote several months apart, documenting everything that he had witnessed.

Fr. Odo Haas was misspelled as "O.O. Hars." Haas was one of the first three people to reach Merton's body. We know of no reliable statement from Haas on what he witnessed. The best source for what Haas witnessed are the letters of Say and Donovan. As we shall explain in Chapter 4, what has been represented as an official statement by Haas is almost certainly a fabrication.

Fr. Egbert Donovan was not mentioned in the police report. Donovan reached Merton's body at the same time as Say and Haas. Donovan wrote a letter to document what he had witnessed, and he thought that the position of the body was inconsistent with Merton's hands ever having touched the fan found lying across his body.

Sr. Edeltrud Weist was misspelled "Nun Arden Tross Wise." Dr. Weist was the first medical doctor to reach Merton's body and she observed a bleeding wound on the back of his head.[34] In addition to misspelling Weist's name, the police report failed to say that she was a medical doctor, describing her only as a witness "who had a knowledge of nursing." Dr. Weist wrote a report with a drawing included, dated December 11, 1968.

Even the police investigator's name was misspelled. Lt. Boonchop Poomvichit was misspelled as "Boonchob Cheongvichit." His signature was on the reverse of the death certificate that had been certified as officially translated by Chan Bhansattabutr, Consular Clerk of the American Embassy, Bangkok, having been duly sworn by Vice Consul Katherine E. Barry.[35]

We have requested the original Thai language police report from the Royal Thai Police. As of this writing, they have not responded. Without a copy of the original Thai police report, we can't say if the misspellings and errors in the report are the fault of the embassy's anonymous translator or the Thai police. The U.S. State Department documents at the National Archives include copies of the Merton death certificate and doctor's certificate in both English and Thai. By curious and suspicious contrast, neither the original Thai police report nor any English translation of

---

[34] M. Edeltrud Weist, Report on the first impressions after Rev. F. Thomas Merton's tragic death given by an eyewitness, handwritten note, Bangkok, Dec. 11, 1968, the Merton Center.

[35] Chan Bhansattabutr, Consular Clerk, sworn statement authenticating the Death Certificate translation, Dec. 16, 1968, from National Archives.

it can be found among State Department documents at the National Archives with the other Thai documents concerning Merton's death.

When names of eyewitnesses are misspelled in a police report, it can indicate that there is an intentional cover-up going on. Misspelled names in police reports make it difficult, if not impossible, for others to locate the witnesses. As an example, Patrick Knowlton was a crucial witness at the scene where the body of President Bill Clinton's deputy White House counsel, Vincent Foster, had been discovered. The U.S. Park Police report misspelled Knowlton's name as "Nolton."[36] At one point, even FBI agents had difficulty locating Knowlton because his name had been misspelled in their own documents.[37]

An even more obvious example of hiding a witness by misspelling his name is the 1949 case of the Bethesda Naval Hospital Apprentice Edward Prise. His name was clearly intentionally misspelled "Price" in the official inquiry into the supposed suicide of Secretary of Defense James Forrestal, a death that was far more likely an assassination. Prise was never mentioned publicly until the year after his death when Forrestal biographers Townsend Hoopes and Douglas Brinkley cast him in the very unlikely role of the witness

---

[36] Ambrose Evans-Pritchard, *The Secret Life of Bill Clinton*, Regnery, 1997, p. 159.

[37] Ambrose Evans-Pritchard, conversation to Reed Irvine, October 28, 1995, https://youtu.be/RE3-TxJajSA

whose testimony provided the strongest support for the suicide thesis.[38]

The Thai police report did not mention the bleeding wound on the back of Merton's head that Dr. Weist had seen or some cuts mentioned in a letter.[39]

The police report, remarkably enough, did not provide any details about the death scene. It only said, "The body was lying down on the floor headed to the North East and there was a stand fan resting on the body..." The police did not say whether he was face up or face down, where the body was lying exactly, what he was wearing, where the fan was lying on his body, or the make and model of the fan. The police only reported that there was a burn on the skin without saying exactly where.

The police failed to follow standard procedure by investigating Merton's death as a homicide. A leading textbook on homicide investigation, *Practical Homicide Investigation, Tactics, Procedures and Techniques*, states that even if a death appears to be suicidal or accidental it should first be handled as a homicide. Every death investigation should be considered to be a homicide by investigators until

---

[38] David Martin, "Daughter of Key Forrestal Witness Surfaces," http://dcdave.com/article5/171011.htm

[39] M. Edeltrud Weist, Report on the first impressions after Rev. F. Thomas Merton's tragic death given by an eyewitness, handwritten note, Bangkok, Dec. 11, 1968, the Merton Center; Six Trappists letter to Flavian Burns, Appendix VIII, *The Asian Journal of Thomas Merton*, New Directions, 1973, pp. 344-347.

there is evidence to rule out homicide.[40] In one case cited in the textbook, a body found in a wooded area was at first properly considered a homicide by investigators. Later an autopsy showed that the man was a hunter who had died after suffering a stroke.

No death investigation is going to be perfect, but there are proper accepted procedures. Christopher Rush, retired New York City police officer and Special Deputy United States Marshall testified to the U.S. Senate:

> According to generally accepted principles of police procedure, an officer called to the scene of a death is expected to treat the scene and the death as a crime, and to conduct the investigation accordingly. Only after the possibility of homicide has been eliminated should the officer proceed to an investigation of whether the death was suicide or accident.[41]

---

[40] Vernon Geberth, *Practical Homicide Investigation, Tactics, Procedures and Techniques*, CRC Press, 2014, p. 16.

[41] Christopher Rush, testimony before Committee on Armed Services, United States Senate, 104th Congress, Sep. 12, 1996, p. 17.

CHAPTER 3

What Happened? The Police Versus the Witnesses

Not only did the Thai police do nothing but guess about what might have caused Merton's death, but they were even worse when it came to determining when Merton died. They had the testimony of two men for that purpose, Fr. François de Grunne, who had entered the cottage in the company of Merton some five minutes ahead of the second man, Fr. Celestine Say. The police report leaves the impression that the death must have occurred an hour or so after the three of them arrived at the cottage, because it states that de Grunne heard a "loud noise" coming from downstairs at 3:00 p.m.

Since Say's testimony did not accompany the police report supplied by the U.S. Embassy, we don't know what he told them. We do know from what he told other people in letters, the implied time of death is wrong. Not only did Say not hear any loud noise in what was essentially the same room as his, but from the moment that he set foot in the cottage, Say detected not the slightest sound from Merton. From every indication, Merton was already dead or unconscious by the time Say entered the cottage. The only question to be resolved appears to be whether Merton's death occurred while de Grunne was still with him or after de Grunne had gone to his own upstairs room.

Curiously, in spite of implying that the death must have occurred at around 3:00 p.m. in the body of the report, in the "Subject" line at the beginning, the police report states, "The incident occurred on December 10, 1968, at about 2:00 p.m....".

One must wonder if this might have been an accidental statement of truth by the Thai police. Later we shall see that John Moffitt also, after studying the evidence, concluded, as we have, that the time of Merton's death was, indeed, close to two o'clock.[42]

Not only does the 2:00 p.m. time of death not fit with the time that the police say that de Grunne heard the noise, it doesn't quite fit their incorrect timing of events at the conference, either:

> On December 10, 1968, at 10:45 A.M. the usual meeting began and Reverend Thomas Merton was the speaker who gave a talk until 11:45 A.M. Then there was a break for lunch until 2:00 P.M., after which they separated to go to

---

[42] John Moffitt, letter to Brother Patrick Hart, February 8, 1970, Moffitt papers.

their lodgings for rest. The meeting was to be resumed at 4:00 P.M. Reverend Thomas Merton went to his room accompanied by Reverend De Grunne from Belgium. Then they separated to their own rooms.[43]

The police report was not accurate in saying Merton and others went to their cottage after 2:00 p.m. Say sat across from Merton at lunch and remembered handing the key to the cottage to Merton. Merton left the dining hall for the cottage at 1:40 p.m. accompanied, as we have noted, by de Grunne. A few minutes later[44] Say followed after them at a distance and could see Merton and de Grunne talking as they walked.[45] Moffitt also remembered Merton leaving the dining room at 1:40 p.m.[46] Since the cottage was a 10-15 minute walk from the main building where they had eaten lunch, Merton and de Grunne arrived at the cottage shortly before 2:00 p.m.[47]

---

[43] The conclusion of police investigation report on the death of Reverend Thomas Merton, author unknown, date unknown, the Merton Center.

[44] Celestine Say letter to John Moffitt, July 1, 1969, Moffitt papers.

[45] Celestine Say, letter to John Howard Griffin, June 25, 1969, Columbia University.

[46] John Moffitt, *A New Charter for Monasticism*, op. cit., p.82.

[47] John Moffitt, letter to John Howard Griffin from Bangkok, 1970, the Merton Center.

The police report also misstated that the meeting was to resume at 4:00 p.m. The meeting was to resume at 4:30 p.m.[48]

The police failed to report that Say followed after Merton and de Grunne, walking a few minutes behind them. If Say had been five minutes behind them, he would have arrived at the cottage around 2:00 p.m.[49] When Say arrived, the door was unlocked, and he wondered if it had been unlocked when Merton and de Grunne got there. Say remembered that he and Merton had found the door to their cottage unlocked previously.[50] Say did not see Merton or de Grunne and went directly to his room across from Merton's.[51] The one other man who shared the cottage, John Moffitt, had gone sightseeing.[52]

The next passage from the police report is especially significant:

> At 3:00 P.M., on the same day, Reverend De Grunne who stayed in an upper room over the scene, while walking into the bathroom, heard a loud noise coming from the lower story which sounded like a heavy object falling onto the floor. Reverend De Grunne rushed to ask Reverend Selistonse, from the Philippines, whose room was adjacent

---

[48] Bangkok Monastic Conference Schedule of events, from Moffitt papers.

[49] Celestine Say, letter to John Moffitt, Dec. 11, 1969, the Merton Center.

[50] Ibid.

[51] Ibid.

[52] John Moffitt, *A New Charter for Monasticism,* op. cit., p.7.

to Reverend Thomas Merton's room, whether he had heard any strange noise.[53]

De Grunne's room was directly over Say's room and not over the room where Merton died.[54] De Grunne is not likely to have been walking into the bathroom upstairs when he heard a loud noise coming from the lower story, because he shared the bathroom on the first floor with Say. As we noted, earlier de Grunne's toilet on the second floor was clogged, although it is possible he could have gone into the bathroom to use the sink.[55]

When Say entered the cottage, he did not see or hear Merton moving around. He went in his room, removed his habit, and then went to the bathroom in the parlor to brush his teeth. While brushing his teeth, he heard de Grunne coming down the stairs. De Grunne banged on the door, and when Say opened the door de Grunne said, "I thought you were Merton." De Grunne then asked Say if he had heard a shout and when Say responded, "no," de Grunne went back upstairs. Say estimated that the time was between 1:55 p.m.

---

[53] The conclusion of police investigation report on the death of Reverend Thomas Merton, author unknown, date unknown, the Merton Center.

[54] John Moffitt, *A New Charter for Monasticism*, op. cit. 1970, p.82.

[55] Celestine Say letter to John Howard Griffin, June 25, 1969, Columbia University.

and 2:15 p.m. when de Grunne came down and banged on the bathroom door.[56]

Say repeated his story of what he had witnessed in four separate letters in 1969: to Abbot Flavian in March, to John Howard Griffin in June, and in two letters to John Moffitt in July and December. Say's story has been consistent.

Merton had a private bathroom on the first floor. Since the other bathroom on the first floor was shared by Say and de Grunne, it doesn't make sense that de Grunne would bang on the door of the bathroom he shared with Say and expect to find Merton. When Say opened the bathroom door why would de Grunne say, "I thought you were Merton," if Merton did not use that bathroom? Why didn't de Grunne simply knock on Merton's door?

De Grunne told Say that since he had not seen him enter the cottage, he thought that Merton was the only person who could have shouted.[57] Since de Grunne told Say that he did not know that he was in the cottage, it is not accurate for the police to report that de Grunne rushed to ask Say if he had heard any strange noise.

Say thought it was unfortunate that de Grunne did not bother to look in on Merton and wondered why he didn't do

---

[56] Celestine Say, letter to John Moffitt, Dec. 11, 1969, the Merton Center; Celestine Say, letter to Flavian Burns, Mar. 18, 1969, the Merton Center.

[57] Ibid.

so.[58] De Grunne could have easily turned his head, according to Say, and looked into Merton's nearby room. If he had come down to check on Merton, why didn't he? Instead, de Grunne went back upstairs.[59]

On leaving the bathroom, Say did not look into Merton's room because, as he said, he was making an effort to respect Merton's privacy, but he still noticed that Merton was not in his bed. He thought Merton was sleeping on the floor because it was cooler or perhaps for penance.[60]

The police report stated that de Grunne had heard a loud noise at 3:00 p.m., contradicting what Say witnessed on three points, the time, the place, and the noise. Say arrived at the cottage and brushed his teeth at 2:00 p.m., not 3:00 p.m.; Say remembered that de Grunne had come to him while he was in the bathroom, not in his room; and Say remembered that de Grunne had asked him if he had heard "a shout," not "a strange noise."[61]

What happened next, according to the police, also differs from what Say witnessed:

---

[58] Celestine Say, letter to John Howard Griffin, June 25, 1969, Columbia University.

[59] Celestine Say, letter to John Moffitt, Dec. 11, 1969, the Merton Center.

[60] Celestine Say, letter to Flavian Burns, Mar. 18, 1969, the Merton Center.

[61] The conclusion of police investigation report on the death of Reverend Thomas Merton, author unknown, date unknown, the Merton Center.

> Then Reverend De Grunne went up to his room to dress, which took about 20 minutes. He left his room to go down to the lower story to Reverend Thomas Merton's room to get the key to use when Reverend De Grunne came back to the compound.
>
> When Reverend De Grunne reached the door of Thomas Merton's room, he called but got no answer. So he looked through the glass louvers into the room. He saw Reverend Thomas Merton lying on the cement floor with a stand fan resting on his body. Reverend De Grunne suspected that Reverend Thomas Merton might be in danger, so he attempted to push the door open to see what had happened, but he could not push the door open because it was bolted from the inside. Reverend De Grunne called for Reverend Selistonse, a witness, staying in the adjacent room, to come to the scene, and at that time Reverend O.O. Hars, from Korea, a witness, also came to the scene. They helped to push the glass louvers of the room apart to reach the inside door bolt and open it. They got in to help Reverend Thomas Merton.

According to Say, after de Grunne went back upstairs he finished brushing his teeth and while returning to his room he noticed that Merton's bed was empty.

Say tried to take a nap but was unable to fall asleep because de Grunne was pacing the floor above his room and was opening and closing his door. After about an hour, at 3:00 p.m., de Grunne came downstairs and left the cottage. He returned shortly and went back upstairs.

Unable to fall asleep, Say decided to take a shower. After showering, he returned to his room and was dressing when he heard de Grunne come down again just before 4:00 p.m., reportedly to ask Merton to go for a swim.[62] He saw de Grunne pause by Merton's door and then de Grunne came and knocked on Say's door. He asked Say if he remembered when he had come down and asked him while Say was brushing his teeth if he had heard a shout. Then de Grunne told Say to come and look at Merton because he was lying on the floor with the fan on top of him.[63]

The behavior of de Grunne in pacing up and down the floor, and opening and banging his door for an hour is an indication of anxiety. It is body language that psychologists call "psychomotor agitation." In failing to report de Grunne's inconsistencies and body language, the Thai police report ignored clues that fairly begged for further inquiry.

If de Grunne had come down and gone out at three o'clock, as Say witnessed, and then returned to the cottage without getting a key from Merton, it makes no sense that he later needed to get the key. The police said de Grunne had come down to get the key from Merton. Say, on the other hand, said that de Grunne had come down to ask Merton if he wanted to go for a swim. The police did not report whether or not the key to the cottage was found in Merton's room after his death.

The police report went on to say, "When Reverend De Grunne reached the door of Reverend Thomas Merton's room, he called but got no answer." Then the police added

---

[62] Celestine Say, letter to John Howard Griffin, June 25, 1969, Columbia University.

[63] Celestine Say, letter to John Moffitt, Dec. 11, 1969, the Merton Center.

that de Grunne "called" for Say. But Say did not report hearing any calls for Merton by de Grunne. What Say told Moffitt was that de Grunne paused near Merton's room, and then came to knock at Say's room.[64]

Say could hear de Grunne on the steps and lingering by Merton's room. If de Grunne had called to Merton and then to Say, Say would have heard de Grunne calling through the partition that was only a screen and curtains. Moffitt wrote in the book, *A New Charter for Monasticism*, that de Grunne knocked at Merton's door.[65] Say did not report hearing any such knocking.

This behavior of de Grunne is very similar to his actions when he came down the first time at 2:00 p.m. to check if Merton had heard a shout, but then he only asked Say and did not attempt to ask Merton. Now de Grunne has come down again supposedly to get a key from Merton, but he only knocks on Say's door. Apparently, de Grunne already knew that Merton could not answer.

It is significant that de Grunne first asked Say if he remembered that he had come down earlier while Say was in the bathroom to ask him if he had heard a shout.[66] In saying this, de Grunne confirmed that Say was in the bathroom when de Grunne first came down and this was around 2:00

---

[64] Ibid.

[65] John Moffitt, *A New Charter for Monasticism,* op. cit., p. 83.

[66] Celestine Say, letter to John Moffitt, Dec. 11, 1969, the Merton Center.

p.m. and not 3:00 p.m. Say brushed his teeth after entering the cottage at around 2:00 p.m.

If de Grunne had, in fact, thought that Merton was in danger, it would have been a needless waste of time for him to ask Say if he remembered being asked about an earlier noise. De Grunne appeared to be more interested in establishing that he had heard the noise than in aiding Merton.

Without any explanation, the police report stated "...at that time Reverend O.O. Hars, from Korea, a witness, also came to the scene." The police report did not mention that de Grunne had left the scene and that Haas had arrived with Donovan only after being told by de Grunne that Merton had had an accident.[67] De Grunne had left the cottage after telling Say that he was going for help.[68] That was around four o'clock. When de Grunne approached Haas and Donovan, he did not immediately ask them for help or tell them that Merton was in danger. He began the conversation by asking if they had had a good swim?[69] After they responded in the affirmative, only then did de Grunne inform them that he heard a sound and decided to check on Merton. Finally, he told them that something had happened to Merton. Haas and

---

[67] Celestine Say, letter to Flavian Burns, Mar. 18, 1969, the Merton Center.

[68] Celestine Say, letter to John Moffitt, Dec. 11, 1969, the Merton Center.

[69] Egbert Donovan, letter to John Moffitt, Dec. 5, 1969, Mott Collection.

Donovan hastened to help Merton. De Grunne continued to go away from the scene toward the main building.[70]

Once again, it looks as though de Grunne's objective was to create in people's minds the notion that he had reacted to a noise, before sharing the more important fact that something had happened to Merton. Establishing a spurious time of death seems to have been foremost in his mind.

The police report made it appear that de Grunne never left the scene and that Donovan never arrived. Donovan is an important witness because he was one of the first to observe the death scene, and it did not look right to him. Donovan told Moffitt that he was puzzled by the fact that they found Merton with his arms lying straight by his side. The position of the arms was puzzling to Donovan because he thought the arms would not be in the position they were found if Merton had in any way touched the fan or pulled it onto himself in falling. Donovan told Moffitt that he thought that if Merton had been able to withdraw his hands from the fan as they were found he could have thrown the fan off of himself, too.[71]

Donovan also commented on the odd pleasantry by de Grunne, asking if they had had a good swim. Donovan wrote that he remembered the detail of his conversation with de Grunne quite accurately because it impressed him as being

---

[70] François de Grunne letter to John Moffitt, July 6, 1969, from Moffitt papers.

[71] Egbert Donovan, letter to John Moffitt, Dec. 5, 1969, Mott Collection.

unusual under the circumstances.[72] Haas also thought de Grunne exhibited odd behavior. Say informed Abbot Flavian that Haas told him later that it was funny the way de Grunne encountered them. De Grunne first asked, "and did you have a good swim?" before telling them Merton had had an accident and was lying on the floor with a fan on top of him. Haas and Donovan rushed to Merton's cottage as soon as they heard that Merton was in trouble.[73] De Grunne, it should be noted, was the first person to call Merton's death an "accident."

Donovan said that he and Haas had moved as quickly as they could to the cottage.[74] After de Grunne alerted Haas and Donovan, he continued on to tell others at the main building.[75] Dr. Weist quickly arrived at the scene and others followed. While others rushed to Merton, only de Grunne distanced himself.

Since the police report left out de Grunne's encounter in which he asked Haas and Donovan about their swim, the police did not mention de Grunne telling them that he had heard a sound and had gone to check on Merton. The police reported that de Grunne only told Say about a noise at 3:00 p.m. Then later he went to Merton's room just to get a key to

---

[72] Ibid.

[73] Celestine Say, letter to Flavian Burns, Mar. 18, 1969, the Merton Center.

[74] Egbert Donovan, letter to John Moffitt, Dec. 5, 1969, Mott Collection.

[75] John Moffitt, *A New Charter for Monasticism*, op. cit., p. 84.

use.[76] There are conflicting stories, then, concerning when de Grunne heard a noise, what noise he heard, and what he did when he heard the noise.

Say wrote that de Grunne came downstairs to go for a swim an hour and a half after he had first come down. It was then that de Grunne found Merton on the floor.[77] An hour and a half from when Grunne first came down would have been shortly before 4:00 p.m. This was very late for de Grunne to go for a swim and ask Merton for the key because the meetings were scheduled to begin again at 4:30 p.m.

There are three versions of how de Grunne discovered Merton on the floor: (1) The police reported that de Grunne heard a suspicious noise at 3:00 p.m. and rushed downstairs. (2) The police reported that de Grunne went to Merton's room to get a key. (3) Say reported that de Grunne went to ask Merton if he wanted to go for a swim.

These three stories cannot all be true, and they may all be false. That first story from the police could not be true because by the time de Grunne reached Haas and Donovan it was nearly 4:00 p.m., which means that he would have waited about 45 minutes before going to check on the noise. But even if that were true, he could not have heard the sound of a cry and heavy object fall at 3:00 p.m. or Say would have

---

[76] The conclusion of police investigation report on the death of Reverend Thomas Merton, author unknown, date unknown, the Merton Center.

[77] Celestine Say, letter to Flavian Burns, Mar. 18, 1969, the Merton Center.

heard it, too. Say heard de Grunne leave the cottage for a short time at 3:00 p.m. And de Grunne had told Say that he had heard a shout at 2:00 p.m.

The second story by the police that de Grunne came down to get the key is also unlikely because, as mentioned earlier, de Grunne had already gone out and returned to the cottage without asking Merton for the key. The third story about asking Merton to go for a swim may also be false, because it would have been too late to go for a swim. By this time, Haas and Donovan were returning from swimming to get back to the conference, which was set to resume at 4:30 p.m.

What is most likely is that de Grunne did not come down to see Merton at all, because he did not call to him or knock at his door. De Grunne only knocked on Say's door. It looks very much like de Grunne actually came down to invite Say to discover Merton on the floor.

When Haas, Donovan, and Say reached Merton's body, they knew immediately that he was dead. Haas reached to remove the fan but recoiled from a shock. Say unplugged the fan. Then Donovan told Say and Haas not to touch anything. They saw it as a crime scene that required the presence of the police. Haas told Say to get his camera and take photographs in case the police asked exactly how they had found Merton.[78] Say took two photographs.

---

[78] Celestine Say, letter to Flavian Burns, Mar. 18, 1969, the Merton Center.

Haas immediately went to tell Weakland, who was in a nearby cottage.[79] Dr. Weist arrived moments later after she heard that Merton was lying dead in his room.[80] Weakland arrived with Dr. Weist and he promptly scolded Say for taking photographs of the scene.[81]

Dr. Weist observed a third degree burn in the upper right abdominal area where the fan switchbox had touched the skin. The burn was three to four inches wide and extended down to the right genital region. Dr. Weist also observed what she took to be "strip-like burns" on his right arm and a bleeding wound on the back of Merton's head. After examining Merton and concluding that he had been electrocuted, Dr. Weist replaced the fan on Merton so that things would look as they had been found for the police.[82]

Although Dr. Weist concluded that an electric shock had caused Merton's death, like the witness Donovan, she was

---

[79] Rembert Weakland, "Merton the Pilgrim," in Paul Wilkes, *Merton by Those Who Knew Him Best*, Harper & Row, 1984, p. 161.

[80] M. Edeltrud Weist, Report on the first impressions after Rev. F. Thomas Merton's tragic death given by an eyewitness, handwritten note, Bangkok, Dec. 11, 1968, the Merton Center.

[81] Celestine Say, letter to John Howard Griffin, June 25, 1969, Columbia University.

[82] Celestine Say, letter to Flavian Burns, Mar. 18, 1969, the Merton Center.

also puzzled.[83] She wrote that she could not determine the reason why Merton had fallen, and she wondered whether he had fainted, had been dizzy, or had had a heart attack.[84] It was a mystery.

According to the police report, Weakland had asked Dr. Nakvachara, Director of Samut Prakarn Hospital, to come to examine the body. The police report concluded:

> However, the Investigating Officer questioned Dr. Luksana Nakvachara, whose views were that Reverend Thomas Merton died because of: 1. Heart failure, 2. And that the cause mentioned in 1. Caused the dead priest to faint and collide with the stand fan located in the room. The fan had fallen onto the body of Reverend Thomas Merton. The head of the dead priest hit the floor. There was a burn on the body's skin and *on the underwear* on the right side which was assumed to have been caused by electrical shock from the fan. (emphasis added)

As a final note on the witness testimony, it would be incorrect to say that Fr. Say heard no sound at all from Merton's room after returning to the cottage. Only after he had observed the fan on Merton and his burned skin did he recall that earlier in the afternoon he thought he had heard some sparking or crackling sound and had noticed an acrid

---

[83] M. Edeltrud Weist, Report on the first impressions after Rev. F. Thomas Merton's tragic death given by an eyewitness, handwritten note, Bangkok, Dec. 11, 1968 p. 1, the Merton Center.
[84] Ibid.

smell.[85] At the time he thought the sound and the smell were coming from outside the cottage.

---

[85] Celestine Say, letter to John Howard Griffin, June 25, 1969, Columbia University; Celestine Say, letter to John Moffitt, Dec. 11, 1969, the Merton Center.

CHAPTER 4

The False Document

In the case of government cover-ups, made up or misrepresented documents are almost standard fare. A notable example is Vincent Foster's somewhat gloomy memorandum to himself, belatedly found in his briefcase days after it had apparently been emptied out in the presence of several people, torn into 28 pieces with no fingerprints on it, and with one piece missing where a signature might have been. That document served for the press as Foster's suicide note, though it isn't addressed to surviving loved ones and gives no indication that anything in it is serious enough that the writer might be even considering taking his own life. Furthermore, three notable handwriting examiners have declared it to be a forgery. [86]

---

[86] Ambrose Evans-Pritchard, *The Secret Life of Bill Clinton: The Unreported* Stories, Washington, D.C., Regnery Publishing, Inc., 1997, pp. 211-216; David Martin, "America's Dreyfus Affair, the Case of the Death of Vincent Foster (Part 1)," November 27, 1996,

A similar document played a central role, from the very first day, in the press and government declarations that recently resigned Secretary of Defense James Forrestal had taken his own life on May 22, 1949, when he fell from a 16th floor window of the main tower of the Bethesda Naval Hospital where he had been confined. In this case the surrogate suicide note was the supposed transcription by Forrestal of a morbid poem by Sophocles, the chorus from *Ajax*, in which the main character in despondence apparently contemplates suicide. That transcription turned out not to be even an attempt at a forgery. Perhaps the writer was confident that it would never see the light of day, because the handwriting doesn't begin to resemble Forrestal's.[87]

A more common type of phony document is a falsified witness statement. Sylvia Meagher's seminal 1967 examination of the Warren Commission Report on the John F. Kennedy assassination is replete with examples of misrepresentation of witness statements by the FBI interviewers.[88] A clear example of a FBI-falsified statement in the Foster case is that of the witness, Patrick Knowlton. Knowlton described to the FBI a car parked at Fort Marcy

---

http://www.dcdave.com/article1/961127.htm. Scroll down to "The Forgery" section.

[87] Hugh Turley, "Handwriting Tells Dark Tale," *Hyattsville Life and Times*, December 2007,
http://www.dcdave.com/article5/090130.htm.

[88] Sylvia Meagher, *Accessories after the Fact*, Vintage Books, New York, pp. 323-326.

Park, where Foster's body was found, that was older and of a distinctly different color from Foster's car, but the FBI interview report stated blandly that Knowlton saw Foster's car.[89]

We have encountered a document in the Merton case that appears to be a combination of the two types of falsifications that we have described. It is apparently not a misrepresentation of what a witness told interviewers; rather, it looks very much like a witness statement that has been entirely manufactured. It has not been as central to the Merton case as the two notes were to the Forrestal and Foster cases, but it is important. It provides the only "evidence" that the bad wiring of the fan might have been such that a person touching it might possibly have been killed on the spot.

It is represented as the written statement of Odo Haas. It would appear to be what he submitted to the Thai police on the day of the death, and that was how it has been characterized in correspondence between those responsible for constructing the narrative approved for public consumption. The document's legibility is poor, so we transcribe it here so that readers might join us in evaluating its authenticity:

---

[89] Evans-Pritchard, op. cit., pp. 158-164; Appendix to Kenneth Starr's Report on the Death of Vincent Foster, http://www.fbicover-up.com/vincent-foster-report.html; *The Vince Foster Cover-up: The FBI and the Press,* https://www.youtube.com/watch?v=eii7LBSziSM.

Report on the Discovery of the Corpse of R.Fr. Thomas-Louis Merton

10 Dec.1968

About 4 p.m. In Bangkok- Swanganivas on Sukhumvit Rd. –Thai Red Cross Haus No. ii

Reporter: Odo Haas, osb, Abbot of Waegevan [sic]

*****

About 4 pm I went by Haus no. 2 together with Rt. Rev. Archabbot E. Donovan/Vincent-Latrobe (USA-Penn.) where Rev. Louis-Thomas Merton was living. There were living with him in the same house: Rev. Celestine Say, om[sic]/Prior of Manila

Rev. Francois de Grunne/St. Andrè-Belgium

MR.Moffitt/Editor of America Magazine

We met Rev. Fr. Grunne [sic] and he told us that about 3 pm he had heard a cry and the fall of a heavy object in or nearby the house. After some time he wanted to go look in the room where Fr. Merton was, off on the right. He saw Fr. Merton lying on the floor as he looked through the screen. The door was locked. He took off immediately to get a key.

The three of us immediately hastened to the door of the room. There we met Fr. Say.

I was going to break the door-window open and it gave way right off so that we could easily open the door.

Fr. Merton lay on the floor before us. He was dressed only in his shorts. He lay between the bed and a stand where his habit was hanging to dry. The feet lay about 40 inches from the feet-end of the bed with the head in the corner of the room in front of the clothes-stand. On his body lay a fan (made in Japan), about 45 inches high. The feet of the fan lay between the legs of Fr. Merton, with the switch on the top seam of the shorts and the fan itself on the face or the head of Fr. Merton.

The toes of both feet seemed to be cramped.

At the point where the switch touched the shorts and the body a wound, a hands-breath[sic] in width, gaped open. The raw flesh was visible and the base of the wound was blood-shot.

The face was deep blue. The eyes were half open. He was the mouth.[sic] On the left side between the body and the arm I observed a pool of fluid. It was not water. I thought it was fluid from the wound or from the body. (Fr. Say advised me to take a picture of the scene. It is doubtful whether it took since it was too dark.) An odor filled the room which, from earlier experience, I had learned to recognize as burnt human flesh.

The fan was still going. And so I wanted to take it off the body right away. In doing so I got a strong electric shock. It kept me from getting free of the fan. Fr. Say pulled the plug of the fan out of the socket as quickly as he could (it was behind the bed in the other corner of the room).

We four together verified the death of Fr. Merton. And so Rt. Rev. Donovan gave him the blessing (presumably general absolution). I did the same.

Immediately I hastened to Rt. Rev. Abbot Primat [sic] R. Weakland who appeared at the scene about 3 minutes later. About 4:10 p.m. the Abbot Primate gave Fr. Merton extreme unction.

(signed) Eyewitness; Odo Haas, osb

    Abbot of Waegwan/S. Korea.

        (The typewritten document was *not* signed. ed.)

53

Considering the fact that this statement was supposedly given within a few hours after the actual event, its clear errors can hardly be explained away on account of the witness's faulty memory. The most obvious error is that de Grunne joined Haas and Donovan after he had informed them of Merton's plight: "The three of us hastened to the door of Merton's room."

We know for certain that that is not true. Everyone else said that the three people who first entered the Merton's room were Haas, Donovan, and Say and that de Grunne had gone on to the main building. De Grunne, himself, in a letter to John Moffitt said that he went quickly to the main building after informing Haas and Donovan of the Merton emergency. Say also wrote to Moffitt that he had noticed that de Grunne did not return after going for help, and reflected that de Grunne must have been hit hard emotionally by what had happened to Merton.

We can also see that this misstatement is not just a slip-up, because near the end of the document the writer says quite definitely, "We four together verified the death of Fr. Merton." The four that he is clearly referring to at that point are Say, Donovan, de Grunne, and himself. One of them could not be Dr. Weist, whom he does not mention in his statement, and it could not be Weakland, who didn't get there until a few minutes later, almost simultaneously with Dr. Weist.

The error looks very much like the sort of inadvertent one that a person would make who was not actually there at the scene. It is very difficult to believe that Haas would have made such a major mistake. Another error of that type concerns the matter of the key that de Grunne supposedly left the death scene to pursue. The door to Merton's room was not secured by a lock that required a key, but by an internal latch. And if getting the key were so important in de Grunne's mind, why would he not have continued on to the main building to try to get it?

Such inadvertent mistakes may be contrasted with the statement's central inaccuracy, which appears to be the main reason that the statement was concocted. We are talking about the "strong electric shock" that the writer says he got that "kept [him] from getting free of the fan" when he attempted to lift it off Merton's body.

That is not what Say reported that he witnessed at the time, saying only that Haas "recoiled" from the shock and that Haas told him that the shock was "not too strong." There is an absolutely fundamental difference between these two descriptions, representing the difference between a would-be killer fan and a fan that one would jerk back from in the manner in which one jerks back from an electric fence. It is extremely hard to believe that a witness like Say, who has proved to be so consistent and reliable in every other way, could possibly have been so wrong about what he saw when Haas touched the defective fan and in what Haas told him about the nature of the shock. Surely Say would not have found such an episode so forgettable that he would never tell anyone else about it, that is, that he had to rush to unplug the fan so that Haas could free himself from it. It is also quite difficult to believe that Haas would describe such an extremely painful and, indeed, life-threatening experience in such a matter-of-fact way.

Whoever wrote this statement—which tellingly lacks Haas's signature and dating at the bottom where a signature is supposed to be—must have realized that reinforcement was needed for the notion that Merton had been killed by a defective fan. The idea had to be planted that the fan might have killed Haas, too, but for the quick thinking of Say to rush to unplug it.

The short statement has other anomalies, likely errors of both the intentional and inadvertent type. In that latter category, the writer has the fan lying on Merton's body with its base between his legs and the blades of the fan on Merton's head. Since the diagonal placement of the fan across Merton's body was so radically different from this, one can hardly believe that this could be the writing of an actual witness.

The writer also says that Say suggested that he take a picture of the scene, but we know that it was Say who actually took photographs, and, according to Say, it was Haas who suggested that he do so. Say, we know, after observing the conduct of the Thai police, became wary of them and decided not to reveal to the police that he had taken photographs of the body for fear that they would confiscate his film. Haas is likely to have shared Say's wariness of the police and would not have divulged that he had taken any photograph for the same reason.

Another likely inadvertent mistake in the statement is that the fan was still running, suggesting that the blades of the fan were still turning. Donovan, however, wrote in a letter to Moffitt, that the blades of the fan were still when they entered Merton's room. It is a good deal more likely that a short-circuited fan would not be running, so Donovan's observation seems more believable.

It is highly unlikely that Haas would have begun his statement by misspelling the hometown of his abbey in Korea. It is equally unlikely that he would have written the initials for the Order of St. Benedict that follows his name in lower case letters. This is never done.

In the intentional misinformation category, the writer reports that de Grunne, as soon as he encountered Haas and Donovan, told them that he had heard "a cry and the fall of a heavy object" at about 3:00 p.m., but, curiously, he hadn't gone to check on it until about an hour later. This fits very well with the "loud noise" that the police report says that de Grunne heard at about that time, but it's very strange that Haas would report such a thing so routinely. Wouldn't he have found it odd that de Grunne would have waited so long to check on such alarming sounds?[90]

---

[90] It also fits with Dr. Weist writing that she had been told that de Grunne heard a shout at about 3:00 p.m., causing her to speculate that this could have been the time of Merton's death. (M. Edeltrud Weist, Report on the first impressions after Rev. F. Thomas Merton's tragic death given by an eyewitness, handwritten note, Bangkok, Dec. 11, 1968, the Merton Center.) De Grunne very likely did tell others what the police say in their report that he told them. For the record, John Moffitt, after studying the evidence, had concluded by

In fact, in a letter to Moffitt, that's not at all how Donovan remembered the encounter. The thing that stood out in his mind was how de Grunne first oddly asked them if they had had a good swim, and only then told them that he had heard a thump, and when he promptly checked he saw Merton on the floor of his locked room. Donovan said that on hearing this from de Grunne, he and Haas quickly went to Merton's cottage. Not only does that account have a greater ring of truth, but it also correctly reports, in agreement with de Grunne and Say, that only Haas and Donovan rushed to look about Merton.

As we have previously noted, Say reported that Haas had told him he thought it most unusual that de Grunne should greet them with a casual query about their swim, but it seems not to have been remarkable enough for mention in this statement that is purportedly by Haas, which is just another reason to doubt its authenticity.

Readers may note that the statement says that Merton was found wearing shorts and that whatever liquid was present was not water. This gives the lie to any notion that Merton was wet from showering when he touched the fan.

1970 that de Grunne could not have heard any shout or sound of an object falling–never mind the time–because de Grunne was upstairs on the opposite side of the cottage with a door closed between the two floors. Merton's body falling onto the terrazzo floor would hardly have made any noise. Neither would the fan falling on top of Merton's body have made much noise. (John Moffitt, letter to Brother Patrick Hart, February 8, 1970, Moffitt papers.)

One might wonder why the perpetrators of a cover-up would manufacture a document that is so incriminating on this point. But we must remember that the wet-from-showering scenario was not yet part of the story that the public had been told. It was not in the police report, and it was not in any news reports and would not be for a few years.

Even though it did not support the shower story, this "Haas statement" was still used to support the approved account, even after the wet-from-showering story had become a part of it, though without direct acknowledgment. No direct reference could be made, precisely because of what the statement accurately said about Merton's body with shorts on it and the absence of water at the scene.

As a final note, if this is indeed a statement that Haas made for the Thai police, and it was in possession of U.S. Embassy at the time that they translated the police report, there is no conceivable innocent excuse for either of them to have mangled the spelling of the names of Haas and Say, as they did in the copy of the police report that was furnished to the abbey. Those names are right there in this statement for them to see.

The statement, in fact, in great contrast to the police report, is downright meticulous about people's names as well as their proper titles and occupations. In that regard, it seems to reflect more the concerns of a fussy bureaucrat than those of a witness at the scene, which is just one more reason to doubt its authenticity.

As we discuss in more detail in Chapter 8, the typewritten witness statement by Dr. Weist has a big problem of its own, that is, that it omits the concluding two paragraphs of Dr. Weist's signed, handwritten version of the statement. The important information thereby left out is that, according to Dr. Weist, Haas told Say that the shock that he had received upon touching the fan was not very strong.

It is hard to escape the conclusion that the folks at the embassy realized how damaging to the electrocution story it was that the fan had only mildly shocked Haas, so they deleted it.

This explanation would be all nice and neat, except for the fact that it was the original handwritten version of Weist's statement that was sent to the abbey with the police report. We obtained our typed copy of it from Weakland, who was not even aware of the police report. Perhaps someone at the embassy messed up when he or she forwarded Weist's handwritten statement and not the typed one. Why would they have even bothered to type it up if it were not designed to be the official one for public consumption?

CHAPTER 5

A Sham Investigation

The police report began by stating that Dr. Luksana Nakvachara, "was the doctor collaborating in the investigation" and that he had arrived at the scene with the police. Dr. Nakvachara completed his report the day of Merton's death without the benefit of an autopsy, before the fan was examined, and before the interviewing of witnesses, which was done on the following day.[91] There was no investigation to determine whether Merton had a history of heart problems or was taking any heart medication. Before any investigation, Dr. Nakvachara concluded that "cardiac failure" had caused "accidental falling into the fan." When investigators know the result of an "investigation"

---

[91] Celestine Say, letter to John Howard Griffin, June 25, 1969, Columbia University.

before it even begins, there is a better word for it. That is "cover-up."

The cause of death is vital. It can determine whether the death is a homicide, by natural cause, a suicide, or an accident. If a death is determined to be an accident there may be criminal exposure or civil liability.

Witnesses at the conference thought that the "heart failure" conclusion by the Thai authorities was simply a choice of convenience. Say told Abbot Flavian at Gethsemani that the Thai doctor "thought [heart failure] a better diagnosis than electrocution to avoid complications in the police report."[92] Biographer Michael Mott said that the opinion of many of those present was that electrocution was deliberately underplayed to protect the Thais and the conference center.[93] One delegate at the Bangkok conference, Sr. Marie de la Croix, wrote that they attempted to say that Merton had died of heart failure to protect the Thai Red Cross and others, and that no one believed the heart attack conclusion.[94] Most everyone knew that Dr. Weist had examined Merton and that she had concluded that he had been electrocuted. De Grunne wrote that it was the fault of the fan, and nothing else. He added that nothing was said

---

[92] Celestine Say, letter to Flavian Burns, Mar. 18, 1969, the Merton Center.

[93] Michael Mott, *The Seven Mountains of Thomas Merton,* Houghton Mifflin Company 1984, p.566.

[94] Marie de la Croix, "The Last Days of Thomas Merton," five page narrative in French., p.5.

about this because blaming the equipment at the conference center would have embarrassed their Thai hosts.[95]

A month after Merton's death, an article was published in the Philippines based on the accounts of Fr. Say and Fr. Bernardo Perez. The story reported that after the coroner came with the police, these Thai authorities gave the cause of death as heart failure only because it was convenient. Such a natural cause conclusion would protect the conference center from bad publicity as well as unwanted investigations.[96]

By making heart failure the primary cause of Merton's death, the Thai officials removed any responsibility for negligence by the Red Cross Center, the fan manufacturer, or others. The natural cause of death eliminated any chance of lawsuits that would have made an autopsy necessary.

The most significant result of declaring that Merton's death was caused by a heart attack was that it made certain that there would not be a homicide investigation. The doctor collaborating with the police ruled out homicide by saying Merton's death was by a natural cause. The suspicious circumstances of the healthy victim found with a bleeding head wound and a strangely electrified fan on top of him were ignored. The doctor declared that Merton had died of a natural cause without any autopsy, as required by law, to

---

[95] François de Grunne letter to John Moffitt, July 6, 1969, from Moffitt papers.

[96] Abraham C. Florendo, "The Final Ascent on the Seven Storey Mountain," *Mirror*, Jan. 18, 1969, pp. 10-11, the Merton Center.

determine what caused his wounds, or if there were additional wounds. The Thai doctor, as previously noted, then falsified his report to make it appear that an autopsy had, indeed, been performed.

The police analysis of the fan

Regarding the fan, police report states:

> The Investigating Officer sent the fan for examination and received the report from the examiner, Pol. Maj. Amnuay Tunprasert, Chief, Chemical and physical Section, Scientific Crime Detection Laboratory, Police Department, which showed that the fan had a defective electric cord installed inside its stand. When the cord contacted the metal stand, it caused an electrical leakage throughout the fan. This flow of electricity was strong enough to cause the death of a person if he touched the metal part.

The police lab report on the fan is very important missing evidence. This report was never made public. The summary police report does not mention the fan manufacturer, Hitachi, or provide any information about the fan model. Say remembered that the brand was Hitachi.[97]

The police say only that "the fan had a defective electric cord installed" without saying anything precise about the defect. The police did not say who installed this defective cord. Was the defective cord installed by the Hitachi Corporation, or did someone sabotage the fan to make Merton's death appear to be an accident?

---

[97] Celestine Say, letter to John Moffitt, July 1, 1969, Moffitt papers.

After the police lab discovered that someone had apparently tampered with the fan by installing a defective cord, or perhaps installing a good cord in a defective manner, it ignored this apparent evidence of foul play. In the same way that the police report had concealed the names of eyewitnesses by misspelling their names, it concealed the manufacturer, Hitachi. If the Hitachi name had been associated with the death of Thomas Merton, the company likely would have sought an autopsy and also would have demanded that the fan be meticulously examined. Japanese electronics have a reputation for high quality, and it is very unlikely that a fan made by Hitachi would have been lethal.

Since Merton had been using the fan with no problems during the first two days of the conference, the existence of the defective cord would appear to be evidence of treachery.[98]

The police reported that its laboratory found that the defective cord "caused an electrical leakage throughout the fan...strong enough to cause the death of a person if he touched the metal part." Other evidence, however, belies this statement by the police.

Haas touched the fan with his hands, and it didn't even come close to killing him. He received a shock and recoiled from the fan, just as one would expect that Merton or anyone else would have done. Say asked Haas whether the shock had

---

[98] Celestine Say, letter to John Howard Griffin, June 25, 1969, Columbia University.

65

been strong when he touched the fan, and Haas told him that it was not too strong.[99]

There is nothing in the police report about who last operated the fan before Merton arrived. Did anyone touch the fan that might "cause the death of a person," before it allegedly killed Merton? There is no report by the police of the maid or other guests being questioned. When Merton and Say had returned the previous day they had found the cottage unlocked. Merton mentioned to Say that his room had been rearranged, and wondered if the maid had done it.[100] The police should have determined exactly who had rearranged Merton's room and at the very least should have attempted to discover who had installed the defective wiring in the fan.

An unfortunate aspect of the accidental electrocution story is that it made Merton responsible for his own demise, either from carelessness or awkwardness, or a combination of the two. The mental gymnastics required was particularly demanding to explain how it was somehow Merton's fault that faulty wiring, as the police said, "had been installed" inside the fan. In August 1969, Moffitt speculated to Griffin that when the fan fell, Merton somehow disarranged the wires.[101] In *A New Charter for Monasticism*, Moffitt quoted

---

[99] Ibid.

[100] Celestine Say, letter to John Moffitt, Dec. 11, 1969, the Merton Center.

[101] John Moffitt, letter to John Howard Griffin, August 31, 1969, Columbia University.

Mother Pia Valeri, O.S.B., and Mother Pia, who also blamed Merton, speculating that he had fainted and that the fan was then damaged and short-circuited as Merton dragged it with him as he fell.[102]

Brother Patrick Hart, when he later wrote about the matter, said only that an examination discovered defective wiring in the fan.[103] He did not reveal the brand name of the fan or what the police had said about the defective electric cord having been installed. Abbot Flavian and Brother Patrick, like the police, were strangely incurious about who had installed the defective cord or when it had been installed. Later, we shall see that the authorized biographer Michael Mott also mentioned the police discovery that defective wiring was installed, but he too failed to take notice of how strongly this fact alone pointed toward homicide.

Did the police rule out homicide?

As mentioned earlier, standard police procedure requires that the possibility of a homicide must be eliminated before investigating a death as a natural cause or accident. The police report does not state how the possibility of homicide was ruled out. There is only this peculiar statement from an anonymous witness in the police report:

---

[102] John Moffitt, *A New Charter for Monasticism,* op. cit., 1970, p. 84.
[103] Brother Patrick Hart, Postscript, *The Asian Journal of Thomas Merton*, New Directions, 1973, p. 258-259.

> Since no one saw Reverend Thomas Merton die, someone there assumed that he fainted and collapsed onto the cement floor, colliding with the stand fan as he did so.[104]

The police report concluded with two perfunctory sentences that offered its only attempt to eliminate the possibility of homicide:

> There were no witnesses who might be suspected of causing the death. There is no reason to suspect criminal causes.

It hardly needs saying that the fact that the witnesses were not suspected of causing the death does not rule out non-witnesses. Eliminating a few possible suspects does not rule out homicide. Moreover, it is very hard to believe that any police investigator worth his salt would have ruled out Fr. François de Grunne at this point as a homicide suspect. In fact, the evidence was such that the Thai police could hardly have been faulted for charging the man with murder. Of course, that would have necessitated the proper investigation that was never conducted, which may well explain why they didn't do it.

We may conclude, then, that the final sentence of the police report is simply false. There was *every* reason to suspect criminal causes. Even without de Grunne's extremely suspicious behavior, Merton's violent unexpected death *per se* is reason enough to suspect homicide. The

---

[104] The conclusion of police investigation report on the death of Reverend Thomas Merton, author unknown, date unknown, the Merton Center.

defective electric cord installed in the fan appeared to be evidence of a crime. The unnatural position of Merton's body prompted the first witnesses not to touch anything and to take photographs to preserve the evidence of foul play. The conflicting statements of witnesses, as well as one very nervous witness whose actions and statements were peculiar, to say the least, amounted to compelling evidence that something was badly wrong.

Summing things up, the Thai police and medical authorities might have called what they did an investigation, but if what we have been furnished by the U.S. Embassy is even close to accurate, their work is best characterized as a sham or a farce. What could be more ridiculous after all, than the notion that a person should have a fatal heart attack and then fall into a fan that happens to be short-circuited? One is more likely to fall onto a venomous snake when struck by lightning. It was such a joke, in fact, that virtually everyone reporting on Merton's death in the English language has chosen either to misconstrue it, to ignore its contents, or, what is most common, to pretend that it doesn't exist.

CHAPTER 6

Police and Clerical Legerdemain

Thai police Lt. Boonchob Cheongvichit and Dr. Nakvachara, as we have seen, handled the autopsy by filing false reports that Merton's body had been taken to the hospital for the autopsy in accordance with the law.

One person at the conference was unconcerned about an autopsy. When we asked Weakland if he expected that an autopsy would be performed in the United States, he said that he had no thoughts about it at the time. That would have been up to the abbey, he thought. The possibility of homicide did not occur to Weakland, because he did not think that Merton was well enough known in Thailand or that anyone would want to kill him.[105]

---

[105] Hugh Turley telephone interview of Rembert Weakland, July 22, 2017.

In March of 1969, Say wrote to Abbot Flavian asking if the cause of death was determined prior to Merton's burial.[106] Abbot Flavian made it appear that it had tried to arrange for an autopsy to be performed in Bangkok. After Merton's burial, Father Matthew Kelty wrote that there had been talk about an autopsy soon after Merton had died, but he was told that that it was too difficult to arrange on the phone to Bangkok.[107] In 1973, Brother Patrick wrote of an attempt to have an autopsy performed, but that it was prevented because of international red tape.[108]

In 1980, Brother Patrick introduced the very peculiar story that there was a Thai law requiring that anyone who had had an autopsy in Thailand had to be buried in Thailand.[109] In effect, what Brother Patrick was saying was that they were told that if they wanted Merton's body back, they could not have an autopsy performed in Thailand. It is very difficult to believe that there ever was such a preposterous law, and Brother Patrick has not identified the source of such supposed information. What, really, does one thing have to do with the other?

---

[106] Celestine Say, letter to Flavian Burns, Mar. 18, 1969, the Merton Center.

[107] Matthew Kelty letter to friends, Abbey at Gethsemani, December 17, 1968, Mott Collection.

[108] Brother Patrick Hart, Postscript, *The Asian Journal of Thomas Merton*, op. cit., pp. 258-259.

[109] John C. Long, "Revival of Theory about Monk's Death Distresses Friend," *Louisville Courier-Journal*, Aug. 3, 1980, p. 1.

Brother Patrick took it upon himself to say that "the monks" wanted Merton buried at the Abbey of Gethsemani more than they wanted an autopsy in Thailand.[110] It appears, rather, that Abbot Flavian and Brother Patrick just wanted Merton buried, period, more than they wanted an autopsy. Abbot Flavian could have requested an autopsy in the United States that could have been very revealing even though the body had been embalmed, but when Merton's body arrived at the abbey, they quickly buried him. On the day of the burial one monk even called Merton's death confused, because they did not really know the cause of his death.[111]

The Thai reports covered up the fact that there had not been an autopsy. As we have noted, officially—though not actually—Merton did have an autopsy in Thailand, and his body was still not buried in Thailand. Just as the Thai officials only gave the appearance of an autopsy, the monks at Gethsemani only gave the appearance of *wanting* an autopsy.

We asked the U.S. Embassy in Thailand about the alleged Thai law that requires persons autopsied in Thailand to be buried in Thailand. Hardly surprisingly, the embassy failed to offer any comment about such a requirement. The embassy only wrote:

> In order to determine the cause of death, the medical examiner on the scene may recommend an autopsy when a U.S. citizen dies outside of a hospital setting. Autopsies are normally performed free of charge by the Forensic

---

[110] Ibid.

[111] Matthew Kelty letter to friends, Abbey at Gethsemani, December 17, 1968, Mott Collection.

Institute at the Police General Hospital in Bangkok or by another forensic institute within 24 hours of receiving the remains. The autopsy reports take at least 45 business days to produce and may fall short of the standard expected in the United States.

Autopsies are not typically performed on U.S. citizens who die in hospitals, except at the request and expense of the next-of-kin. Hospitals are normally able to provide a cause of death, which is required for issuance of a Thai death certificate.[112]

Another early report about Merton's death stated that a Thai law required an autopsied body to be buried within 24 hours, but apparently not necessarily in Thailand. This report came from an article published in the *Philippines Free Press*, written by Bernardo Perez, O.S.B.[113] The U.S. Embassy in Bangkok may have been the source of the strange Thai law requiring autopsied persons to be buried within 24 hours. Weakland said that he was told by the embassy that if the body were to be autopsied it would have to be buried quickly in Thailand.[114]

Abbot Flavian should have noticed the false statements on the Thai documents that an autopsy had been performed.

---

[112] Email to Hugh Turley from American Citizen Services, U.S. Embassy Bangkok, Thailand, May 23, 2017
https://th.usembassy.gov/u-s-citizen-services/death-of-a-u-s-citizen/

[113] Bernardo Perez, O.S.B., "The Death of a Monk," *Philippines Free Press*, April 2, 1969, p.12.

[114] Hugh Turley telephone interview of Rembert Weakland, July 22, 2017.

Once the Thai government failed to examine Merton's body, the responsibility fell to the leadership of the Abbey of Gethsemani to order an autopsy to determine the cause of Merton's death.

The excuse from Brother Patrick that if Merton were to have an autopsy the law required that he be buried in Thailand is not credible for two reasons: First, the Thai document states, "The remains were brought to the Hospital for the purpose of an autopsy by medical doctors and investigative authority in accordance with law." If an autopsy was in accordance with the law, a few monks in Kentucky could not overturn Thai law to prevent an autopsy. Second, the Thai documents *officially* state that the autopsy had been performed in accordance with the law, and Merton was not buried in Thailand.

We sent Brother Patrick a self-addressed stamped envelope and asked the origin of his story that there was a Thai law that would have required Merton to be buried in Thailand and why the abbey did not order an autopsy in Kentucky. He did not respond.

In 1984, Weakland offered a new reason for the absence of an autopsy. He said that the decision had to be made within 12 hours of the death, that he could not legally authorize it, and that they could not get the required written permission from Abbot Flavian within the time limit.[115] He contacted the abbot at the Abbey of Gethsemani, and Abbot

---

[115] Rembert Weakland, "Merton the Pilgrim," in Paul Wilkes, *Merton by Those Who Knew Him Best*, Harper & Row, 1984.

Flavian made the decision to ship the body back without waiting for an autopsy.[116] Sr. de la Croix contradicted Weakland and said that she believed that the abbey had been contacted and that they refused to believe the heart attack conclusion and demanded an autopsy.[117] She left the conference believing that an autopsy was to be done by U.S. Army doctors.

Abbot Flavian wrote in a published account in 1984 that he had spoken to the U.S. Embassy in Bangkok and was told that Merton had died of an accident. The abbot said that since he knew that there would be questions, he requested that there be an autopsy, and he left it at that.[118] The abbot did not say to whom he made his request. By stating only that he requested an autopsy, the abbot deceptively gave the impression that there had been one, when he knew there hadn't been.

The fact of the matter is that the Thai police did not need permission from Weakland or Gethsemani to do an autopsy, which would have been essential for a proper death

---

[116] Hugh Turley telephone interview of Rembert Weakland, Oct. 3, 2012.

[117] Marie de la Croix, "The Last Days of Thomas Merton," op. cit., p.5.

[118] Flavian Burns, "Merton the Monk," in Wilkes, op. cit. It is curious that the U.S Embassy should have told Abbott Flavian that Merton died of an accident, if they, indeed, did so, when their official Report on the Death of an American Citizen, mentioned in Chapter 1, stated that the cause of death was "sudden heart failure" and makes no mention of any accident.

investigation. A more plausible reason why they did not have an autopsy was that it might have found additional injuries not consistent with the official cause of death.

Blaming Thailand for not performing an autopsy does not excuse Abbot Flavian for not seeking the truth about Merton's death by ordering one. The abbey buried Merton's body immediately when it arrived in Kentucky and shifted the blame for the absence of an autopsy onto Thailand. Abbot Flavian had the opportunity to order an autopsy, so he is every bit as responsible as the Thai police for the public not knowing the true cause of Merton's death.

Thai and U.S. cooperation

Michael Mott, in his biography of Merton, wrote that the Thai police bungled the Merton death investigation. People might wonder what would motivate the Thai authorities to cover up Merton's murder. What benefit could there have been for Thailand?

In the 1950s and 60s Thailand cooperated with the U. S. government in covert operations. The United States gave Thailand protection from external threats, and Thailand gave the United States bases for bombing raids in Vietnam and Laos. Thailand also provided rest and relaxation (R&R) for U.S. servicemen fighting in the region. The Thai government clearly felt that any resulting decline in moral values was more than offset by the economic benefit.

> Between 1950 and 1975 Thailand received from Washington approximately $650 million in economic aid...A further $940 million was ear-marked for Thai

defence and security, averaging annually over 50% of Bangkok's own expenditures on its armed forces. On top of this, an additional $US 760 million was paid out by Washington in operating costs, including the purchase of military equipment for Thailand and the payment of Thai troops serving in Vietnam...With over $US 2 billion in total assistance from Washington just between 1965 and 1975, Thailand was the second largest recipient of American aid in Southeast Asia next to Vietnam.[119]

Between 1965 and 1968, the majority of the 1,500 weekly bombing raids that dropped 80% of the bombs on Laos and North Vietnam had emanated from U.S. air bases in Thailand. Without these Thai bases, the U.S. B-52s would have flown from Guam, 2,000 miles from their targets, at a cost to the United States of $8,000 per round trip.

Arriving in Thailand, Thomas Merton landed, in effect, in the middle of the Indochina War that he opposed. The Thai government was closely allied with the United States in pursuing the war. Thais were on the CIA payroll and collaborating with the agency that ran the Phoenix Program training camps in Thailand. The prostitution and nightclubs in shantytowns around the military bases were just another part of their support of the war. Helping to dispose of a nettlesome monk who was interfering with the war effort would have been little more than routine business.

---

[119] Arne Kislenko, "A Not So Silent Partner; Thailand's Role in Covert Operations, Counter-Insurgency, and the Wars in Indochina," *The Journal of Conflict Studies*, The Gregg Centre for Study of War and Society, Summer 2004.

The Thais and Americans were not only collaborating in waging war; they were also partners in a huge drug business. The CIA worked more closely with the Thai police, in fact, than they did with the Thai military.

> In the late 1940s, there was a possibility that heroin addiction might decline to insignificant levels in the United States. Within a decade, however, drug syndicates flourished, Asia's poppy fields spread, and heroin refineries multiplied in Marseilles and Hong Kong. The reason for this rebound in the heroin trade lies, at least in part, in a succession of CIA alliances with drug traffickers--Corsican syndicates in Marseille, Nationalist Chinese forces in Burma, and corrupt Thai police.[120]

> During the 1950s, Thai police, the Nationalist Chinese army, the French military, and the CIA adopted policies that allowed Southeast Asia's mass opium addiction to survive and even thrive.[121]

Not only was the CIA at the very least facilitating the trafficking of drugs in Thailand in 1968, but it was also a heavy presence in a place where a considerable amount of child trafficking was going on. *The Hastings Women's Law Journal* reported that during the Vietnam War in the late

---

[120] Alfred W. McCoy, *The Politics of Heroin: Complicity in the Global Drug Trade*, Lawrence Hill Books, an imprint of Chicago Review Press, 2003, p. 17.
[121] Ibid., p. 128.

1960s, sex tourism and child prostitution had become popular in the Philippines and Thailand.[122]

The CIA is capable of things so unspeakably evil that the average person would probably prefer not even to know about them. In September 2002, Pakistani intelligence agents took two boys, Yousef al-Khalid, 9, and his little brother Abed al-Khalid, 7, from an apartment in Karachi, Pakistan, and later handed them over to the CIA. The CIA then flew the boys to a secret location in the United States for interrogation.[123] The father of the abducted children, Khalid Sheikh Mohammed, subsequently confessed under torture to the crimes of 9/11, plotting to blow up the Panama Canal, plotting to kill Pope John Paul II, and to numerous other crimes. The fate of his two children held by the CIA is unknown, and no one is asking about them.

If the CIA had targeted Merton for assassination, it surely knew that it could count on its friends in the Thai police to do whatever was necessary to facilitate and conceal it. Falsifying documents to make it appear that an autopsy had been performed or declaring that an assassination was "cardiac failure" would have been more business as usual.

---

[122] Kathy J. Steinman, "Sex Tourism and the Child: Latin America's and the United States' Failure to Prosecute Sex Tourists," *Hastings Law Journal*, Jan. 1, 2002, Vol. 13, p. 56.

[123] "Olga Craig, CIA has 2 Sons of the 9/11 Architect," *Washington Times*, p. 1, March 9, 2003; David Martin, "Do We Still Have Khalid Sheikh Mohammed's Sons"
http://www.dcdave.com/article5/070318.htm

CHAPTER 7

Things Not Seen and Things Imagined

Without any evidence to rule out homicide, Merton's death should have been, and still should be, viewed as a homicide. A professional investigator's handbook cautions that people do horrifying things to one another, and they often use extreme measures to hide their actions. All possibilities should be considered and focus directed on the evidence. The truth is often beyond the "obvious." Evidence can be misunderstood or misinterpreted, but it does not lie.[124]

The police conclusion that "the dead priest" fainted is absurd and not based on the evidence. Dead people cannot faint. Had Merton died and then collided with the fan, it would have been far more likely that he would have landed on top of the fan instead of the fan landing on top of him. If

---

[124] Dean A. Bears, *Practical Handbook for Professional Investigators*, CRC Press 2014, Ch. 9 Death Investigation, p. 227.

Merton had grabbed the fan, there should have been some evidence of it.

Dr. Weist described the burns that she observed, and she did not report burns on Merton's hands. Say was very clear, "I don't remember seeing the hands of Merton burned at all" and he added, "Definitely, I do not remember seeing any burn in his palms."[125] Donovan could not confirm or deny the burns on Merton's hands. He was certain that if Merton had been touching the fan or had pulled it onto himself in falling, his hands would not have been in the position where they were found.[126]

De Grunne was unable to recall anything specific. When Moffitt asked him if he saw burns on Merton's hands, de Grunne said only that there were too many people in the room for him to see anything when he returned from the main building.[127] De Grunne, the first to see Merton on the floor, offered no comments on his observations of Merton's body.

Evidence that is not present can be as important as evidence that is present in determining what happened. The evidence does not support the popular story that Merton

---

[125] Celestine Say, letter to John Moffitt, Dec. 11, 1969, the Merton Center.

[126] Egbert Donovan, letter to John Moffitt, Dec. 5, 1969, Mott Collection.

[127] François de Grunne, letter to John Moffitt, November 28, 1969, Moffitt papers.

grabbed the fan. If Merton did not place the fan on himself, then someone else placed it on him.

Dr. Nakvachara explained the fan being on top of Merton simply by declaring that the victim placed the fan on top of himself when he died of a heart attack. There is no evidence to support this. There is also no evidence to rule out the possibility that someone else placed the electrified fan on top of Merton. The first priority in the investigation should have been to look into that possibility.

Missing evidence can be revealing. In the highly suspicious death of Deputy White House Counsel Vincent W. Foster, Jr., according to the testimony of witness Patrick Knowlton, Foster's car was not at the park where his body was found. [128] The absence of Mr. Foster's car was corroborated by the descriptions given by other witnesses. The fact that his car was not there proves that he did not drive to the scene and commit suicide.

In the case of Merton's death, there is no evidence that he grabbed the fan. Say did not hear a "shout" or the sound of a "heavy object falling," because these sounds, in all probability, never happened. The stories of these sounds appear to have been invented by de Grunne. But he could not keep his story straight about what sound he heard or when he heard it, completely destroying his credibility.

---

[128] Volume 2 Appendix, The Report on the Death of Vincent W. Foster, Jr. by the Office of Independent Counsel In re: Madison Guaranty Savings & Loan.

Missing, too, is evidence that Merton was alone when he died. Who might have been responsible for the bleeding wound in the back of Merton's head? The Thai police didn't have to address that question because, as we have noted, they left out any mention of it, as did the death certificate and doctor's certificate.

One witness, Donovan, was suspicious of the death scene from the beginning, and he is left completely out of the police report.

At the request of Weakland, two Trappist monks, Abbot Joachim Murphy, O.C.S.O., from New Zealand, and Fr. Anselm Parker, O.C.S.O., from Australia, along with Dr. Weist, dressed Merton and placed him on his bed.[129] Weakland wrote that there had been a gash on the back of Merton's head, but later he said that he never saw it.[130] Rather, he only remembered that Dr. Weist had told him that there was such a wound.[131] Since no autopsy had been performed, we do not know if there were additional injuries or what might have caused the bleeding head wound. The police simply ignored this vital evidence.

The most important missing evidence is the autopsy. If Merton had suffered wounds that were inconsistent with the official cause of death, this evidence is missing, because the

---

[129] Celestine Say, letter to Flavian Burns, Mar. 18, 1969, the Merton Center.
[130] Rembert Weakland, "Merton the Pilgrim" in Wilkes, op. cit.
[131] Hugh Turley telephone interview of Rembert Weakland, June 10, 2017.

police and the abbey leadership did not even bother to look for it.

The day following Merton's death, plants that were in front of the windows of the cottage were removed and the soil was changed. An interpreter told Fr. Say that this was done because the Thai people were superstitious.[132] The entire cottage was scrubbed from top to bottom. If there had been any evidence or footprints of an assailant it was immediately destroyed.

The partition that separated Merton's room from the parlor was completely removed. Merton's bed and furnishings were replaced with a couple of tables and a dozen chairs making the space appear to be a meeting room. Photographs of the cottage taken the day after Merton's death are available at the Merton Center at Bellarmine University. Any evidence remaining at the crime scene had been destroyed less than 24 hours after Dr. Nakvachara had declared the cause of Merton's death "cardiac failure."

Since Merton's death, quite a bit of new "evidence" has been manufactured. In one instance, the manufacture seems to have been accidental. That is the evidence of Merton's badly burned face.

"Evidence" of Merton's badly burned face

Fr. John Eudes Bamberger said that there were burns over the right side of Merton's face from the fan, so that the Abbot

---

[132] Celestine Say, letter to Flavian Burns, Mar. 18, 1969, the Merton Center.

of Gethsemani could not identify Merton when he viewed the body.[133] He wrote that in April of 2012, and this invites the question: Who first reported that Merton's face was badly burned?

The police did not report any burns on Merton's face. The Thai doctor's report did not mention any facial burns. None of the first witnesses, Haas, Donovan, de Grunne, or Say, mentioned seeing any burns on Merton's face. Doctor Weist, who examined Merton's body, including his eyes with a flashlight, did not say that there were burns on Merton's face. How could Merton's face have been so badly burned as to make him unrecognizable to Abbot Flavian when no one else noticed even the slightest burn?

The answer is to be found in a typographical error in Mott's biography of Merton, published in 1984. The error surfaced sixteen years after Merton died and has since become another of the "facts" about Merton's "accidental death." In his endnote number 464, Mott misquoted the following statement by Dr. Weist: "I was convinced that it was due to an electric shock by the fan." Mott mistakenly transcribed the word "fan" as "face." Mott's error made it appear that Dr. Weist thought Merton's death was caused by an electric shock by the "face."

Mott was the authorized biographer with access to documents that no one else could see, so his writing was accepted as fact. His small typographical error in transcribing what Dr. Weist had written became the popular

---

[133] Fr. John Eudes Bamberger, email to Hugh Turley, April 2, 2012.

"truth" for those repeating Mott's story of Merton's accidental death.

In 2006, Marquette University Press published a Merton biography by Joan C. McDonald in which she paraphrased Mott's account of Merton's death. McDonald, as is more than apparent, could not have studied the source documents on Merton's death. If she had done so, she would have discovered Dr. Weist's report. The depth of her research was only to look at Mott's endnotes in which she found Mott's error in quoting Dr. Weist about a shock by the "face." McDonald paraphrased the error to make it her own. She wrote that the physician who examined Merton pronounced him dead by a shock "to" the face. Dr. Weist's "shock by the fan," became Mott's "shock by the face," and McDonald fashioned this into "shock to the face."[134] We shall examine more about McDonald's biography of Merton later.

Mott's popular biography became the accepted source for what had happened. The burns on Merton's face did not appear in the literature until after the publication of Mott's book. After Mott, the burns on Merton's face were mentioned by others, but rarely were the burns so bad that they made Merton unrecognizable.

In 1993, Sister Bernadette M. Smeyers wrote about the vigil kept with Merton's body. She did not remember Merton's face being disfigured. Smeyers wrote about reciting

---

[134] Joan C. McDonald, *Thomas Merton A Personal Biography*, Marquette University Press, 2006, p. 441.

the psalms and rosary and how comforting it was to see the peaceful expression on Merton's partially burnt face.[135]

In 1998, another sister wrote that Merton's face had become very dark, but that his face was the same and recognizable as Thomas Merton.[136] And another sister wrote that Merton appeared to be sleeping, very calm, almost smiling.[137] Moffitt wrote that there wasn't any sign of pain on Merton's face.[138] Weakland, who anointed Merton, said his face was not burned at all.[139]

Dr. Weist's drawing of the crime scene is evidence that the fan had not burned Merton's face:

---

[135] Sister Bernadette M. Smeyers, "Thomas Merton and Bangkok a Few Reminiscences," 8-15 December 1968, *The Merton Seasonal*, Summer/Autumn 1993, p. 16.

[136] Sr. Teresita D'Silva, O.S.B., "Bangkok Diary" - Dec. 1968, *The Merton Seasonal*, Winter 1998, p. 9

[137] Marie de la Croix, "The Last Days of Thomas Merton," op. cit. p.5.

[138] John Moffitt's Reflections on the death of Thomas Merton to John Howard Griffin and Brother Patrick Hart (not to be shared with others), undated, Mott Collection.

[139] Hugh Turley telephone interview of Rembert Weakland, June 10, 2017.

Dr. Weist's drawing of the fan on top of Merton

As we shall see later, photographic evidence shows conclusively that no part of the fan was near Merton's face or that his face was burned.

In the short note written by Fr. Eudes in 1968, on the tag on Merton's coffin, he said that he was readily able to identify Merton's bloated and swollen body. Fr. Eudes wrote nothing about any burns on Merton's face in 1968. In the same year that Mott's book came out, a very nice essay by Fr. Eudes about Merton was also published. Fr. Eudes clearly knew Merton well. He wrote about identifying Merton's body and about the note that he had written in 1968.[140] He made no mention of any burns on the face. Fr. Eudes is also trained as a physician, so he surely would have noticed burns on the right side of Merton's face when identifying him.

---

[140] John Eudes Bamberger, "Merton the Monk," in Wilkes, op. cit.

What could explain Sr. Smeyers writing about Merton's burned face and Fr. Eudes writing, in due time, that Merton had burns over the right side of his face so that the abbot could not recognize him? Perhaps after reading some of the articles and books following Mott's biography, they believed that there was a shock on the face. Having seen Merton's face, they may have convinced themselves that if others had seen burns on the face, they must have seen burns, too. Sr. Smeyers seemed less sure, writing that the face was only partly burned. Fr. Eudes, although speaking with the authority of a physician who had identified the body, still managed to get it wrong as well. It is human nature to see and believe what others believe, and sometimes that includes errors.

Most people are inclined to go along with whatever is popular, and Mott's authorized biography of Merton was very popular. The story that Merton accidentally killed himself, in fact, has become a popular story. St. Augustine wrote:

> Truth is loved is such a way that those who love some other thing want it to be the truth, and precisely because they do not wish to be deceived, are unwilling to be convinced that they are deceived.

People loved Mott's authorized story that Merton had accidentally electrocuted himself in such a way that they wanted it to be the truth. It is easier to go along with the popular view than to suffer the disapproval of others. Sr. Smeyers and Fr. Eudes may have convinced themselves that they saw burns where there clearly were none.

The strongest evidence that there were never any burns on the right side of Merton's face is a photograph taken by Say immediately upon the discovery of the body and before anything was disturbed. The right side of Merton's face is clearly visible in the photograph, and the fan is not near his face. This photo is irrefutable evidence that the right side of Merton's face was not burned. Originally it was underexposed, but with digital imaging technology the photograph was made visible in 2017. We shall say more later about what this important photograph shows.[141]

---

[141] Celestine Say, photograph taken of Merton's body on December 10, 2017, John Howard Griffin Collection, Box 14, folder 511, Butler Library, Columbia University.

CHAPTER 8

François de Grunne

As for Fr. de Grunne, he gave me the creeps.
– Dom Celestine Say[142]

As poor witnesses and suspicious characters in the Merton death case go, no one compares to Fr. François de Grunne. At the very least, one may describe him as enigmatic, if not downright strange.

Not only do we have his many contradictions with others, and even himself, but he "was nervous and fidgeting the entire time" when he was interviewed by Thai police, according to Celestine Say in a letter to Abbot Flavian.[143] Later, writing to Griffin, Say described de Grunne during the

---

[142] Celestine Say, letter to John Howard Griffin, June 25, 1969, Columbia University.
[143] Celestine Say, letter to Flavian Burns, Mar. 18, 1969, the Merton Center.

police interview as being "extremely nervous."[144] After Say was interviewed, the police asked de Grunne to stay and he "almost blew his top."

The fact that the abbey leadership withheld from Moffitt de Grunne's statement to the police makes it even more difficult to get a handle on the man and what he observed from the time he was the last person to see Merton alive until he was the first person to see his dead body. The statement of Say, the other key witness at the cottage where Merton died, is also unavailable, but, as we have seen, the letters that he wrote about what he observed have been a veritable gold mine.

Most intriguingly, Michael Mott, in the passage of the Merton biography in which he talks about de Grunne hearing a cry and the sound of something falling around 3:00 p.m. and de Grunne responding to it by going downstairs and knocking on Merton's door, references the Thai police report, but then he adds that more support for this account can be found in the letters that de Grunne sent to John Moffitt in 1969. This reference sent us on a mission to the library of the University of Virginia, where Moffitt's papers are housed.

We found eleven letters, all written in very good English. Nine of them have 1969 dates, the first on January 10 and the last on November 28. They are extraordinary and they are revealing, but not at all in the way that we had hoped that they would be. The contrast with what Say has written is stark. Say, quite understandably, seems to have been

---

[144] Celestine Say, letter to John Howard Griffin, June 25, 1969, Columbia University.

traumatized by the experience of the great Thomas Merton having died mysteriously in the room right next to him. He writes in meticulous detail about it. One gathers that he is trying desperately to make sense of it. That is in no way the case with de Grunne.

The first of de Grunne's letters, the one dated January 10, is in response to a December 30 letter from Moffitt (which we do not have), and it finds de Grunne almost giddy with excitement. He is thrilled at having heard from Moffitt, happy that Moffitt had a nice trip to Japan—apparently on his way back from the conference—and delighted at what a great success the Bangkok conference was. He concludes with a reference to the delightful time that he had with Moffitt there and wishes him a happy New Year.

One gathers that the death of a mosquito, smacked on the face of a conference attendee, might have made as much of an impression on de Grunne as did Merton's death. The typewritten letter is a page in length, and Merton's name doesn't appear in it.

It's almost as peculiar and apparently unfeeling as his inquiry to Donovan and Haas if they had had a good swim before informing them that Merton appeared to be in a bit of trouble back in his room. The only difference between the de Grunne of the letters and the de Grunne of December 10, 1968, is that the earlier agitation or nervousness is absent. The de Grunne of the letters appears to be at full peace with the world. He continues in the same vein with a letter to Moffitt on January 28, which is mainly touristy, reflecting happily on the many beautiful sites they saw and photographs they took during their Southeast Asia sojourn, with a mention of the two other favorite topics he likes to discuss with Moffitt, Hinduism and Moffitt's poetry.

Moffitt is treated to more of the same from de Grunne with three similarly cheerful and chatty letters in February of 1969. De Grunne's first mention of Merton is in a letter in March, but it is only in general terms, referring to Moffitt's writing about Merton, along with some theological conjecture. Still, he says nothing about Merton's untimely death. That doesn't come until July 6. It is clear that he is responding to a direct inquiry from Moffitt about what he witnessed on December 10, and here the note of agitation reappears. He apologizes without explanation for the fact that he is able to answer in only the most cursory fashion and then proceeds to downplay his own involvement in the Merton death drama.

Rather than tell Moffitt what he had witnessed, de Grunne recommends that Moffitt ask Mother Pia, who was not a witness in the cottage, as the authority on Merton's death, and, as we have seen, that is what Moffitt did.

De Grunne minimized his importance by telling Moffitt that all that he had heard was a sound and there were lots of noises from a nearby house. He told Moffitt that he was not especially concerned about that noise, but that he later went to check to see if *Say* was all right, since he had heard him taking a bath and splashing!!! De Grunne added that he had later gone to ask Merton for the key to the cottage, and when no one answered, he peeked inside and saw the fan lying on Merton.[145]

We hardly need to remind readers that this account not only fails to lend support to the police report as Mott claims that it does, but it is also inconsistent with everything everyone else had said previously about de Grunne's words and actions, including de Grunne, himself.

Also, in contrast to the narratives of Say, Donovan, and Weist, de Grunne's letter to Moffitt fails to mention the times of any events. De Grunne does not say what time he and Merton arrived at the cottage, when he heard the sound, or when he discovered Merton on the floor.

Say narrowed the time down of when de Grunne asked him about the shout while brushing his teeth to between 1:55 and 2:15 p.m. It was an hour and a half later, he said, when de Grunne found Merton on the floor.

De Grunne told Moffitt only that it was upon the occasion of his going to Merton's room to ask for the key, sometime after he had heard the now nondescript and negligible noises, when he discovered Merton on the floor. The room was locked and no one answered, so he looked inside and saw Merton on the floor with the fan. He then went to tell Say and others.

De Grunne declared in his letter to Moffitt that the cause of Merton's death was the fan and nothing else. As evidence, he said that that is what Mother Pia had told him.

---

[145] François de Grunne, letter to John Moffitt, July 6, 1969, Moffitt papers.

Others were puzzled and expected that an autopsy would determine the cause of death. Only de Grunne knew without any doubt that the fan alone had caused Merton's death, and never, in any correspondence that we have been able to find, did he demonstrate any interest in whether or not there had been an autopsy.

After placing the blame for Merton's death on the fan, de Grunne said that nothing had been said about it because no one wanted to blame the Thai people for their defective fan after they had been so hospitable.[146] De Grunne reinforced his tale by adding that trucks loaded with smaller fans arrived on the last day of the conference to replace all the large killer fans. Moffitt would learn that this story by de Grunne was not true, because Griffin later wrote to him that in the spring of 1969, Penn Jones, Jr. (more about him later) photographed the room where Merton had died. A Hitachi fan was there that looked just like the fan that lay across Merton in Say's death-scene photograph.[147]

Not only did Jones see no evidence of the fans' replacement, but no other witness reported the replacement of all the fans, either. Prudently, neither Moffitt nor Mott repeated this story publicly.

Moffitt appeared to do his best to use the rapport that he had established with de Grunne to attempt to get a straight

---

[146] François de Grunne, letter to John Moffitt, July 6, 1969, Moffitt papers.

[147] John Howard Griffin, letter to John Moffitt, December 5, 1969, Moffitt papers.

answer from the last man to see Merton alive and would have even heard Merton's last words. On November 28, 1969, de Grunne responded to an inquiry by Moffitt about when he and Merton arrived at the cottage. In a characteristic brusque and unhelpful answer, de Grunne told Moffitt that he could not recall the time that he and Merton had gone to the cottage, but he did not think that it was late.[148]

Unfortunately, there is no record of what de Grunne and Merton talked about when they were walking to the cottage, nor have we been able to find out if Moffitt ever asked de Grunne that. What we do know is that Merton's last words on earth were not, "I will now disappear," which he said at the conclusion of his presentation. Rather, Merton's last words were whatever he said to de Grunne as they entered the cottage, as witnessed by Say from some distance behind them.

That November 28, 1969, letter was apparently the last one that Moffitt would get from de Grunne for a long time. We found one later letter, dated February 18, 1973, and it doesn't get close to any topic related to Merton.

One other outlier might be worthy of comment. That is the letter dated August 6, 1968, which would have been several months before the Bangkok conference. It is unclear from the letter if Moffitt and de Grunne already knew one another or if de Grunne is just responding with praise for something that Moffitt has written. If they knew one another,

---

[148] François de Grunne, letter to John Moffitt, November 28, 1969, Moffitt papers.

we have to wonder how it was that this Belgian monk and New York magazine editor might have made one another's acquaintance. We also have to wonder how it happened that they should occupy the same cottage with one another and with Merton and that Moffitt should have chosen to take off that fateful afternoon to go sightseeing. Merton was hosting a discussion session beginning at 4:30 p.m. that afternoon, and he was the conference's main attraction. As a journalist covering the conference, Moffitt would have seemed to have a responsibility to be there, but he said that he didn't return to the conference center until 5:30 p.m.[149]

Griffin and Moffitt confided in each other that there were significant differences between the accounts of Say and de Grunne. Griffin wrote to Moffitt that Say was very suspicious of de Grunne. After Say had told Griffin that de Grunne gave him the creeps, Griffin defended de Grunne, telling Moffitt

---

[149] John Moffitt, *A New Charter for Monasticism*, op. cit., p.7. Moffitt had gone to visit a pagoda with Sr. Marie de la Croix and five others from the conference (John Moffitt, letter to Brother Patrick Hart, February 8, 1970, Moffitt papers). Sr. Marie reported, however, that they returned from the visit to the pagoda at 4:00 p.m., which seems more likely, since the conference was to resume at 4:30, and they would not have wanted to miss any of it (Marie de la Croix, "The Last Days of Thomas Merton," five-page narrative in French). If Moffitt was not candid about his actual time of return, one must wonder why and also where he was when Merton's body was discovered and who told him about the death.

that he had read a great deal by him and had found him to be an impressive and stable person.[150] It is hard to believe that Griffin had read a great deal of de Grunne's writings because he actually wrote very little. Griffin's professed admiration for the most unreliable witness makes Griffin himself appear dubious.

Further insight into de Grunne's nature is revealed in a confidential letter from Moffitt to Griffin that we found among Griffin's papers at Columbia University. Moffitt told Griffin that Fr. Jean Leclercq had been his overnight guest and Leclercq confirmed his view that Say could be trusted completely while de Grunne was unreliable. Moffitt confided to Griffin that de Grunne had a history of mental instability and was an extremely nervous man.[151] It is not surprising that in a letter to Griffin, Say used the same words, "extremely nervous," to describe de Grunne.[152]

Moffitt also shared with Griffin some new information about de Grunne concerning the day prior to Merton's death. Moffitt revealed that on that day, de Grunne had also paced nervously back and forth and was opening and closing his door. Moffitt told Griffin that de Grunne was extremely

---

[150] Celestine Say, letter to John Howard Griffin, June 25, 1969, Coumbia University; John Howard Griffin, letter to John Moffitt, August 18, 1969, Moffitt papers.
[151] John Moffitt, letter to John Howard Griffin, August 31, 1969, Columbia University.
[152] Celestine Say, letter to John Howard Griffin, June 25, 1969, Columbia University.

distraught the day before when there was nothing to be distraught about.[153]

Moffitt could have been mistaken that de Grunne had nothing to be distraught about the day before. His actions were that of a distraught, or at least a very wrought up person, the afternoon of Merton's death before the body was discovered. If de Grunne knew that Merton's death was coming in advance, he could very well have been distraught, or at least anxious.

In closing his letter to Griffin, Moffitt returned to the subject of de Grunne and Leclercq, saying that *de Grunne's mental history had been that of an unstable man.* Moffitt, as de Grunne's friend, also tried to excuse de Grunne's behavior. Moffitt speculated that de Grunne might have had feelings of overwhelming guilt for not having acted swiftly to save Merton.

Moffitt may have correctly concluded that de Grunne's behavior indicated feelings of guilt, but his speculation as to why de Grunne would have such feelings did not entertain the possibility of foreknowledge of Merton's death. Advance knowledge would go a long way toward explaining his behavior the day before and the day of Merton's death before the body was discovered.

We made several attempts to contact The Abbey of St. Andre in Bruges, Belgium, de Grunne's home abbey, to learn what had become of him. They have told us virtually nothing about François de Grunne, not even to say if he is still living.

---

[153] John Moffitt, letter to John Howard Griffin, August 31, 1969, Columbia University.

De Grunne has simply disappeared and his life after the conference remains a mystery.

One Benedictine monk explained the silence from The Abbey of St. Andre by saying that, sadly, even in his own community, there have been some men whom they would prefer the public not know about.[154] This source has also learned that when de Grunne returned from Bangkok in 1968, he told the monks at St. Andre that his room was next to Merton's, and after dinner Merton went to his room to rest. After a while de Grunne heard a cry once and nothing more, so he felt no need to investigate further. That was all De Grunne told them.[155] This second-hand account, if accurate, would be yet another contradictory story from de Grunne.

---

[154] Confidential source to authors.
[155] Confidential source to authors.

Part 2. The Authorized Conclusion: Accident

The Real Rashomon Effect

"I'll always tell the truth," he said.
"I swear and hope to die."
And that is what he always did
When he had no reason to lie.

David Martin

Celestine Say with Thomas Merton on the morning of
December 10, 1968, the day of Merton's death

CHAPTER 9

The Myth around Merton's Death

The popular belief of how Merton died

The official Thai conclusion of heart failure has been, for all practical purposes, ignored. The official website of the Abbey of Gethsemani, in a statement by Brother Patrick Hart, states flatly, "Merton died by accidental electrocution in Bangkok, Thailand."[156] The first American news reports are the origin of the story that Merton was accidentally electrocuted. A few years later, the accidental electrocution of Thomas Merton became associated with a shower or bath, probably to make the electrocution appear more plausible. For years, secondary sources have told and retold this story of Merton's death. A search of books, articles and newspapers yields examples like these:

---

[156] http://www.monks.org/index.php/monks-pages/thomas-merton

- "Merton slipped on the wet bathroom floor after he took a shower and he grabbed a fan for balance and was electrocuted."

- "…when climbing out of his bath he was accidentally electrocuted by a fan."

- "…electrocuted by a fan after taking a shower."

- "…Merton took a shower and while doing this accidentally electrocuted himself,"

- "Around 1:30 in the afternoon Merton showered and was electrocuted trying to move a large electric fan…"

- "…He had taken a shower and was electrocuted accidentally when he bumped into an old electric fan…"

- "…he touched a live wire in a floor lamp after taking a shower and died by an electric shock on December 5th"

Authors routinely construct their own creative descriptions of Merton's death using any words they prefer, such as bath, tub, shower, grabbed, slipped, touched, moved, lamp, fan, wire, etc. Exaggerating and getting dates wrong are acceptable scholarship. The only formula that authors need follow is to say that Merton accidentally killed himself.

There is absolutely no evidence that Merton took a bath or shower. All the evidence, in fact, is to the contrary. The origins of these false stories are instructive.

No shower in early reports

The first news reports of Merton's death did not include any mention that he had taken a shower. The official reports from the Thai authorities said nothing about a bath or a shower. The popular story that water was involved in Merton's electrocution was likely invented because it is common knowledge that touching an electric appliance while in a bath or shower can be fatal. On the other hand, a fatal electrocution from simply touching a household appliance is virtually unheard of. The story that Merton was electrocuted from touching a fan while wet from a shower is particularly vile and insidious because it manages to blame a likely assassination victim of killing himself through his own carelessness.

January 18, 1969, one month after Merton died, the first detailed article about his death was published, and that was in the Philippines. The account was based on the accounts of two Filipino priests who had attended the Bangkok conference, Fathers Bernardo Perez and Celestine Say.[157] The story reported that the cause of death, according to the

---

[157] Abraham C. Florendo, "The Final Ascent on the Seven Storey Mountain," *Mirror*, Jan. 18, 1969, pp. 10-11, the Merton Center.

Thai authorities, was heart failure. The article said nothing about Merton taking a shower. Later accounts by John Moffitt also made no mention of any shower.

Moffitt published two articles on Merton's death, the first was in *The Catholic World* and the other was in his report on the Monastic conference, *A New Charter for Monasticism*. [158] *The Catholic World* article, published in July of 1969, filled in some of the details. However, it included a number of errors and omissions. Moffitt reported the Thai doctor's conclusion of a heart attack and added the possibility that Merton had somehow been electrocuted, without speculating how.

Although he was a journalist, Moffitt's reporting on Merton's death might best be described as a day late and a dollar short. He did not say how he had heard that Merton had been electrocuted, and he offered no theory as to how the fan had landed on top of him. Moffitt prefaced his remarks on Merton's death by saying that since he was living in the same cottage where Merton had died, it may be appropriate for him to tell what he knew of the accident. Moffitt knew that the Thai doctor concluded heart attack as the cause, yet Moffitt called Merton's death an accident. Moffitt was unable to say how the accident occurred, and he offered no evidence that would rule out homicide.

---

[158] John Moffitt, "Thomas Merton the Last Three Days," *The Catholic World*, July 1969, pp.160-163. Moffitt also briefly mentioned Merton's death in an article, "New Charter For Monasticism," *America*, January 18, 1969.

Moffitt gave more details about Merton's death in his 1970 book, referenced at the beginning of Chapter One, but he furnished no new useful information. A few things are worth mentioning in Moffitt's reports. None of them said that Merton took a shower. The shower story had not yet surfaced. In fact, in 1970, Moffitt told Brother Patrick of the Gethsemani Abbey in a letter that the best evidence showed that Merton did not take a shower.[159]

In none of his published accounts did Moffitt mention the bleeding wound on the back of Merton's head, although he knew about Dr. Weist's report describing such a wound.

Moffitt concluded his final description of Merton's death by quoting Mother Pia. She believed that no one could be certain of the cause of Merton's death. Mother Pia thought that maybe the cause was a heart attack or perhaps electrocution and probably both. She speculated that Merton fainted and when falling he dragged the fan and somehow broke it so that it became short-circuited. She was satisfied that it was just a mysterious death and blamed Merton's clumsiness for damaging the fan and killing himself.

Abbot Flavian Burns and disinformation

Brother Patrick and Abbot Flavian contacted Moffitt between his two accounts of Merton's death. First, Brother

---

[159] John Moffitt, letter to Brother Patrick Hart, February 8, 1970, Moffitt papers.

Patrick wrote to Moffitt complimenting him on his article.[160] Brother Patrick said that Moffitt's *Catholic World* article helped him to correct a few difficulties in his thinking. It is hard to imagine how it helped Brother Patrick's thinking because Moffitt's article relied on statements from François de Grunne that were in conflict with Celestine Say's more consistent and reliable account.

It should be noted that in his article Moffitt concealed the names of the key witnesses Say, Haas, and De Grunne by calling them "the prior," "the abbot," and "the monk." Otherwise in his article, Moffitt gives the names of conference attendees quite specifically. Moffitt shared the cottage with two of the witnesses, and he knew exactly who they were, but he kept this information from the readers of *The Catholic World*. Moffitt also concealed the fact that the accounts of the two witnesses, Say and de Grunne, were very different. Moffitt also wrote erroneously that Haas entered Merton's room through a front window.

When Brother Patrick wrote to Moffitt, the abbey had already received the police report. Only people that Abbot Flavian and Brother Patrick deemed authorized could see certain materials like the police report and the death scene photograph that the abbey held.

On December 15, 1969, Abbot Flavian wrote a letter to Moffitt offering his guesses for the cause of the accident, and he introduced the idea that perhaps Merton bathed and tried

---

[160] Brother Patrick Hart, letter to John Moffitt, August 22, 1969, Moffitt papers.

to move the fan closer to his bed.[161] He told Moffitt that the best they could do was to guess, without telling Moffitt that he had a Thai death certificate with a heart-failure cause of death. Abbot Flavian guessed that the shock knocked Merton down and the force of the fall freed his hands from the fan.

Abbot Flavian, with his "guesses," was trying to induce Moffit to write things that the abbot had to have known were not true. Abbot Flavian had Say's letter that he had received in March with the photograph, so he would have known that Merton did not bathe in the shorts that he had on in the death-scene photograph. The police report had arrived at the abbey in August. That report, as contradictory of the witnesses as it might have been, was in agreement with them in that it made no mention of any possibility that Merton might have taken a shower at any time after he had returned to the cottage.

Abbott Flavian told Moffitt that he had made his guesses only after reading and rereading the reports of those who first found Merton. But Say made no mention of Merton bathing in his letter to Abbot Flavian, nor did de Grunne, Haas, Donovan, or Dr. Weist say anything about Merton having showered before he was found dead. Nevertheless, Abbot Flavian told Moffitt that his guess was that Merton undressed, possibly bathed, and tried to move the fan. The abbot knew that Merton was not undressed in the sense of when a person

---

[161] Flavian Burns, letter to John Moffitt, December 15, 1969, Moffitt papers.

is bathing. The meaning of the term "undressed" in terms of when a person is bathing means to be naked.

Abbot Flavian also told Moffitt that there was no fuse system at the cottage where Merton was staying. But the police report and eyewitness reports said nothing about fuses. Abbot Flavian was feeding Moffitt false information about a bath and a fuse system. The abbot did not provide Moffitt with any evidence from any documents or sources to support his guesses that Merton bathed and that there were no fuses. The abbot made no mention of the photograph. Moffitt and Abbot Flavian had both seen Say's photograph of Merton dressed in his shorts.

Moffitt's own separate knowledge probably made him favor Mother Pia's guesses over Abbot Flavian's guesses that Merton possibly bathed in his final theory on Merton's death, published in 1970. It is to Moffitt's credit that he did not buy in to the abbot's suggestions of Merton undressing and bathing or that there weren't any fuses. The abbot's private suggestions that Merton took a shower or bath remained private.

Nevertheless, against all evidence, the story that Merton showered and accidentally electrocuted himself would eventually become the authorized story, believed by almost everyone. Abbot Flavian's story that there was no fuse system was never mentioned again. That whopper was probably too easily verifiable as false, so it was abandoned.

Given the choice between the heart attack conclusion of the Thai authorities and the accidental electrocution of the original press reports, the abbey leadership came down foursquare on the side of the latter. In fact, they went even further, blaming Merton for causing the accident when in 1973, they would put out the story publicly—and over Moffitt's objections— that Merton had taken a shower and had accidentally electrocuted himself.

CHAPTER 10

Building on the Myth

The Asian Journal of Thomas Merton

The Asian Journal of Thomas Merton, copyrighted by The Trustees of the Merton Legacy Trust and New Directions Publishing Corporation in 1973, provided the first public report that Merton had taken a shower before his accident. Edited by Naomi Burton Stone, Brother Patrick Hart, and James Laughlin, the book is the record of Merton's final trip to Asia from his diaries. Appendix VIII of the book is represented as a copy of a letter from six Trappists to Abbot Flavian Burns, dated December 11, 1968, informing the abbey of Merton's death. We mentioned earlier that this letter, purportedly by six Trappists at the Bangkok conference, was mailed out by the abbey on December 19, 1968, in response to requests for details about Merton's death. The copy of this letter in the book gives their names for the first time. The letter only speculated about possible causes and stated that the exact cause of death was hard to determine.

This speculation only underscores the fact that the monks had buried Merton on December 17 without knowing the cause of his death. However, Brother Patrick Hart strongly suggested in the postscript—with "new evidence"—that the cause of Merton's death was a settled fact.

The Trappists

The first mention of the possible shower by Merton appeared in that December 11, 1968, private letter to Abbot Flavian at Gethsemani from the "six Trappists," which, as noted earlier, the abbot made at least semi-public eight days later. Appendix VIII is represented as a verbatim copy of that letter, but in fact, it is not.[162] It differs only in its obviously intentional omission of three important words. The original unpublished letter said that Merton was found, after he had taken a mid-day nap, lying on his back on the floor *in his pajamas*.[163]

In a volume in which the story that Merton was wet from a shower was to be introduced, those pajamas on the dead body really had no place, so the three-word prepositional phrase revealing that Merton was not naked when he was

---

[162] Six Trappists letter to Flavian Burns, December 11, 1968, Appendix VIII, *The Asian Journal of Thomas Merton*, New Directions, 1973, pp. 344-347.

[163] Six Trappists letter to Flavian Burns, unpublished, December 11, 1968, the Merton Center.

found was simply removed, with no ellipsis left to mark the spot.

It's a great shame that it was taken out, because this is one of the few things in the newly highlighted letter that is accurate, at least as far as it goes. When we read "pajamas," we envision the nightclothes we wear when the weather is cold, covering the arms and the legs. In fact, it is quite likely that the shorts that Merton was wearing when his body was found were too long to be boxer-style underwear and were, in fact, the short bottoms of summer pajamas.

The letter mentioned wounds that were not consistent with electrocution or heart attack, specifically, the bleeding wound on the back of Merton's head and cuts on his right side and arm. The head wound is often dismissed as being caused by the floor when he fell. Though implausible, it might have been possible, but an autopsy was clearly called for to determine the cause of the head wound. The cuts to the arm and side are not so easily dismissed as being caused by the floor, however.

The letter, otherwise, is greatly oversold, clearly trotted out at this time only because it mentions the possibility that Merton took a shower. None of the six was an actual witness to the death scene, and the letter said only that Merton—most improbably—could have taken a shower before he had a heart attack while next to the fan and had somehow knocked it onto himself, or that he had been shocked to death by the fan while barefooted on a stone floor.

Such speculation may be considered as only natural for someone lacking precise knowledge of the case, because the idea of a person being fatally electrocuted by a household appliance in the absence of water is so outlandish. At this point the natural question that must come to anyone's mind should be, "But what did the autopsy show was the cause of death?" The letter, however, didn't tell us that there was no autopsy and neither did the covering "informational" letter that Abbot Flavian sent out with it on December 19, 1968.

The letter also failed to mention the names of any of the key witnesses or of the Thai investigative authorities.

Representing the letter to be from the six Trappist delegates was misleading, because, as we have noted, there were seven Trappists left at the conference after Merton died. One of the Trappists said that the conclusion that Merton's death was caused by a heart attack was only for convenience to avoid problems for the conference center and others and that no one believed it.[164]

Sr. de la Croix expected that an autopsy would be performed, and she knew that Dr. Weist had said that the cause of death was electrocution. Griffin, authorized by the abbot to see the police report and other private documents, contacted Sr. de la Croix by letter on August 8, 1969, to introduce himself as the official biographer. Griffin told her that he had access to the police report and other documents at the abbey.[165] He had read her 5-page memoir, "The Last Days of Thomas Merton," and he wanted to learn if she had

---

[164] Marie de la Croix, "The Last Days of Thomas Merton," op. cit., p. 5.
[165] John Howard Griffin, letter to Sr. Marie de la Croix, August 8, 1969, Columbia University.

any photographs of Merton's room or any other information. Griffin was interested to know if any witnesses were suspicious about Merton's death. He also wrote to Say and to de Grunne.[166]

Some statements in the letter by the six Trappists are clearly false. They wrote that when Merton was found, the fan was positioned across his chest. The abbot knew this was not true from the photograph that he had received from Say.

The letter from the Trappists also erred in saying that after Merton had gone to his room a shout was heard by others who were in the cottage but, after checking, they thought that they had only imagined the cry. Abbot Flavian also surely knew that this was false, because he had the summary police report and the letter from Say that he had received in March. Those documents made it unmistakable that only de Grunne said that he had heard a shout or a cry. There were no others. The only other person in the cottage was Say, in essentially the same room as Merton as far as the transmission of sound was concerned, and he never heard any such sound.

Not only the abbot, but also the editors of *The Asian Journal of Thomas Merton*, which included Brother Patrick Hart, surely knew that what was in this letter about the positioning of the fan and about the real or imagined shout was not accurate, and yet they permitted this misinformation to be printed without correction. Compared to their own wanton erasure of the evidence that Merton's body was at

---

[166] John Howard Griffin, letter to John Moffitt, August 11, 1969, Columbia University.

least partially clothed when it was found, though, these failures on their part may only be counted as peccadillos.[167] And the questionable nature of this letter hardly ends with these blatant errors, as we shall see later.

Brother Patrick Hart

Brother Patrick Hart, Merton's friend and secretary, wrote in 1973 in the postscript to *The Asian Journal of Thomas Merton* that the abbey had received a call from the U.S. Embassy in Thailand at noon on December 10, 1968, confirming that Thomas Merton had died of accidental

---

[167] If one looks at this letter as an attempt to provide information to a bereaved family, its shortcomings are even more obvious. The loved ones would be screaming for answers. Instead, the letter provides mainly maddening speculation, without even giving any clear idea as to what the speculation is based upon. Worse than that, it offers no avenue for learning more. In their desperation for more information, family members would want most of all to know who they might get it from. On that key point, the letter is silent, just as it is silent on the vital matter of an autopsy and the findings of the Thai police and medical authorities. The letter should be open ended, but, on the contrary, the writers give the impression that they are satisfied to accept the death as a mystery. One must wonder how they could know that the recipients of the letter would share their point of view and not react more naturally with anger and frustration.

electrocution at 2:00 p.m.[168] (Bangkok is 12 hours ahead of the abbey's time.) If true, this information places the embassy right in the forefront of the promotion of the accidental electrocution story, as though it were almost planned in advance to be the cause of death. It contradicts the finding of the Thai authorities that heart failure caused Merton's death, and it also contradicts what the Thai police's star witness, François de Grunne, told them about hearing a sound at around 3:00 p.m., indicating that something serious had happened in Merton's room at that time (although it is in accord with the 2:00 p.m. "time of the incident" in the police report's "Subject" line).

However, there are very good reasons to believe that what Brother Patrick wrote is not true. Before publishing, he had sent a draft version of his postscript to John Moffitt for review.[169] In the draft, he says that the abbey had learned from the phone call that the death had occurred at about 3:00 p.m. Bangkok time.[170]

This was in February of 1970, and by that time, Moffitt had seen the death scene photograph, the police report, and had carefully studied descriptions from eyewitnesses, so he was well qualified to offer advice. He also seemed to realize

---

[168] Brother Patrick Hart, Postscript, *The Asian Journal of Thomas Merton*, op. cit., p. 259.

[169] Brother Patrick Hart, letter to John Moffitt, February 5, 1970, Moffitt papers.

[170] Brother Patrick Hart, draft foreword and postscript for Asian Journal of Thomas Merton, January 1970, Moffitt papers.

that what Brother Patrick had written was not based upon any actual statement to the abbey from the embassy, because he proceeded to argue for changes in what Brother Patrick had written that the embassy had said. First, he suggested that Brother Patrick not say so declaratively that the cause of death was "accidental electrocution." Rather, he suggested, the statement should be qualified with an "apparently." Brother Patrick ignored that recommendation. Then, most crucially, Moffitt presented a well-reasoned argument based on the best available evidence that Merton had to have died closer to 2:00 p.m. after Merton and de Grunne had arrived at the cottage at about 1:50 p.m.[171]

Instead of offering what would seem to be the natural response that he could not very well change what he had been told by the embassy, Brother Patrick took Moffitt's advice on this one and simply changed the time of death, *as notified by that U.S. Embassy telephone call*, to an hour earlier than the time he had written in his draft.

More evidence that this information is not based upon a call from the U.S. Embassy is that Brother Patrick is also at odds with Abbot Flavian's account of the telephone conversation.[172] Abbot Flavian says that the call was from the abbey to the embassy and not the other way around. As mentioned earlier, Abbot Flavian also wrote that the embassy told him that Merton had died of an accident, with

---

[171] John Moffitt, letter to Brother Patrick Hart, February 8, 1970, Moffitt papers.

[172] Flavian Burns, "Merton the Monk," in Wilkes, op. cit.

no mention of electrocution, and he had no time of death in his report on the phone conversation.

That the embassy should be calling the death an accident at this early stage of the game would still be incriminating of them, considering the conflict with what the Thai authorities would report, but we also have to wonder if even what Abbot Flavian reported was true. After all, the Report of the Death of an American Citizen (Exhibit 8) issued by the embassy three days later on December 13 stated simply that the cause of death was "Sudden Heart Failure (according to official Death Certificate)."

Moving the time of death from 3:00 p.m. to 2:00 p.m. put Brother Patrick at odds with the apparently "authorized narrative," as reflected in the Thai Police Report, the U.S. Embassy Report on the Death of an American Citizen, and with Michael Mott's Merton biography eleven years later, and it still did not completely resolve Brother Patrick's conflict with Moffit. Moffitt had spent considerable time studying the witness accounts and had made up a chart with the times of the events. He had concluded that Merton left the dining hall at 1:40 p.m. to return to the cottage with de Grunne. Against Moffitt's advice, Brother Patrick ignored the best evidence and wrote that Merton returned to the cottage around 1:30 p.m., apparently so this would allow time for Merton to take that crucial shower before the new, adjusted time of death at 2:00 p.m.

Merton could not have returned to his cottage about 1:30 p.m. At 1:30 p.m. Merton was still in the main building at lunch. He did not leave to return to the cottage with de

Grunne until 1:40 p.m. and the cottage was a 10-15 minute walk so he would have returned closer to 2:00 p.m. Brother Patrick should have known this from having read the eyewitness accounts. He made it appear that Merton arrived at the cottage much earlier than he did.

Moffitt provided Brother Patrick with evidence that Merton did not take a shower, asking Brother Patrick what proof there was that Merton had, in fact, showered. In supporting his query, Moffitt quoted Say: "His body was not wet, and I thought that perhaps he must have been preparing to go to the bathroom for a shower."[173] Moffitt certainly knew from everything that Say had heard in the cottage that if Merton had taken a shower, Say would have heard it. Moffitt also knew that de Grunne, the other witness present in the cottage, never said Merton took a shower. Disregarding the evidence and sound reasoning from Moffitt that Merton had not showered, Brother Patrick left that misinformation in his postscript published by the Merton Legacy Trust.

Against Moffitt's much more knowledgeable counseling, Brother Patrick wrote with an authoritative voice that Merton had returned to the cottage around 1:30 p.m. and promptly took a shower. To make it appear to be a matter of fact, he prefaced his shower statement by saying that he had

---

[173] John Moffitt, letter to Brother Patrick Hart, February 8, 1970, Moffitt papers.

reviewed eyewitness accounts in addition to the official medical and police reports.[174]

As we have previously pointed out, the Thai police report had been sent to Abbot Flavian from the U.S. Embassy in Thailand on July 30, 1969. However, it was not until 1973 that its existence was revealed to the public, when Brother Patrick did so, apparently to build himself up as an expert on Merton's death.

Brother Patrick carefully crafted his narrative to establish the story that Merton was responsible for accidentally

---

[174] Brother Patrick Hart, Postscript, *The Asian Journal of Thomas Merton*, op. cit., pp. 258-259; We had wanted to use a long quote from Brother Patrick at this point in the narrative in which he states categorically that Merton took a shower. The use of such direct quotations requires permission from the publisher. We were granted permission, but only after payment of a fee, which, though customary (if optional), struck us as a bit above the going rate for such things, so we withdrew our request. More ominous from a legal standpoint was the publisher's added remark that any suggestion on our part that Brother Patrick has been less than completely truthful would incur the displeasure of the Merton Legacy Trust and the publishing company. We responded that we would gladly include whatever evidence the publisher would like to furnish in support of Brother Patrick's veracity, but, as of the time of publication, we have received no response. Brother Patrick's malleability over the question of what he says he was told by the embassy, in itself, suggests that his publisher has taken upon itself a very difficult assignment.

electrocuting himself. In the process, much like Moffitt, he left out the names of all of the witnesses by calling them two monks, the abbot, someone, a Korean prioress, and so on.

Brother Patrick even concealed the names of his Abbot, Flavian Burns, and Father John Eudes Bamberger who had identified Merton's body. Brother Patrick wrote only that when the casket was opened several of the monks identified Merton's body. It is hard to believe that Brother Patrick did not intentionally conceal the names of all of the witnesses.

Brother Patrick hid more than the names of witnesses. Truth can be concealed by errors of omission. That's why, when witnesses are sworn in a court of law they swear to tell the *whole* truth. Brother Patrick implied that he learned that Merton's death was caused by accidental electrocution based on his reading of the medical and police reports and the accounts of several eyewitnesses.

Brother Patrick had read the official Thai documents, so he knew that the doctor's certificate said that the primary cause of death was "acute cardiac failure," the death certificate said that the primary cause of death was "sudden heart failure," and that the police report said the primary cause was "heart failure." Brother Patrick simply covered up the official Thai cause of death. These inconvenient documents, we have discovered, are no longer to be found at the Abbey of Gethsemani.[175]

---

[175] Hugh Turley telephone interview with the abbey archivist, Brother Lawrence Morey, O.C.S.O., February 7, 2018. Br. Morey said the death certificate and doctor's certificate are not at the Abbey and

No witnesses or official reports said that the cause of death was "accidental electrocution." Dr. Weist concluded only that Merton was electrocuted, but she never called it an accident. Dr. Weist could not determine the cause of the electrocution. When it was decided to authorize the cause of death to be accidental there could have been concern about liability and negligence, but proving legal responsibility might have required that an autopsy be performed. Blaming the accident on Merton ingeniously removed any potential blame for the accident on others. As quickly as the authorized cause of death became an accident, the accident was concurrently blamed on Merton for taking a shower and then touching the fan.

We asked Brother Patrick, "What evidence exists that Merton actually took a shower?" Brother Patrick responded that there was no direct evidence of anyone saying that, but it was Bangkok at noon, it was very hot and steamy, and therefore Merton undoubtedly had taken a shower. [176] Brother Patrick admitted that he had no actual evidence for his shower story. However, it is a story that has been repeated in nearly every subsequent article and book that mentions Merton's death.

---

suggested we try might try the Merton Center. The Merton Center had not seen these documents until we provided them our copies from Archbishop Weakland and the National Archives in 2017.

[176] Brother Patrick Hart, voicemail to Hugh Turley, May 31, 2017, 2:14 pm.

In his effort to convince people that Merton electrocuted himself, Brother Patrick said that Merton apparently touched the fan to turn it on, but he omitted the fact that Merton's fan was on nearly 24 hours a day, so it's unlikely that he needed to turn it on. [177] In any event, if Merton did touch the fan to turn it on, it would likely have been a routine occurrence. Say wrote that "Merton used the fan a lot."[178] How was it, then, that this time this previously harmless household appliance killed him?

Furthermore, the first people to reach Merton's body said that he was dressed in his shorts.[179] Merton would not have showered with shorts on, and he would not have put on his shorts if he had been wet. The placement of words by Brother Patrick made it appear that Merton could have been wet from a shower by saying Merton took a shower and then while barefoot he apparently touched the fan. The implication was that Merton was still wet and naked. Brother Patrick left out the important facts that Merton was dressed in shorts, no water was on the floor, the shower was in the bathroom outside of Merton's room, and neither of the two monks present in the cottage witnessed Merton taking a shower. One of those monks, Fr. Say, thought Merton might have been preparing to take a shower, after Merton's body

---

[177] Celestine Say, letter to Flavian Burns, Mar. 18, 1969, the Merton Center.

[178] Celestine Say, letter to John Howard Griffin, June 25, 1969, Columbia University.

[179] Ibid.

was discovered wearing his shorts. Furthermore, Merton's body was not wet.[180]

Obviously Say would not think Merton was going to take a shower if Merton had already taken a shower. It is evident that Say had not witnessed Merton taking a shower. Say recalled that he could hear Merton's bare feet on the floor whenever he walked around.[181] Say never heard Merton moving from the time he entered the cottage around 2:00 p.m. The fact that Say never heard Merton moving indicates, as we have previously observed, that Merton was very likely killed quickly after he entered the cottage and removed his habit.

Until Brother Patrick publicly announced that he had read a police report, the report was known only to a few, Abbot Flavian, Brother Patrick, Moffitt, and Griffin. Griffin told Sr. De la Croix that he had read it, probably to win her confidence, but he did not give her a copy of the report.

The news media, which routinely covers police matters and especially, we should expect, when they involve the death of an important public figure, consistent with their lack of curiosity at the time of Merton's death, took no interest in Brother Patrick's revelation that there was a police report on Merton's death. This is in spite of the fact that *The Asian Journal of Thomas Merton* itself did receive plenty of press coverage from reviewers across the United States. The reviewers simply duly repeated the story that Merton was accidentally electrocuted in Bangkok by an electric fan. One

---

[180] Ibid.

[181] Ibid.

reviewer wrote that Merton's final journal entry was two days before his accidental death by electrocution.

These book reviews were the most news coverage of Merton's death since 1968. They all followed the script that the death was by accidental electrocution. None of the reviewers observed that the letter from six Trappists said that Merton had wounds that are not normally associated with accidental electrocution, to be precise, the bleeding head wound and some cuts.

Perhaps some journalists noticed these anomalies and that Brother Patrick had concealed the names of all of the witnesses, but they figured this was not a matter that they should pursue if they wanted to remain employed.

One big thing ignored by the press was the existence of the police report and that only persons authorized by the abbey leadership had been allowed to see it. Even bigger than that is the fact that although they widely publicized the book, they didn't tell us that in the almost four years that had elapsed since his death, this was the first public report of Merton having taken a shower. Later writers of books simply repeated it as a fact, never hinting that it had belatedly originated nearly nine thousand miles from the scene with Brother Patrick Hart, who essentially made the story up.

Then the press ended its coverage as quickly as it did when Merton had died. It would be eleven more years before the national press would revisit Merton's death with the publication of Michael Mott's biography. In the meantime, as we shall see in the next chapter, the Catholic press returned to Merton's death in 1980.

Brother Patrick's ecumenical allies

In 1976, in their short biography, *Thomas Merton: The Daring Young Man on the Flying Belltower*, Cornelia and Irving Sussman repeated Brother Patrick's story that Merton had taken a shower and that his door had to be broken down, and they added some embellishments of their own.[182] They wrote that Merton's "shouts," (plural) were ignored by his fellow monks in the cottage out of respect for his privacy, and they tell us falsely that Merton normally shared his room with two other people. They didn't name them, of course, nor did they name or number the "abbots" who had come some two hours after the shouts to break through the upper panels of the door to make the gruesome discovery. The fan, they tell us correctly, was found lying across Merton's supine body, but they stray from the truth by telling their readers that Merton had horrible burns across his *chest*. (The burns were across his pelvic region directly under the fan.) Like others before and since, including Brother Patrick in his *Asian Journal of Thomas Merton* postscript, and in contrast to the observations of Fr. Say, they also describe the shock that the unnamed witness received upon touching the somehow still-running fan as "severe."

The Sussmans also write falsely that the Thai doctors concluded that Merton had died of heart failure *caused by the electrical shock*. What they pointedly fail to tell us is that

---

[182] Cornelia and Irving Sussman, *Thomas Merton the Daring Young Man on the Flying Belltower*, Macmillan Publishing, 1976, pp.157-158.

whatever conclusion the doctors or the police authorities reached, they did it without the benefit of an autopsy.

The authors acknowledge that a shock of the sort that Merton received is not usually fatal, but then they engage in flights of fancy, speculating that Merton's heart might have been weakened by the effects of a lingering cold or even by the fact that he had been deprived of his precious solitude. They even hint at murder, noting that some have suggested that the CIA might have gotten into the room ahead of Merton and somehow arranged the "accident," but they quickly assign that possibility to the "rumor" category.

Few writers who have written about Merton's death have conveyed as much misinformation as the Sussmans have. The really remarkable thing about their account, though, is that everything they wrote apparently had the blessings of Brother Patrick Hart. In their acknowledgments, they single out Brother Patrick as a person who had read their manuscript and even suggested changes. It's obvious, though, that any changes that he might have recommended were hardly in the interest of the truth about Merton's death.

In their acknowledgments, the authors, who also wrote among other things *How to Read a Dirty Book; Or, the Way of the Pilgrim Reader*, also credit John Howard Griffin for his assistance. The Sussmans were particularly close to Griffin, corresponding with him extensively over a number of years. On March 31, 1976, Griffin wrote them with glowing praise for their new Merton book, telling them as well that he did not think the book had any factual errors.[183]

---

[183] John Howard Griffin, letter to Irving and Cornelia Sussman, March 31, 1976, Columbia University.

CHAPTER 11

The Catholic News Service's Straw Men

One method to conceal truth is to plant a false story that is easily debunked and then replace it with your own false story. The press often employs this strategy, and a good example is seen in the Merton cover-up. In May of 1980, *The Tennessee Register*, the diocesan newspaper of Nashville, published a story by Joseph Sweat alleging that the CIA had murdered Merton.

On May 19, 1980, the National Catholic News Service circulated Sweat's story based on anonymous "friends" of Merton, with obvious errors that could easily be refuted. The story said Merton was in the city of Bangkok, bathing in his hotel room, when an agent knocked an electric fan into Merton's bathtub. The story said that Bangkok authorities who investigated Merton's death were unsure whether the fan fell in the tub or Merton touched it while getting out.[184]

---

[184] Joseph Sweat, "Friends of Thomas Merton See CIA Hand In His Death," National Catholic News Service, May 19, 1980.

The Catholic wire service spread this false story to a broader audience, reaching even England and Canada.

The National Catholic News Service acts like the Associated Press, and diocesan newspapers subscribe to the service to publish articles. Why did the National Catholic News Service plant this self-discrediting story about Merton from anonymous sources? One may deduce the answer from how it was used.

The National Catholic News Service had set the table for the false story to be debunked, only to be replaced by another more palatable false narrative. This is one of the *Seventeen Techniques for Truth Suppression*, popular on the Internet, known as "Knock down straw men." That is #4 in the techniques, often opening the door for #2, "Wax indignant." (See Appendix 1)

The *Catholic New Times* of Toronto published a response to Sweat's story from John Howard Griffin that appeared on June 8, 1980. Griffin pointed out the glaring errors in the story, concluding that there were no grounds for speculation that the CIA had murdered Merton. It ran a photograph of Griffin with the headline "Report on Merton's Death False." Griffin said that an electrical short in a Hitachi fan had caused Merton's death.[185]

On August 3, 1980, a stronger rebuttal to Sweat's story came in the Sunday edition of the *Louisville Courier-Journal* in a front-page story by John C. Long, titled "Revival of theory

---

[185] John Howard Griffin, "Report on Merton's Death False," *Catholic New Times*, June 22, 1980, p. 2.

about Monk's death distresses friend." Brother Patrick was featured as the distressed friend of Merton upset by the rumors spread by Sweat, and he called it irresponsible journalism and nonsense.[186]

After condemning Sweat's article, Brother Patrick and the *Courier-Journal* "set the record straight" with their own errors. They said that the official reports had concluded that Merton had died of a heart attack caused by an electric shock.[187] This error is the exact opposite of the Thai official reports. The Thai reports, as we have seen, said that heart failure caused him to fall into the electrified fan.[188]

Another technique for truth suppression is to baldly and brazenly lie. The *Courier Journal* introduced the error that water was involved in Merton's death by saying that the only thing in Sweat's article that agreed with the eyewitnesses was that Merton had been bathing and was shocked by an electric fan.[189] But, as we have seen, no witness at the scene and none of the Thai official reports said Merton had been bathing.

Brother Patrick quite presumptuously declared that no one at the Abbey of Gethsemani ever thought that the CIA had been involved in any way with Merton's death. Brother

---

[186] John C. Long, op .cit.

[187] Ibid.

[188] The conclusion of police investigation report on the death of Reverend Thomas Merton, author unknown, date unknown, the Merton Center.

[189] John C. Long, op. cit.

Patrick, a Christian, came to the defense of an organization known for secrecy, torture, and, yes, assassination. Brother Patrick defended the CIA by accusing his friend Merton of accidentally killing himself. He did this in very nearly the same manner as one of Vince Foster's sisters. In a story different from what she originally told the police, the sister defended the authorities and the press by blaming her brother in his very suspicious death.[190] While it should carry hardly any weight at all, the press, with its implied "How dare you?" cry, makes it carry the greatest weight.

The article reported that Brother Patrick was troubled by Sweat's use of anonymous sources and his many errors, resulting from his failure to check out the facts. According to Brother Patrick, the facts could be found in *The Asian Journal of Thomas Merton*, published in 1973, which contained a letter from six people who were at the scene and a well-researched narrative by Brother Patrick, himself.[191]

Brother Patrick complained about anonymous sources and then recommended his own account that does not name any of the witnesses. Sweat had the basic facts wrong, but as we have seen, the facts in *The Asian Journal of Thomas Merton* are also incorrect, including several errors by Brother Patrick. And the six people who were "at the scene" were not at the actual death scene. The scene of Merton's death was at least

---

[190] Hugh Turley, "*The Washington Post*, Vince Foster's Sister, and Donald Trump,"
http://fbicover-up.com/sheila-foster-anthony.html
[191] John C. Long, op. cit., p. 20.

a 10-minute walk from the main building. The six described themselves as the six delegates at the Bangkok conference and not the six delegates at the scene.

As noted earlier, Brother Patrick admitted to us that he has no evidence that Merton had taken a shower. The journalist John C. Long reported that Brother Patrick called Sweat's article irresponsible journalism, which, indeed, it was, but Long was equally irresponsible. Why didn't Long ask Brother Patrick what evidence he had that Merton had taken a shower? Long had an obligation to his readers to check the facts, but he, unfortunately, is typical of American journalists, who only masquerade as people interested in the truth.

The *Courier-Journal* elevated Brother Patrick, as the secretary to Gethsemani's abbot and the spokesperson about Merton for the abbey, to be the authority on Merton's death. In that capacity, Brother Patrick was troubled that Sweat and the staff of other newspapers that ran Sweat's story did not confirm the facts with the abbey.

Sweat's article said that there was a report from the Bangkok authorities who had investigated Merton's death, and it called the death an accident, but they were unable to determine whether the fan fell into the tub or Merton touched it. Brother Patrick and the *Courier-Journal* did not use the official reports of the Thai authorities to challenge Sweat's story from "Bangkok authorities" about the tub, even though the Brother Patrick had them. Sweat's self-styled critics ignored the police and medical reports, of course,

141

because they did not conclude that the death was an accident, and they said nothing about a bath or shower.

In 1973, Brother Patrick had written in *The Asian Journal of Thomas Merton* that attempts to have an autopsy in Thailand were unsuccessful because of international red tape. Now, in response to the Sweat article, as reported by Long, he introduced the bizarre story that Thai law required that anyone autopsied in Thailand be buried in Thailand. Long simply reported it as fact, making no apparent attempt to confirm it.

Long further reported, with Brother Patrick as his authority, that an unnamed monk who had tried to move the fan had not been not fatally shocked because he had been wearing shoes and was dry, while Merton was wet and stepping out of a shower.

We can't make this point strongly enough. If Merton had simply died from an accident it would not be necessary to exaggerate and to invent stories like these. Brother Patrick argued that more evidence against an assassination was that Merton's room was locked from the inside, so that monks had to break the door to get inside.[192] This false story that the monks had to break the door is in both the *Courier Journal* article and in Brother Patrick's narrative in *The Asian Journal of Thomas Merton*.

The door was latched from the inside, but it was easily unlatched without breaking the door. Donovan said that the door had been locked but that on touching a panel it swung

---

[192] John C. Long, op. cit., p. 1.

open. It was not secured and swung on two pins.[193] Another witness wrote to Abbot Flavian, "then abbot Odo [Haas] happened to push the upper panel of the door and found that it was like a window that opened inwards. He climbed in and unbolted the door."[194] As the person at the abbey in charge of furnishing the facts about Merton's death to the public, Brother Patrick, in all likelihood, would have been aware of this letter.

Planting the false story that Merton's door had to be broken as "proof" against the possibility of assassination actually makes assassination appear more likely. The *Courier-Journal* article reported that Brother Patrick said that there were no facts to support the assassination theory and that "the monks" and the CIA thought that it was complete nonsense.[195] The story by Sweat picked up by the National Catholic News Service, blaming the CIA without any evidence, was the vehicle for Brother Patrick to take up the cudgels for the appalling CIA and blame Merton for causing his own death.

In 1980, the authorized biographer Mott at first joined Brother Patrick in saying they had to break down the door to get in the room, and he dismissed Sweat's story, saying that the circumstances made it almost impossible for anyone to

---

[193] Egbert Donovan, letter to John Moffitt, December 5, 1969, Mott Collection.

[194] Celestine Say, letter to Flavian Burns, Mar. 18, 1969, the Merton Center.

[195] John C. Long, op. cit., p. 1.

have assassinated Merton.[196] A few years later, after reading the accounts of witnesses, Mott changed his mind, writing in his 1984 book that Merton's room was not secure from the entrance to the cottage, from the window, or Merton's door.[197]

On August 15, *The Catholic Review* of Baltimore kept the CIA speculation going with another National Catholic News Service syndicated article by Stephenie Overman. The Overman article gave Sweat an opportunity to respond to Brother Patrick and the *Courier-Journal* article. Sweat said that he personally had no theory, but he thought the speculation by his anonymous sources was plausible and fascinating. The article repeated Sweat's CIA accusations with the denunciations from Brother Patrick and the CIA.[198] The Catholic press acted in concert with the Associated Press and others by not obtaining the official Thai documents, including the police report, and they continued to ignore what eyewitnesses had seen and heard.

We are forced to conclude that the Catholic press participated in covering up the murder of Merton by planting false information and rumors. John Moffitt, an editor at the

---

[196] Shirley Williams, "His Biographer Feels a Kinship with Merton" *Louisville Courier-Journal*, Aug. 24, 1980 p. 95.

[197] Michael Mott, op. cit., p. 568.

[198] Stephenie Overman, "Merton-CIA? Speculation Continues on Possible Assassination of Famed Trappist over Vietnam War Opposition," National Catholic News Service, *The Catholic Review*, August 15, 1980.

Catholic magazine *America,* suppressed the information that he knew about inconsistencies and contradictions among witnesses.

The Catholic press, it would appear, does not offer alternative news but, rather, serves to complement the secular official media. The Catholic news media, including the popular Eternal Word Television Network (EWTN) does not question the official narratives of important events like 9/11, or the assassinations of John F. Kennedy, Robert F. Kennedy, Martin Luther King, and Thomas Merton. They even stood idly by when in 2005 syndicated columnist George Will, through *The Washington Post* and other newspapers, spread British writer Simon Winchester's completely unfounded slander of the Church that after the massive 1755 earthquake in Lisbon, priests "roamed the streets" of Lisbon having people hanged as heretics out of suspicion that they were responsible for the tragedy.[199] Catholic news, unfortunately, looks very little different from *The New York Times,* Associated Press, FOX, and PBS at their most propagandistic, with the added window dressing of some *Vatican News* to make what they are dishing out more digestible.

---

[199] David Martin, "No Source for Winchester's Hanging-Priests Calumny,"
http://www.dcdave.com/article4/051117.htm

CHAPTER 12

The Not-to-Be-Shown Photograph

I was afraid the police might later confiscate my films, but luckily they didn't come to hear about it.
– Fr. Celestine Say[200]

Brother Patrick Hart may have been the first to add electricity-conducting water to public discourse on Merton's death, but he did not make it popular. The shower story became popular with Michael Mott's *New York Times* best-selling biography of Merton that was runner-up for the Pulitzer Prize. The abbey's Merton Legacy Trust appointed Mott as the official biographer in 1978 after Griffin, the original appointee, became too ill to continue.

Griffin told Moffitt that only Merton's biographer had access to certain materials, and that the most closely guarded

---

[200] Celestine Say, letter to John Howard Griffin, June 25, 1969, Columbia University.

document was a photograph. The photograph showed clearly that Merton had not died from touching a fan as he emerged naked from a shower, so a strategy was employed to conceal it.

Say took two photographs of Merton's body exactly as the body was found. Upon entering Merton's room, Donovan told Say and Haas "not to touch anything," and Haas turned to Say and told him to "take a picture."[201] They had taken the photographs to show the police exactly how they had found the body. Indoor lighting primarily illuminated the room, and Say did not have a flash, so he took the two photographs at different shutter speed settings, of $\frac{1}{4}$ and $\frac{1}{8}$ of a second.[202] After Say had taken the two photographs Weakland arrived and told him stop taking pictures. Consequently, those two were the only photographs that Say took.[203]

When the police arrived, they hastily concluded that Merton had died of a heart attack, and Dr. Nakvachara told Say that this was a convenient conclusion to avoid "problems." Since Say and others were made suspicious by the scene when they found Merton, the heart attack conclusion may have caused Say to lose confidence in the Thai investigation. Say did not volunteer his photographs to the Thai authorities.

---

[201] Ibid.; Celestine Say, letter to Flavian Burns, Mar. 18, 1969, the Merton Center.

[202] Celestine Say, letter to John Howard Griffin, June 25, 1969, Columbia University.

[203] Celestine Say, letter to Flavian Burns, Mar. 18, 1969, op. cit.; Celestine Say, letter to John Howard Griffin, June 25, 1969, op. cit.

He feared that the police would have confiscated his film if they had known that he had the pictures.[204] Say's roll of film included personal photographs, including one of himself with Thomas Merton that he would not have wanted to risk losing. Therefore, he returned to the Philippines with the two vital photographs in his possession.

When Say developed the film, only one photograph was usable. The underexposed photograph was too dark. He mailed Abbot Flavian the one good photograph on March 18, 1969, and wrote, "Abbot Odo turned to me and suggested that I take a picture, just in case the police would ask how we found him."[205] In the same letter, he asked about the results of Merton's autopsy. Say understandably, but mistakenly, believed that an autopsy had been performed, because he thought that the abbot would surely be interested in determining the actual cause of Merton's truly mysterious death.

Abbot Flavian shared the photograph with Griffin, the authorized biographer. Griffin immediately recognized the importance of Say's photographs and appeared to take steps to prevent them from ever being published. In early June of 1969, Griffin informed Say that he was the authorized biographer and that he had seen the photograph. Griffin praised Say for taking the historic picture, writing that he was very appreciative that Say had had such presence of mind to

---

[204] Ibid.

[205] Celestine Say, letter to Flavian Burns, Mar. 18, 1969, op. cit.

take the photograph and to send it to the abbey.[206] He told Say that he was counted among those who knew how important it was that the photo *not be published* and that the Merton Legacy Trust would protect it. Griffin beseeched Say to give him the original negative strip as well.

Griffin was working closely with Abbot Flavian and Brother Patrick, and he copied them on his correspondence with Say. Griffin requested that Say send him the entire strip of negatives. It was nearly impossible, he told Say, to copy one negative. Griffin wanted everything. He assured Say that after making copies, he would return the originals to Say if he needed them.[207]

Say replied to Griffin on June 23 that he preferred to send the original negatives to Abbot Flavian as a gift. He told Griffin that he trusted the abbot to decide what to do with the negatives. Say reminded Griffin that the photographs were taken immediately after they found Merton's body and that *nothing had been disturbed*. He told Griffin that the "print you have with you shows the fan's position before it was moved. The police snaps show the position after they had replaced the fan. Sister Edeltrud, a doctor, removed the fan to examine Merton."[208]

Say closed his letter to Griffin by telling him that he would send the negatives to Abbot Flavian by registered mail and

---

[206] John Howard Griffin, letter to Fr. Celestine Say, June 4, 1969, Columbia University.

[207] Ibid.

[208] Celestine Say, letter to John Howard Griffin, June 25, 1969, op. cit.

that the strip contained three frames.[209] On June 26, Say sent the negatives to Abbot Flavian by registered mail from Manila.

The knowledge that Say had taken the photographs before anything in the room had been disturbed made it all the more crucial to Griffin for the negatives to be secured. On June 30, Griffin wrote to Abbott Flavian and Brother Patrick and sent them a copy of Say's June 23rd letter. Griffin emphasized that Say had taken the photographs at the instant Merton's body was discovered with the fan just as they found it. Griffin told them that the photographs and negatives *should not be published for a very long time, in all probability never.*[210]

There was one difficulty. The following day, July 1, Say sent another copy of the photograph to Moffitt and told him that the abbey and Griffin also had a copy.[211] Say told Moffitt that Griffin requested the negatives but that he had sent them to the abbot. Say asked Moffitt not to publish the photograph without permission from the abbot. Moffitt would later write to Griffin in October telling him that he had received the never-to-be-shown photograph from Say of Merton with the fan. In December, Moffitt received another letter from Say

---

[209] Ibid.

[210] John Howard Griffin, letter to Brother Patrick Hart and Abbot Flavian Burns, June 30, 1969, Columbia University.

[211] Celestine Say, letter to John Moffitt, July 1, 1969, Moffitt papers.

telling him that the negatives had been sent to Griffin, but he had actually mailed the negatives to Abbot Flavian.[212]

It seems that Moffitt was not part of the inner circle. At first the approach was to remain silent about Say's photographs and negatives. In time, the tactic changed to undermine the significance of Say's photograph so that people would disregard it. One copy of the photograph originally sent only to the abbot and Moffitt made its way to the Merton Center at Bellarmine University. Little attention has been paid to this photograph, because scholars have readily accepted a false story that it had been taken only after the scene had been disturbed. Later we shall describe in more detail how Mott falsely stated that the room had been disturbed before Say took photographs, successfully making Say's photographs appear to be insignificant.

The evidence is irrefutable that Say's photographs were taken before anything was disturbed. "I took only two snaps of Merton right after I found him dead," Say wrote. The photograph, he said, "shows the fan's position before it was moved."[213] He stopped his photography at about 4:10 p.m. when Weakland arrived.[214] Dr. Weist moved the fan and examined Merton.

---

[212] Celestine Say, letter to John Moffitt, Dec. 11, 1969, the Merton Center.

[213] Celestine Say, letter to John Howard Griffin, June 25, 1969, op. cit.

[214] Celestine Say, letter to Flavian Burns, Mar. 18, 1969, the Merton Center.

Moffitt, to his credit, spent a lot of time studying the statements and letters from the eyewitnesses, and he made a chart to show the timeline of the events. According to Moffitt's chart, between 4:05 p.m. and 4:10 p.m. Say entered the room, unplugged the fan, and took two pictures. Moffitt's next entries state that Weakland told Say not to take photographs, and Dr. Weist examined Merton.[215] Say wrote to Moffitt that he stopped taking photos when Weakland and Dr. Weist arrived and that she then examined Merton and pronounced him dead.[216] Griffin confirmed to Moffitt that Say had taken the photographs *before* Dr. Weist arrived and disturbed the scene.[217]

Say entered the room right behind Haas and he wrote that Merton was dressed "in his shorts."[218] Say's photographs are definitive evidence that Merton was not naked. None of the witnesses who first found Merton said that he was naked, and as Say's photographs confirm, they found Merton in his shorts.

Moffitt and Griffin agreed that there was never a moment when anyone could have dressed Merton in shorts for modesty's sake, because Say took his photographs

---

[215] John Moffitt, letter to Brother Patrick Hart, February 8, 1970, Moffitt papers.

[216] Celestine Say, letter to John Moffitt, July 1, 1969, Moffitt papers.

[217] John Howard Griffin. letter to John Moffitt, September 3, 1969, Moffitt papers.

[218] Celestine Say, letter to John Moffitt, Dec. 11, 1969, the Merton Center.

immediately.[219] Griffin and Moffitt speculated that if anyone had arranged Merton's body by putting shorts on him, this would have to have been done prior to the discovery of his body. Of all the speculation by Griffin and Moffitt, this is the most intriguing because it considers the possibility of the body being arranged and the scene being staged. They went no further in this direction, however.

No one placed shorts on Merton, but, as we shall see, the evidence very strongly suggests that someone *did* place the fan on him.

After the negatives from Say arrived at the Abbey of Gethsemani, they remained a closely guarded secret, known only to a few. It appears that Griffin, the original authorized biographer, removed the historic negatives from the abbey. There would not have been a need to take the negatives from the abbey if they had they been insignificant pictures taken by Say after the scene had been disturbed. The negatives were removed because they were of great importance. Griffin held the negatives until he later died of complications from diabetes on September 9, 1980, in Fort Worth, Texas. He was 60 years old. Griffin apparently filed the negatives away, and no one understood their importance. They disappeared for 48 years until they surfaced again in 2017.

Some of Griffin's papers are at the University of Texas in Austin. Other papers, specifically related to Merton, are stored in the Rare Book and Manuscript Library of the Butler

---

[219] John Moffitt, letter to John Howard Griffin, October 4, 1969, Columbia University.

Library at Columbia University in New York City where Merton spent significant years in his early life.

One can imagine our excitement when, on the basis first of Internet research, we received upon our request a large pdf file from the Butler Library that showed, in addition to various Merton-related papers, a little negative with three indistinguishable photographs on it. These had to be the negatives of the long-suppressed death scene photographs, we reasoned. Griffin must have saved them, and then when he became too ill to continue work on the Merton biography, he forgot about them and the conspirators' need to keep them away from public view.

We had to see those photographs, but we were a bit wary about requesting a copy of them or of developed photographs for fear of alarming the librarian and possibly causing access to them to be denied to us on "sensitivity" grounds. At that point, we felt that it was a pretty sure thing that the folks at the library had no idea of the crucial evidence that they had there gathering dust in folder 511 of Box 14 since 1994.

Hugh Turley concluded that the only thing to do was to take a drive up to New York from his home in the Maryland suburbs of Washington, DC, and to have a look for himself. Sure enough, inside folder 511 were the Merton death scene negatives. The filmstrip was protected inside a cellophane wrapper from the 1960s. On the wrapper someone had written "Merton-Say <u>Confidential.</u>" The envelope from Say to Abbot Flavian was also inside the folder and on the envelope was a handwritten note from "b Lawrence" to Abbot Flavian saying that Brother Patrick was concerned about the negatives. The note said that the negatives were for Griffin.

The filmstrip had three frames exactly as described by Say in his letter to Griffin. This was the original strip of negatives sent to Abbot Flavian by Say in June of 1969, forty-eight years earlier. One photograph on the filmstrip was of several conference attendees with Merton. This was the last photograph that Say took of Merton alive.

Turley made his own copy on the spot, calling up a blank white background on the laptop computer that he had brought with him and photographed the strip of negatives against that backdrop. Later he would use a computer application that would turn the negatives into serviceable photographs, even the underexposed photograph of Merton's dead body taken from a different angle.

As it turned out, his makeshift photography development proved to be unnecessary. Upon our later request, the digital imaging technician at the Columbia University Library produced excellent high-resolution digital photographs. The underexposed photograph was clearly visible for the first time.

Soon after we received the photographs, an assistant director at the library wrote us and asked what the content of the photographs were, so they would know what they were looking at. As we suspected, they did not know what they had in their collection and requested our help with a description so that it could be added to their image repository.

Abbot Flavian, Brother Patrick, Say, Griffin, Moffitt, and eventually the Merton Center only saw the one photograph. The underexposed photograph had been too dark and could not be seen until now. Using 21st century digital imaging, the library has made good pictures of both of Say's shots taken at different angles.

The most striking thing about these photographs is the position of Merton's body. This is what so alarmed Donovan, that he told Say and Haas not to touch anything. The suspicious scene is also what prompted Haas to tell Say to get his camera and take photographs.

Merton's body is lying perfectly straight as if ready for a coffin. Merton's body is not at all in the position one might imagine of a person who has fallen accidentally, stepping out of a shower. When a person falls to the floor, by fainting, heart attack, or a blow to the head, his knees typically buckle and he falls in a heap. One does not fall flat on his back lying perfectly straight with his arms at his side. One hardly has to be an expert in crime scene analysis to see that these photographs make it clear that the press, the abbey leadership, the Thai police, and, as we shall see, biographer Michael Mott have not accurately characterized what happened to Thomas Merton. The photographs also make it evident why anyone promoting a story that a naked, wet Merton died from touching a suddenly lethal fan had to keep them secret.

Even to the most untrained eye, the photographs show what looks like a crime scene staged to look like an accident. Professional assassins may be skilled at killing, but they may not be experienced at staging a crime scene, and the job had to be done very quickly before Fr. Say arrived. Hastily staged crime scenes look like what they are, staged crime scenes.

Unfortunately, such is the state of things, when the authorities cover up evidence of a crime, a poorly staged crime scene hardly matters, because no one is able to find out about it. It has taken a very long time for their perspicacity to bear fruit, but the quick thinking of three monks has, at long last, made the Merton death different. They could see that something was not right when they discovered Merton's body, which is why they took the photographs, and later, as we have surmised, they saw that something was not right with the police investigation, which is why they did not, as they had planned, share them with the police. [220]

---

[220] The saving of these crucial crime scene photographs by witnesses with the good sense not to turn them over to the police might be contrasted with what happened to the photographs of Deputy White House Counsel Vincent Foster's body, as recounted by former lead investigator for Kenneth Starr, Miguel Rodriguez: "To be honest with you I think that ah, I think that the photographs that were taken for [sic] several people don't exist any longer or they have never been turned over to reviewing officials. At least seven were missing and that was established at one point. At least five that were taken by one particular person are gone, and don't exist in addition to the thirteen. In other words, I had a person look at 13 photographs and that person told me, 'Mine are not here.' That person's photographs are missing, at least that much." http://www.fbicover-up.com/miguel-rodriguez.html

As we have seen, Celestine Say unknowingly erred, though, in giving his photograph and his negatives to Abbot Flavian in the belief that he would be interested in the truth about Merton's death. However, providence intervened and placed the negatives safely at the Butler Library at Columbia University where we found them in July of 2017.

The photographs show Merton lying very much like we saw in Dr. Weist's crude drawing, although his arms are closer to his side and his legs are straighter. The top of his head is near the corner of the room very near two clothes racks where his habit is hanging.

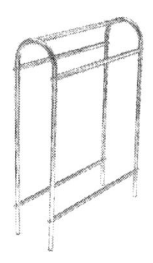

The two clothes racks are standing at a right angle to one another parallel to the walls. They appear to be made of metal, possibly aluminum. They are similar in design to the one pictured above.

The photographs show that Merton is very close to the clothes racks where his habit is hanging. The sleeve of Merton's habit is touching his head, and his left shoulder is just under the bottom rod of the clothes rack. It is unlikely Merton slid under the clothes rack after he fell on the floor. It is more likely that the rack had been placed just over Merton's left shoulder. The rack may have been knocked over during a struggle and then set up by the assailant, who placed the fan on Merton. The haphazard placement of Merton's habit on the rack also suggests that the rack had been knocked over and then stood up again.

Merton is wearing large white shorts with a tight pattern of black spots. The fan crosses his body diagonally from the middle of his left thigh to his right side as depicted in the Weist drawing. The fan crosses the bottom hem of his shorts at the middle of his left thigh and falls across his crotch to the waistband of the shorts on his right side. There is a white box on the shaft of the fan coming down from the area behind the rotary blades.

At the area where the white box part of the fan is resting on Merton's side, just above his waistband, is a dark area where he was badly burned.

This somewhat curved rectangular box appears to be about 16 inches long and 3 by 4 inches around. It appears to be made of white plastic. The fan looks modern for 1968, and, as we have noted, witnesses said it was manufactured by Hitachi.

The point where the box extends up from the shaft is resting on Merton's pelvis and farther up the edge of the box is at Merton's ribs. The fan's rotary blades are over the floor, to the right of Merton's right arm that is lying on the floor. His hands are palm down.

One photograph by Say was taken near the base of the fan, looking up from Merton's feet that are not pictured. The base of the fan was lying to the left of Merton's left ankle. The second photograph was taken facing Merton's right side and the face of the fan is facing the camera. The fan face is closer to the camera, to Merton's right, to the right of Merton's right arm.

The proximity of Merton's body in the corner of the room by the clothes racks suggests that he may have been attacked while facing the corner and removing his habit. He would have been most vulnerable when pulling the habit off over his head.

The photographs by Say are not at all how people might have imagined that Merton was found, based on the false stories that he was naked and stepping out of a shower. Say's pictures flatly contradict the authorized and popular stories about Merton's death. They also contradict the heart attack conclusions of the Thai police. Say's photographs show the truth, and that is doubtless why Michael Mott, as we shall see, concocted a story to undermine their effect.

Dr. Weist and Donovan were puzzled by the position of Merton's body. We may speculate that someone placed the arms and legs straight in order to roll Merton onto his back. The fan was placed on top of him to make it look like an accident. Merton was likely dead before his body was electrocuted. Exactly how he died, possibly a blow to the back of the head, a gunshot with a silencer-equipped weapon, or strangulation likely would have been determined by an autopsy, so there had to be no autopsy.

In spite of fact that the one crucial photograph by Say has been at the Merton Center for quite a long time, apparently no one has paid any attention to it. People have also ignored Say's letters, especially the letter to Abbot Flavian on March 18, 1969, that had the crucial photograph enclosed.

CHAPTER 13

Michael Mott's Authorized Story of the Death

Michael Mott, the authorized biographer who succeeded Griffin, vitally covered up the truth about Merton's death in several ways. He presented false information, concealed evidence, and altered the true sequence of events. Of all the evidence that Mott concealed, the most important was related to the Say photographs.

Mott should have had access to all of the significant materials, but he never referenced several important documents, including a letter from Say to Griffin dated June 25, 1969, in which Say made it clear that Merton never took a shower. Mott used other documents selectively, ignoring evidence that did not support the authorized story. Most importantly, he rearranged the chronology of events to make it appear that critical events happened differently.

Ignoring the virtually incontrovertible evidence to the contrary that we have described, Mott actually gave reinforcement to Brother Patrick's unsupported story that Merton had taken a shower. In fact, his biography became the popular source that Merton had showered. Mott speculated that Merton came out of a shower naked or wearing his shorts and that his feet may have still been wet when he slipped and then grabbed, or tried to move, the fan.[221]

Does anyone come out of a shower wearing shorts? Mott, though, was probably forced to offer that unlikely occurrence as a possibility out of fear that the photograph that he knew about would be discovered, and that it would become known that it had been taken immediately upon the discovery of Merton's body.

Mott's suggestion that Merton's wet feet may have caused him to slip and that this, in turn, may have caused him to grab the fan and kill himself may not be as farfetched as the Thai police conclusion that Merton suffered a heart attack, causing him to fall into a lethal fan, but it may be even more dishonest. Mott knew that there was absolutely no evidence to suggest that Merton took a shower. Rather, all the evidence said he didn't.

Mott also suggested that it was not known for sure if Merton was found naked or in his shorts. Witnesses found Merton dressed in shorts and several documents stated that

---

[221] Michael Mott, *The Seven Mountains of Thomas Merton*, op. cit., p. 567.

Merton was wearing shorts. Mott ignored these documents. But worse than that, he and those at the abbey who authorized his work had seen the photograph of Merton dressed in shorts, taken at the time his body was discovered. Mott had to have known that what he was writing was not true. What, dear readers, does that tell you?

No eyewitness ever said that Merton had been found naked. Mott's insinuation that Merton could have been naked was a device to support the shower story. Say was only a few feet from Merton and witnessed everything in the cottage. He did not witness Merton taking a shower. Say wrote to Griffin in that ignored June 25, 1969, letter, "His body was not wet, and I thought that perhaps he must have been preparing to go to the bathroom for a shower."[222] There was no towel or evidence that Merton had showered. De Grunne, unreliable as he may be, was in the cottage the entire time with Merton and he said nothing about Merton taking a shower, either. Brother Patrick, who had access to the witness accounts and police reports, admitted there was no evidence that Merton had actually taken a shower, even though he has written that he did.[223]

In the final analysis, it is Mott who is undressed by his gratuitous speculation that Merton may have been naked at the time he died of electrocution. He is not alone in his

---

[222] Celestine Say, letter to John Howard Griffin, June 25, 1969, Columbia University.

[223] Brother Patrick Hart, voicemail to Hugh Turley, May 31, 2017, 2:14 pm.

exposure. The abbey leadership and the Merton Legacy Trust, as authorizers of Mott's work, in effect, attested to its veracity and therefore must share responsibility for his errors and falsehoods.

Mott's most important and obviously willful falsehood is about the timing of the crucial photograph. The photograph of Merton in his shorts was enclosed in the letter from Say to Abbot Flavian. The negatives of the photos taken by Say were later sent by registered mail to the abbot in June of 1969.

Mott had Say's letter in which he told the abbot that he had taken the photographs just as they had found Merton. The chronology of events is repeated in other documents. Mott had to know that this is what really happened:

1. Haas, Say, and Donovan entered Merton's room.
2. Haas told Say to take pictures and he took two photographs.
3. Haas summoned Weakland from a nearby cottage.
4. Weakland arrived and told Say to stop taking pictures.
5. Dr. Weist also arrived and moved the fan to examine Merton.

In his letter to Griffin, Say was emphatic that his photographs were taken of the death scene as it was found undisturbed, before anyone had moved the fan. Mott purposely and with obvious malice aforethought ignored Say's letter to Griffin and proceeded to rearrange the order of the events to discredit Say's photographs and make them seem unimportant.

Here is how Mott changed the order of the events in the authorized biography:

1. Haas, Say, and Donovan entered Merton's room.
2. Haas called Weakland from the nearby cottage and he arrived in minutes with Dr. Weist.
3. Dr. Weist examined Merton and pronounced him dead.
4. Say then took photographs *after* Dr. Weist had moved the fan.
5. Weakland told Say to stop taking pictures.

After Mott changed the order of events, he stated the new result and emphasized that the pictures were taken as a record of the then disturbed room.[224] Having made Say's photographs seem unimportant, Mott then ignored them. Mott never divulged that Say had sent a photograph to the abbot or that Griffin had implored Say to give him the valuable original negatives.

Mott also tried to dismiss a drawing of the crime scene by Dr. Weist who, by her account, was the first person to "move the fan somewhat aside." Mott implied that her drawing was not accurate, because the fan had been moved a number of

---

[224] Michael Mott, *The Seven Mountains of Thomas Merton*, op. cit., p. 566.

times. Say's photos prove that her drawing was a very close depiction of how the fan was found on Merton.

Hardly anything in Mott's account withstands scrutiny. Say wrote, "Abbott Odo [Haas] turned to me and suggested that I take a picture, just in case the police would ask how we found him." This only makes sense if Say's pictures were a record of how they found Merton. Mott's story that the pictures were taken as a record of the room after it had been disturbed makes absolutely no sense. It would have been pointless for Say to have taken photographs to preserve a record of an already disturbed room. Mott's chronology is incredible, very much like his story that Merton might have come out the shower with his shorts on or that he might have been knocked to the floor by a lethal fan while naked. But, as the authorized story, Mott's tale has been repeated over and over as though it were the unvarnished truth.

It probably goes without saying, but if Say's photographs had been taken after the scene had been disturbed, Griffin, Brother Patrick, and Abbot Flavian would not have been so anxious to get the full negative film strip and to make certain that the photographs would never be published. Mott's false story about when the photographs were taken only underscores their importance.

Mott's paragraph with his reconstruction of Merton's shower has only one endnote to support it, number 465, in the middle of the paragraph. The endnote references a letter from Say to Abbot Flavian, and the only detail in this letter in support of the paragraph was that Merton's fan was on almost 24 hours a day. The letter from Say offers no evidence that Merton showered, had wet feet, slipped, grabbed, or moved the fan.

As we have pointed out repeatedly, nothing the witnesses said even begins to suggest that Merton showered or slipped or touched or moved the fan, nor do the death scene photographs support that thesis. The authorized biographer added these details for the sole purpose of supporting his accidental electrocution thesis. Mott's placement of the sentence about the fan being on night and day, supported by endnote 465, made it appear the other details he added were supported by Say's letter, which they were not.

After neutralizing Say's photograph, Mott continued to suggest that Merton had been naked. Mott said that there had been some cleaning up soon after Merton's body had been discovered. He added that there had been confusion about different pairs of drawers. There is absolutely no evidence to support any early cleaning up after the discovery of Merton's body. Mott would have people believe that shorts were placed on Merton to make him respectable. As evidence Mott wrote that the burn on Merton extended under his shorts while the material was not burned. However, the police report stated there was "a burn on the body's side and on the underwear."

Mott misrepresented the chronology of other events when Merton died. We have already made it clear that the events happened in this order:

1. Merton and de Grunne returned to the cottage shortly before two o'clock.

2. Say arrived at the cottage moments later, removed his habit, and proceeded to brush his teeth.
3. De Grunne came downstairs while Say was brushing his teeth and asked him if he had heard a shout. At this time, around 2:00 p.m., Say did not see Merton in his bed.
4. De Grunne left the cottage at around three o'clock and returned shortly after.
5. Just before four o'clock, de Grunne knocked only at Say's door and told him that Merton was in trouble.
6. De Grunne then left the cottage, and after telling Haas and Donovan that Merton had had an accident, he continued on to the main building.
7. When Say entered Merton's room with Haas and Donovan, Say saw Haas recoil after touching the fan.

Mott, on the other hand, produced a chronology whose larger purpose was to promote the accidental electrocution theory using the police report and the fake Haas document:

1. Merton and de Grunne returned to the cottage at a time not mentioned.
2. A few minutes before three o'clock, de Grunne heard a cry and the sound of a falling object and came down and knocked at Merton's door.
3. At this time, Say was brushing his teeth. Say told de Grunne that he did not hear a noise. Say did not see Merton in his bed at this time, which was about 3:00 p.m.

4. One hour later, a few minutes before four o'clock, de Grunne knocked at Merton's door and told Say that Merton was in trouble.
5. De Grunne went for help and told Haas and Donovan that Merton had had an accident.
6. De Grunne returned to the cottage with Haas and Donovan to join Say. The four men opened the door to Merton's room.
7. Haas was held to the shaft of the fan by an electrical shock.

Mott did not reference the fake Haas document in his endnotes, but the document is in his papers at Northwestern University. The fake Haas document is the only known source for de Grunne returning to the cottage with Haas and Donovan to join Say and for Haas being stuck to the fan. Mott faithfully followed the version of events from the shoddy police report and the fake document, which said that de Grunne had heard a sound at three o'clock.

Mott avoided any accounts by witnesses that did not support the authorized version of events. He was careful not to mention Brother Patrick's narrative from *The Asian Journal of Thomas Merton* when he wrote that Merton had showered, because this would have contradicted Mott's implied time of Merton's death of around three o'clock. John Moffitt had carefully studied the accounts of witnesses and had advised Bother Patrick that the time of Merton's death had been at approximately two o'clock. Moffitt was convinced that there was no cry or sound of anything falling at three o'clock, because Say certainly would have heard it.

Mott wrote that some twenty individuals gave information about the events surrounding Merton's death and the aftermath, but he was careful not to reveal who most of them were or what they actually had to say. The documents that he worked with were essentially secret, known only to Mott, Moffitt, and key people at the abbey, since Griffin had died in 1980. When we sent the official Thai documents that we got from the National Archives and from Weakland to Dr. Paul Pearson at the Merton Center, he told us that he had not seen them before.

The cover letter from the Embassy in Bangkok that was sent to the abbot with these documents is in Mott's papers at Northwestern University. The letter mentioned that the Foreign Service Report of Death, Death Certificate, and other documents were enclosed, so Mott would have known that these documents were sent to the abbey.

Jerked sideways and held to the shaft?

In furtherance of the accidental electrocution story, Mott might not have gone so far as Brother Patrick did in writing explicitly that Merton had taken a shower, but he embraced completely the equally unsupported story that the witness, Fr. Odo Haas, was "paralyzed" by the electric current and became stuck to the shaft when he tried to remove it from Merton's body. That story comes completely from the fake Haas document, which we discussed in Chapter 4. Interestingly, Mott doesn't reference that document because it describes Merton's body as wearing shorts when it was found, virtually ruling out any possibility of a shower.

One might be inclined to excuse Mott for relying so heavily on such an unreliable source because he could not conceive of the possibility that anyone at the U.S. Embassy in Thailand would concoct it. But, as the successor to John Howard Griffin as Merton's authorized biographer, he was privy to all of the relevant correspondence that convincingly contradicted the dubious Haas statement.

John Moffitt, for his part, did a lot of speculating to find ways to explain Merton's suspicious death. In August of 1969 he suggested to Griffin that if Haas had been stuck to the fan, Merton could have been stuck too.[225] In Moffitt's theory to explain how the fan became electrified, he said that Merton broke the fan and somehow disarranged the wires. Two months later, Moffitt changed his thinking and concluded that Haas could not have been stuck to the fan. Moffitt then wrote to Griffin that Haas was shocked and his hands were not stuck to the fan, because Say had written that Haas recoiled from a shock upon touching the fan.[226]

Griffin hardly needed any reminding, because four months earlier he had received a letter from Say with precisely those words, that Haas "recoiled from a shock upon

---

[225] John Moffitt, letter to John Howard Griffin, August 31, 1969, Columbia University.

[226] John Moffitt, letter to John Howard Griffin, October 4, 1969, Columbia University.

touching the fan."[227]   Later in December of 1969, Moffitt received another letter from Say in which Say wrote that when Haas tried to remove the fan he "recoiled from a shock."[228]

It is a natural reaction to recoil from an electric shock. Almost everyone has had the unpleasant—but far from deadly—experience at one time or another.   Though privately Moffitt had written to Griffin that Haas was seen recoiling from the fan, publicly he wrote that when Haas tried to move the fan he received a strong shock and the current paralyzed his hands. [229]

Mott even went beyond the fake Haas document by writing that when Haas touched the fan he was jerked *sideways* by a shock, and he was held to the shaft of the fan

---

[227] Celestine Say, letter to John Howard Griffin, June 25, 1969, Columbia University.

[228] Celestine Say, letter to John Moffitt, Dec. 11, 1969, the Merton Center.

[229] John Moffitt, letter to John Howard Griffin, October 4, 1969, Columbia University; *A New Charter For Monasticism: Proceedings of the Meeting of the Monastic Superiors in the Far East, Bangkok, December 9 to 15, 1968*: John Moffitt, ed., Notre Dame, 1970 p.84; Had Griffin lived, one can be certain that his Merton biography would not have been any more honest than Mott's. In an October 6, 1969, letter to Moffitt, he referenced the dubious "Haas statement" that his hands were stuck to the fan by the jolt and said that it was "of course" consistent with recoil, which is the precise opposite of the truth. Moffitt papers, University of Virginia.

until Say unplugged it.[230] Mott may have borrowed the word "jerk" from the police report that stated that when, "Haas touched the fan, which rested on Reverend Merton, he was seen to jerk away." Mott has just added the "sideways" for dramatic effect, but the police report's "jerk away" is just another version of Say's "recoil."

Mott's endnote number #459 that he offered to support Haas being jerked sideways and held to the shaft is the letter from Celestine Say to Abbot Flavian. The letter does not say anything about Haas being jerked sideways or being held to the shaft. The only part of Mott's story supported by Say's letter is that Say unplugged the fan.[231] Say even repeated to the abbot in that letter what he had told Griffin, that Haas had "recoiled from the shock."

Mott made up the story that Haas was jerked sideways, not only to exaggerate the force of the shock, but also to imply that Haas had moved the fan. Mott did not miss the opportunity to undermine the importance of Say's photographs.[232]

This is just one more of Mott's tall tales that others have parroted. Even Merton's friend Jim Forest wrote that a shock

---

[230] Michael Mott, *The Seven Mountains of Thomas Merton*, op. cit., p. 565.

[231] Celestine Say, letter to Flavian Burns, Mar. 18, 1969, the Merton Center.

[232] Michael Mott, *The Seven Mountains of Thomas Merton*, op. cit., p. 567.

jerked Haas sideways, and he was held to the shaft of the fan.[233]

Even if Haas had been paralyzed and held to the shaft—which he was not—people should wonder why he wasn't killed by a heart attack from the shock like Mott has given us to believe that Merton was? Shouldn't Haas also have succumbed to the full 220 volts of direct current?

Some, including Brother Patrick Hart, have anticipated this apparent contradiction, arguing that Haas likely had shoes on while Merton was barefooted. One false story requires another false story to support it. Being barefooted, though, won't do it. Who can recall ever being warned about handling household appliances when they don't have shoes and socks on? Being barefooted on a dry terrazzo floor, of course, is not inherently dangerous when one is handling household appliances, and that is why it was necessary to invent the shower story.

It is a very interesting fact that Brother Patrick, the inventor of the shower story, who in the same essay in 1973 said that the abbot who attempted to move the fan off Merton's body had received a "severe" shock, changed his account in 1998. In his introduction to *The Other Side of the Mountain*, which is Volume 7 of *The Journals of Thomas Merton*, which he edited, he repeats almost verbatim his story from 1973 of how Merton was killed, except this time he describes it as a "slight" electric shock.[234] Though he would

---

[233] Jim Forest, *Living with Wisdom*, Orbis Books, 1991, p. 215.
[234] *The Other Side of the Mountain, The End of the Journey*, Patrick Hart, O.C.S.O., editor, Harper, San Francisco, 1998, p. xix.

never admit it, the logical conclusion of Brother Patrick's more recent denial that Haas received a strong shock, much less that he became stuck to the fan, is that he must now agree with the authors that the "Haas statement" is a fake, with everything that that implies.

With even Brother Patrick onboard, in stark contradiction to his earlier confident assertion, no fair-minded person can come to any other conclusion than that the shock that Haas received was the familiar mild one that almost everyone has felt at one time or another, and it was not even close to being lethal. What is really important is that someone's installation of a defective cord in the Hitachi fan gave Haas that little shock and caused him to recoil. Could it be any more obvious that the defective cord was installed—just as the fan was laid across his body—not to kill Merton but to make his assassination appear to be an accident? The big questions to be asked—and the ones the police should have been asking—are who installed the cord and who moved the fan.

Reviews of the authorized biography

The Washington Post's review of Mott's biography echoed Brother Patrick that the cause of death was Merton's own carelessness in accidentally touching a defective electric fan when he was still damp from taking a shower. *The Post* added that Mott said that there were other improbable theories, including a bizarre theory that Merton had been murdered.[235]

The behavior of *The Washington Post* is instructive and quite familiar to anyone who has followed the *Post's* cover-ups.[236] In this case, they simply repeated the false story that Merton was still damp from showering, while belittling skeptics with adjectives like "bizarre and unlikely." The use of such loaded language is another of the techniques for truth suppression.

But what could be more bizarre and unlikely than a household product like a fan killing someone? This is why the false stories were invented that Merton was still damp from showering. Even more improbable is the idea that touching a Hitachi fan would kill a person. One is far more likely to be murdered than to be killed by a fan.

The Post was hardly alone. Mott's authorized biography was highly acclaimed in book reviews throughout the national press. Fr. John Jay Hughes, church historian and priest of the Archdiocese of St. Louis, reviewed Mott's book for the *St. Louis Post-Dispatch*. Fr. Hughes praised the book as virtually unassailable in his view because Mott had full access to all the sources.[237] The book, he declared, was

---

[235] Nancy Wilson Rose, *Washington Post* book review of Michael Mott's biography of Merton, December 16,1984.

[236] David Martin, "Vince Foster, Tommy Burkett, and Fake News," April 20, 2017, http://www.dcdave.com/article5/170420.htm

[237] John Jay Hughes, "Thomas Merton's Dynamic Center of Calm," *St. Louis Post-Dispatch*, Dec. 23, 1984, p. 27.

authoritative because it was painstakingly researched and well documented. But, giving Fr. Hughes the benefit of the doubt, he did not know what he did not know. Anyone who has followed our account up to this point is immeasurably better informed on the circumstances surrounding Merton's death than Fr. Hughes could have been.

It is highly unlikely that Fr. Hughes knew that Mott withheld the fact that Abbot Flavian had received the photograph with the letter from Say explaining when and why that key crime scene photograph was taken. He also could hardly have known that Mott also left out any mention of the important July 1, 1969, letter from Say to Moffitt that also included another copy of the photograph. Say told Moffitt that Griffin had also seen the picture and that Griffin had requested the negatives, but that they had been sent to Abbot Flavian.

Of course, Mott also left out any mention of a visit to the Philippines by Griffin's friend and associate, Penn Jones, Jr., a noted writer about the John F. Kennedy assassination, during which Jones told Say that he thought there was a strong possibility that Merton was murdered.[238] We shall say more about that later.

Edward C. Sellner, Professor of Theology at the College of St. Catherine, also called Mott's book well researched.[239] The sheer number of the endnotes is, indeed, impressive, but

---

[238] Celestine Say, letter to John Moffitt, July 1, 1969, Moffitt papers.
[239] Edward C. Sellner, "Merton's Soul Matured in the Caldron of Earthly Battles," *Minneapolis Star Tribune*, Feb. 3, 1985, p. 105.

endnotes need to be compared to the source documents to determine if the book is truly well-researched. It is evident from his review that Sellner, like Hughes, was clueless about the important documents that Mott did not use.

Even in their ignorance, if they were truly critical readers and thinkers, Hughes and Sellner and any of the many other reviewers who praised Mott's work and took it at face value might have noticed the many problems in his account of Merton's death. Most readers would have learned for the first time from Mott that the Thai police investigators had concluded officially that Merton had died from a heart attack and fallen into a fan—one that had been running quite well night and day without harming a soul—that turned out to have had faulty wiring installed, leaving post-mortem burns on his body. Mott slips around that revelation by offering his own conjecture that if Merton had indeed died from a heart attack, it had been caused by the lethal shock that the fan had given him. Mott even mentioned the bleeding wound in the back of Merton's head that Dr. Weist had noted in her examination. He explained that away by asserting that it must have been caused by Merton's fall onto the (level) floor.

Clearly, the situation screams for an autopsy. How credulous does one have to be not to suspect that a bleeding wound in the back of Merton's head offers a better clue as to what killed him than does a fan improbably lying across his even more improbably positioned body? The police had to examine the head wound, but we are given no indication that they did so. A small caliber handgun with a silencer attached, one that produces no exit wound, is a favorite assassin's weapon. Would an autopsy have discovered a bullet in Merton's brain or that there had been a sharp lethal blow to the head with a weapon of some sort?

Mott even informed his readers that no autopsy had been performed while verbally wringing his hands and offering a variety of weak excuses for the failure. Honest and even slightly astute reviewers should have noticed that something is amiss here, even if they didn't know, as we do, that Mott had concealed the fact that the Thai authorities falsely claimed that they had done an autopsy.

Furthermore, Mott conceded that murder could hardly be ruled out, considering the fact that the Thai police had made no effort to determine if anyone else had been in the room when, as he further revealed, access to the first-floor room by window and by door was relatively easy and that the bushes and even the topsoil outside Merton's window had been removed the next day (due to "superstition"). Then he proceeded to rule out murder by concluding that no one around there at the time could have had any motive for it. Drawing on #3 of the Seventeen Techniques for Truth Suppression, after actually making a pretty good case for murder in spite of himself, he dismisses such suspicions as simply "rumors."

Mott even dropped clues that the witness de Grunne was a suspicious character. He described de Grunne's pacing around in the room above Say while Say was trying to sleep and later he makes excuses for the fact that the first thing out of his mouth when rushing to "get help" for the stricken Merton is to ask Haas and Donovan if they had had a good swim by saying that the apparently inappropriate words must have been a product of his nervousness. Nervousness? That is hardly the right emotion for the moment, but Mott otherwise treats de Grunne as a perfectly reliable and believable witness, although, as we know, and Mott surely knew, that de Grunne had contradicted other witnesses and himself, as well.

A particularly disappointing example of a reviewer who should have known better was D. Q. McInerny. In his short review, he praised Mott's efforts highly, making no mention of Mott's treatment of Merton's death.[240] However, in his early biography, *Thomas Merton, the Man and His Work*, published in 1974, he wrote cryptically that everything pointed toward accidental electrocution as the cause of the death, without mentioning the fact that the Thai investigators had concluded otherwise and that there had been no autopsy.

McInerny was well qualified as a Merton scholar to review Mott's book. A philosophy professor, he has also written books about logical thinking and Thomistic ethics, that is, the ethics of St. Thomas Aquinas. Unfortunately, though, he failed to apply what he has taught others about Aristotle and Aquinas to his review of Mott's book. McInerny knows that a first principle of rational reasoning is that a thing cannot be and not be at the same time and same respect.

---

[240] D.Q. McInerny, Review of *The Seven Mountains of Thomas Merton* by Michael Mott, *Catholic Historical Review*, Oct. 1986, pp.681-683.

In his doctoral dissertation in 1969, McInerny wrote that Merton was found lying on the floor in his pajamas.[241] Mott, on the other hand, wrote that Merton may have been naked.[242] How could McInerny ignore the contradiction between what Mott wrote and what he had, himself, written?

Particularly in light of his praise for Mott's book, one must wonder about McInerny's earlier failure to report that the Thai investigators had concluded that Merton had died of heart failure and that there had been no autopsy. The very best thing one can say about McInerny's work in this instance was that he was guilty of what Aquinas would call consequent ignorance.

Consequent ignorance is when we choose, for sinful reasons, to remain ignorant of things we can and ought to know.[243] McInerny's offense was even greater if he knew these facts and withheld them from the reader while writing that everything pointed toward accidental electrocution.

People who are persuaded by accounts like Mott's are people who want to be persuaded.

Hughes, Sellner, McInerny and the other reviewers, unfortunately, appear to be among such people. Mott provided new information that should have raised questions, but he bottled the new wine in the old "accidental-electrocution" bottle that people had been made to believe

---

[241] D.Q. McInerny, "Thomas Merton and Society: A Study of the Man and His Thought Against the Background of Contemporary American Culture," Doctoral Thesis, 1969, p. 26.

[242] Michael Mott, *The Seven Mountains of Thomas Merton*, op. cit., p.567.

[243] D.Q. McInerny, *A Course in Thomistic Ethics*, 1997, pp. 40-42.

was the truth for going on 16 years when his book came out. His comforting conclusion simply reinforced what people already thought that they knew.

Mott's authorized story became the standard, and others would repeat his story. Mott brushed aside the idea that Merton might have had opponents who wished him harm, and he said that the failure to have an autopsy was only regrettable. Mott either ignored or papered over evidence that might make people doubt the authorized narrative.

Virtually every writer that came after him lined up to praise Mott's authoritative authorized biography. His became the authority to invoke in accordance with #7 of The Seventeen Techniques for Truth Suppression. Behind him lay the authority of the Merton Legacy Trust and the leadership of the Gethsemani Abbey, who had authorized his work.

The national press revisited Merton's death to praise Mott's authorized biography and crown him as the authority on Merton. The press reviews repeated, "accidental death," "electrocuted by a defective fan" and even a shock by a "defective lamp."[244] The influential *New York Times* reported

---

[244] Patrick Henry, "Finding Virtue in Merton," *Philadelphia Enquirer*, Dec. 23, 1984, p. 129; Frank P.L. Somerville, "In Search of Merton and His Mountain," *The Baltimore Sun*, Feb. 11, 1985, p. 9; United Press International (UPI) *The Daily Chronicle*, Dekalb, Il, Dec. 28, 1984, p. 7.

that Merton's death was a "freak accident."[245] The bottom line, repeated again and again, was that Merton's death was an accident. Mott's book was the capstone on the cover-up.

---

[245] Kenneth E. Briggs, "Merton Portraits," *The New York Times*, Dec. 20, 1984, p. C21.

Wise Monkeys?

Why haven't they looked into Merton's demise?
Here's what's occurred to me:
Our scholars have all averted their eyes
Out of fear of what they might see.

David Martin

CHAPTER 14

In Michael Mott's Wake

The shower, the shock, and the shout

Before Mott's biography was published in 1984, the generally accepted version of Merton's death was the account of Brother Patrick and the letter from the six Trappists from *The Asian Journal of Thomas Merton,* published in 1973. This version was repeated in 1980 by Cornelia and Irving Sussman, whom we have already discussed, and by Merton's friend Jim Forest. Forest published a pictorial biography of Merton and wrote that Merton had taken a shower, received an electric shock from a fan, and died of heart failure. Forest said nothing about Merton's bleeding head wound, although he did mention the cuts that were reported in the letter by the six Trappists but curiously made nothing of them. [246] An unauthorized biography, published in 1980, by Monica Furlong retold the story from the six Trappists.[247]

After 1984, though, virtually everyone followed Mott's lead. In 1999 in *Heretic Blood: The Spiritual Geography of Thomas Merton,* Michael Higgins described Merton crying out after grabbing a faulty fan when wet upon emerging from a shower, only to be discovered fatally injured by the shock he received from the powerful 220 volts of electricity. Unaware of the fraudulent ultimate source of the information, he duly described how Haas had also become stuck to the fan by the severe shock until Say had unplugged it.

Paul Elie's book, *The Life You Save May Be Your Own: An American Pilgrimage,* won the PEN/Martha Albrand Award for First Nonfiction in 2004 and received the National Book Critics Circle Award nomination. Elie graphically described a scene of instant electrocution, as though he had been there to witness it. Merton cried out in agony when he grabbed the

---

[246] Jim Forest, *Thomas Merton a Pictorial Biography*, Paulist Press, 1980, p.98.

[247] Furlong quoted directly from December 11, 1968, letter by the six Trappists to Abbot Flavian, leaving out the words, "in his pajamas" and referenced the Thomas Merton Study Center. Furlong may have taken the quote from *The Asian Journal of Thomas Merton* that she also references in her book without noticing those three words "in his pajamas" are only in the copy of the letter at the Thomas Merton Study Center.

lethal fan after slipping on the wet floor when he emerged from a shower, wrote Elie, but the cry was ignored.[248]

Elie went even farther than Mott in dismissing the possibility of murder, without even explicitly entertaining the thought. Mott wrote accurately that the door to Merton's room was locked, but Say, Haas, and Donovan quickly realized that they could reach through the door's louvered windows and unlatch it from the inside. That means, of course, that Merton's killer could have latched it in the same way. Elie tells us, though, that the door had to be broken down.

James Harford's book, *Merton and Friends, A Joint Biography of Thomas Merton, Robert Lax, and Edward Rice*, published in 2006, repeated that Merton was electrocuted after getting out of a shower and touching a defective fan.[249]

Joan C. McDonald took a creative approach in writing about Merton's death in *Tom Merton a Personal Biography*, published by Marquette University Press in 2006. McDonald presented the details of his death in the first person, as Thomas Merton. The story was the same, but it seems that McDonald thought the story would be more believable if people could hear it in Merton's own words, and here we paraphrase: "Hence, I stepped out of the bath, still wet,

---

[248] Paul Elie, *The Life Your Save May Be Your Own: An American Pilgrimage*, Farrar Straus & Giroux, 2003, p. 422.

[249] Jim Harford, *Merton and Friends: A Joint Biography of Thomas Merton, Robert Lax, and Edward Rice*, Bloomsbury Academic, 2007, p. 193.

tracking water across the floor, touched the fan, and I felt the electrical shock up my arm straight to my heart." McDonald's actual words, scream and all, can be found on page 437 of her book.

In McDonald's final pages, she describes the death of Merton again by retelling the Mott account, including all of his errors and omissions. Mott's errors do not need to be listed again, but there was one error by Mott that McDonald was able to expand upon.

McDonald's research clearly included reading Mott's endnotes. This resulted in her misfortune of copying an error from Mott's endnote #464. As mentioned earlier, Mott mistakenly transcribed the word "fan" as "face" in his endnote. McDonald, trying not to copy Mott's account exactly, put this error into her own words and wrote that Dr. Weist declared the cause of Merton's death was by electric shock to the face. McDonald was first among scholars to state that the cause of Merton's death was by electric shock to the face.[250]

McDonald also restated Mott's pernicious chronology that Dr. Weist had examined Merton's body *before* Say had taken several photographs. Repeating Mott's propaganda to make Say's photographs appear useless, McDonald proved herself to be a useful idiot who might have made Vladimir Lenin smile.

If McDonald had done proper research, she could have learned that Say took his photographs *before* Dr. Weist

---

[250] Joan C. McDonald, *Thomas Merton A Personal Biography*, op. cit. p. 441.

disturbed the scene by moving the fan and examining the body. McDonald also would have known that Say took exactly two photographs, not several, another error she repeated from Mott.

Even though Mott had quoted Dr. Luksana Nakvachara correctly from the police report with his conclusion that heart failure had caused the shock, McDonald goofed and got it backwards and wrote that Dr. Nakvachara said the shock induced the heart failure. It is easy to see how McDonald could get confused here, because, although Mott quoted the doctor accurately, he then reversed it in writing his own conclusion. With so many errors in print it is not surprising that people might get a little mixed up.

In one of the most recent books, published in 2008, Robert Waldron in *Thomas Merton: Master of Attention* leaves out the ignored shout and Haas's supposed bout with the lethal fan, but the emergence from the shower is there and he stresses the power of those 220 volts, as though that fact alone was sufficient to explain Merton's instant death.[251]

Paul Elie returned to the subject in 2015 on the 100th anniversary of Merton's birth with an article in *The New Yorker*, revealing that he had learned nothing since he wrote his book more than a decade before. Once again, he tells us

---

[251] Robert Waldron, *Thomas Merton: Master of Attention*, Paulist Press 2008, p. 13.

about the shower, the slipping on the wet bathroom floor, and the grabbing of the instantly lethal fan.[252]

The story has been told so many times now, and with such an air of authority, that it's hard for anyone not to believe it. The plain fact of the matter, though, is that from the best evidence we have been able to gather from the witnesses, Merton took no shower and he made no shout. His body did, indeed, receive a mild shock that caused Haas to recoil. Such a shock administered to a dead body over a period of more than an hour would certainly cause damage to the skin, and that appears to be what Dr. Weist observed on the part of Merton's body that was in contact with the fan.

Lawrence Cunningham in his 1999 book, *Thomas Merton and the Monastic Vision*, repeated Brother Patrick's disinformation that Merton had taken a shower around 1:30 p.m. and tried to move a fan, while barefooted, on a damp floor. He was unsure if the shock caused a heart attack or a heart attack caused him to fall over the fan. Cunningham also repeated the weird story that Abbot Flavian wanted an autopsy in Thailand, but Thai law would have required Merton to be buried in Thailand if that were done. Cunningham, a theologian, added that this was necessary for religious reasons.[253]

---

[252] Paul Elie, *Thomas Merton and the Eternal Search*, The New Yorker, March 5, 2015.

[253] Lawrence S. Cunningham, *Thomas Merton and the Monastic Vision*, 1999, p. 179.

Thinking that Cunningham, a professor of theology (emeritus) at the University of Notre Dame, might be something of an expert on such questions, we asked him what specific religious reasons required Merton to be buried in Thailand if there had been an autopsy there. Cunningham responded that he wrote that based on conversations with Brother Patrick. Professor Cunningham said that it was all rather vague to him, but he thought that the religious reasons might have been because Merton was a monk!!![254]

Weakland flipflopped on the Merton shower story

Archbishop Weakland is the only witness who was present who has ever said that Merton had his shorts on and looked like he had just showered.[255] The former archbishop wrote this in a section of a book about Merton in 1984, the same year that Mott's biography of Merton was published. At that time, Weakland was surely compromised because of a homosexual affair and a church pedophile embroglio, neither of which had yet come to light. We shall have more to say about that later. He also wrote that flames were coming out of the fan and that Merton's contorted hands made it appear that he had suffered as he died. No one else ever claimed to have seen any flames coming out of the fan. The photographs by Say disprove Weakland's story of contorted hands.

---

[254] Lawrence S. Cunningham, email to Hugh Turley, May 24, 2017.

[255] Rembert G. Weakland, "Merton the Pilgrim" in Paul Wilkes, op. cit.

Twenty-five years later, after Weakland had been publicly exposed, his story of Merton's death changed. In 2009, he published his memoirs. In that book he returned to the death of Thomas Merton, but he did not repeat the popular story that Merton had showered. As one of the last surviving witnesses, Weakland surely knew that the shower story was not true. This time Weakland broke ranks with virtually everyone outside Thailand, repeating the cause of death as stated on the Thai doctor's certificate. Improbable as it may sound, he wrote, "Death was caused as a result of fainting – due to acute cardiac failure and electric shock due to accidental falling against the electric fan to the floor."[256]

Merton's friends

Jim Knight and Ed Rice were suspicious when Merton died. Ed Rice always firmly believed that there was some dirty work at the crossroads.[257] As we have seen, though, they were among the very few to express any suspicion, apart from the most immediate witnesses.

On August 15, 1969, Moffitt shared with Griffin his displeasure that a person had sincerely written that Merton had been assassinated in connection with the murders of Martin Luther King and President Kennedy.[258] Three days

---

[256] Rembert G. Weakland, *A Pilgrim in a Pilgrim Church, Memoirs of a Catholic Archbishop*, op. cit., p. 166.

[257] Interview by Hugh Turley of confidential source.

[258] John Moffitt, letter to John Howard Griffin, August 15, 1969, Columbia University.

later Griffin replied that he also had heard the assassination story and totally and instantly disregarded it.[259] Consider the fact, however, that one of the people bandying about the story that the Kennedy and King assassinations might be related to Merton's death was none other than Griffin's close friend and associate, Penn Jones. It makes one wonder what game Griffin might have been playing.

On July 1, 1969, Moffitt received word from Say that a reporter named Jones had visited the Philippines and had told him that it was probable that Merton had been murdered and that there was a connection to the Kennedy and King assassinations.[260] We shall have more to say about Jones later.

Griffin also told Moffitt that he was amazed that very few people close to Merton, including some at the abbey, were comfortable that the death was as stated.[261] The private admission by Griffin that some of the monks at the abbey were uncomfortable has never been admitted publicly.

Some of those close to Merton seemed unconcerned. Naomi Burton Stone was an original trustee of Merton's literary estate. According to the Merton Center website, Stone was Merton's literary agent and a close friend who became something of a mother or sister figure. Five months

---

[259] John Howard Griffin, letter to John Moffitt, August 18, 1969, Moffitt papers.

[260] Celestine Say, letter to John Moffitt, July 1, 1969, Moffitt papers.

[261] John Howard Griffin, letter to John Moffitt, August 18, 1969, Moffitt papers.

after Merton died, she wrote to Moffitt telling him no one could know if Merton suffered a heart attack, was electrocuted, or what.

It did not seem to bother her that there had been no autopsy or, apparently as far as she knew, even a police report. The cause of Merton's death remained unknown, and yet, she seemed not to consider the possibility of murder. Stone told Moffitt, with a tone of great incredulity, that on some recent television program she had heard it baldly stated that Merton was a murder victim.[262] Imagine that.

In 2015, James T. Baker published a play, *Under the Sign of the Waterbearer: A Life of Thomas Merton*, to commemorate the centennial of Merton's birth. Baker, who knew Merton, said that he wrote this play soon after Merton died, revising it in 2015. Baker wrote that Merton bathed in a tub and with his feet wet, touched a wire exposed on a fan, was thrown to the floor by the shock, and the fan fell on top of him. No card-carrying Mertonian, it would seem, could write about Merton's death without including the water necessary to make the story at least a little bit believable. Even more was that the case for a dramatist with an immediate audience to consider. Baker, the distinguished professor of history at Western Kentucky University, with his 2015 play had even gone so far as to put Merton back into the bathtub of Joseph Sweat's baseless, debunked article.

---

[262] Naomi Burton Stone letter to John Moffitt, May 7, 1969, Moffitt papers.

Professor Baker also has Merton's body not being discovered for several hours. To our knowledge, no one admonished Baker for his play's lack of verisimilitude, because he stuck with the authorized story line that Merton caused his own death and not the CIA or anyone else. No one, neither the police, Merton's biographers, his friends, nor anyone else had exhibited the slightest interest in discovering who might have been responsible for the installation of that faulty wiring in the previously safe and functional Hitachi fan.

Part 3.
The Enemies of Truth

Hear the serpents' lies,
The concealed community's lucifugous lies
That eviscerate the social compromise.
Arrogantly thinking they needn't obey
The rules by which the rest of us play,
By word and by deed they chip away
At the country's very foundation,
At the base of our civilization.
Where, pray tell, is there room
In a decent, law-abiding nation
For inveterate practitioners of intimidation,
Disinformation, assassination,
Covert opinion manipulation,
Agents provocation,
And human experimentation?
Why must we simply assume
The national need for an occupation
That lives on equivocation?
On lies, lies, lies,
Black loathsome lies,

White gauzy lies
That stupefy and paralyze,
While we meekly tolerate
Subversion of the Fourth Estate,
And those who send up warning cries
They slather with their unctuous lies,
Paranoia feeding,
Suspicion breeding,
Justice impeding
Lies, lies, lies, lies,
Lies, lies, lies.
Clumsy, corrupting,
Ugly, disgusting,
Impudent, putrid, lies.[263]

---

[263] Verse three of "The Lies (Poe Meets Orwell)" by David Martin, http://www.dcdave.com/poet1/p030698d.html

CHAPTER 15

Murder by the Book

In the 1950s, the CIA published a manual with its different classifications of assassinations:

> The techniques employed will vary according to whether the subject is unaware of his danger, aware but unguarded, or guarded. They will also be affected by whether or not the assassin is to be killed with the subject. Hereafter, assassinations in which the subject is unaware will be termed "simple"; those where the subject is aware but unguarded will be termed "chase"; those where the victim is guarded will be termed "guarded."
>
> If the assassin is to die with the subject, the act will be called "lost." If the assassin is to escape, the adjective will be "safe." It should be noted that no compromises should exist here. The assassin must not fall alive into enemy hands.
>
> A further type of division is caused by the need to conceal the fact that the subject was actually the victim of assassination, rather than an accident or natural causes. If such concealment is desirable the operation will be called "secret"; if concealment is immaterial, the act will be called "open"; while if the assassination requires publicity to be effective it will be termed "terroristic."

Following these definitions, the assassination of Julius Caesar was safe, simple, and terroristic, while that of Huey Long was lost, guarded, and open.[264]

The CIA document further states, "For secret assassination...the contrived accident is the most effective technique. When successfully executed, it causes little excitement and is only casually investigated." [265] The suspicious airplane crashes of United Nations Secretary-General Dag Hammarskjöld, Congressman Hale Boggs Sr., U.S. Secretary of Commerce Ron Brown, John F. Kennedy Jr., Senator Paul Wellstone, and the odd fatal skiing accident of Congressman Sonny Bono are other possible examples of secret assassinations.[266]

Secret assassinations have been concealed as "suicides" in the case of Deputy White House Counsel Vincent Foster and the murder of America's first Secretary of Defense, James V. Forrestal. For further reading on the Forrestal assassination see "Who Killed James Forrestal?" by David Martin.[267]

Dale Peterson, the CIA's chief of media relations, was quoted in the *Courier-Journal* as giving his assurance that the

---

[264] Operation PBSuccess, CIA, A study of assassination, online at George Washington University,
http://nsarchive.gwu.edu/NSAEBB/NSAEBB4/ciaguat2.html
[265] Ibid.
[266] David Martin, "The Cover-up of Sonny Bono's Murder," http://www.dcdave.com/article5/080406.htm
[267] David Martin, "Who Killed James Forrestal?" November 10, 2002, http://www.dcdave.com/article4/021110.html

CIA was not involved in Merton's death.[268] Would Peterson have said anything different if the CIA had successfully executed a simple, safe, and secret assassination of Merton?

When asked how the CIA verified that none of their operatives murdered Merton, Peterson said that the CIA does not kill U.S. citizens. Peterson tacitly admitted that the CIA murders people. The reality is that the CIA kills lots of people, including Americans.

On November 28, 1953, an American citizen, Frank Olson, was dropped from a 10th floor window of the Statler Hotel in New York City.[269] A description of Olson's murder is in the CIA's assassination manual, "The most efficient accident, in simple assassination, is a fall of 75 feet or more onto a hard surface. Elevator shafts, stair wells, unscreened windows, and bridges serve well...a private meeting with the subject may be arranged at a properly-cased location...Care is required to ensure that no wound or condition not attributable to the fall is discernible after death."[270] In Merton's case, there was no autopsy to determine whether the bleeding head wound or any other additional wounds were crucial factors in his death.

---

[268] John C. Long, op. cit. p. 20.

[269] Michael Ignatieff, "C.I.A.; What Did the C.I.A. Do to His Father?" *New York Times*, April 2, 2001.

[270] Operation PBSuccess, CIA, A study of assassination, online at George Washington University,

http://nsarchive.gwu.edu/NSAEBB/NSAEBB4/ciaguat2.html

Olson was a scientist employed by the CIA serving as an army officer at Fort Detrick in Frederick, Maryland. In the early 1950s, he traveled to Germany and witnessed terminal human experiments on German, Norwegian, and Russian prisoners from World War II. Olson was horrified by the unspeakable evil he had seen. When Olson tried to resign from the Agency he was drugged with LSD and murdered. Olson's death was related to the CIA operation called ARTICHOKE that preceded the infamous MKUltra mind control project.[271] He also might have been killed because of fears that he would divulge the use of biological weapons by the United States in the Korean War.[272]

In 1975, Frank Olson's family discovered that they had been lied to about Olson's "suicide" from a 10th floor window.[273] President Ford apologized for the CIA's role in Olson's death, and the death was then called an "accident." The widow accepted a $750,000 settlement. The CIA Director William Colby also met with the Olson family in his office and apologized. Colby promised the family a full accounting, but Colby never delivered on his promise.[274]

---

[271] http://www.frankolsonproject.org/Statements/FamilyStatement2002.html

[272] Sophie Gilbert, "*Wormwood:* Obsession, Lies, and a CIA Cover-up," *The Atlantic*, December 18, 2017, https://tinyurl.com/y6ubc9jg

[273] Report to President by the Commission on CIA activities within the United States, June 1975, p. 227.

[274] Matthew Hay Brown, "Six Decade Later, Son Seeks Answers to Death of Dietrick Scientist," *Baltimore Sun*, December 8, 2012.

Olson's son Eric eventually requested a new autopsy and discovered that his father had been murdered. The autopsy found that someone had struck Olson in the head, probably with a hammer, before throwing him out of the window.[275]

The same William Colby had run the CIA's notorious Phoenix Program, known for torture and assassinations in Southeast Asia, including Thailand, between 1968 and 1972.[276] This CIA killing machine was in full operation, then, when Merton was killed.

American intelligence has had a long presence in the U.S. Embassy in Thailand. Gen. William Donovan, known as the founding father of the Central Intelligence Agency, was appointed to head the American diplomatic mission in Bangkok in 1953. The CIA operated on a large scale in Bangkok.[277] The U.S. Consulate secretary came to the Red Cross Conference Center to claim Merton's possessions and arrange for the U.S. military to take Merton's body. Seven months later, the embassy would be the source of that anonymously translated Thai police report with no author,

---

[275] Kevin Dowling and Phillip Knightley, "The Olson File, a Secret that Could Destroy the CIA," *Night and Day Magazine*, *The Daily Mail*, Aug. 23, 1998, reprinted Dagens Nyheter, Stockholm, Sweden, June 12, 1999.

[276] Seymour M. Hersh, "Moving Targets," *The New Yorker*, Dec. 13, 2003.

[277] E. Bruce Reynolds, "Staying Behind in Bangkok: The OSS and American Intelligence in Postwar Thailand," *Journal of Intelligence History*, Vol. 2, 2002, p. 21.

205

date, title, or signature and presumably of the fake Haas document.

Archbishop Rembert Weakland said that there were rumors when Merton died that the CIA had killed him because he was opposed to the Vietnam War, but Weakland didn't think that the government had any interest in Merton.[278] Weakland was mistaken. In 1958, the CIA illegally intercepted a letter from Merton to Russian writer Boris Pasternak. The letter was opened, copied, resealed and sent on to Pasternak.[279] Merton was on a CIA watch list to have his mail to the Soviet Union monitored.[280]

In 1968, a local group calling itself Catholic Concerned Citizens sent a letter to the Kentucky Un-American Activities Committee urging state legislators to declare Merton a "dangerous radical" and a prime target for investigation. A copy of the letter was sent to the FBI in Washington, D.C., but the FBI was already watching Merton's activities as well as a number of peace groups that were using his name.[281]

---

[278] Hugh Turley telephone interview of Rembert Weakland, Oct. 3, 2012.
[279] Ira Simmons, "People Seek Insight into Monk," Gannett News, *The Times,* Shreveport, Louisiana, Apr 1, 1989, p. 10.
[280] Michael Holtzman, "James Jesus Angleton, The CIA & the Craft of Counterintelligence," U Mass Press, 2008, pp171-172.
[281] Ira Simmons, op.cit.

Homicide by electrocution

Homicides by electrocution are extremely rare, but they are not unknown. [282] A case study specifically on electrocution as a method to conceal a homicide was published in the *Journal of Indian Academy of Forensic Medicine*. Initially, the police concluded that the death was accidental electrocution. Later, a careful autopsy showed that it was a homicide.[283] The actual cause of death was strangulation, supplemented by an injury to the head. The wounds from the electricity, it turned out, were post-mortem. The CIA is particularly adept at killing people, and, as we have discussed, they use a wide assortment of methods.

---

[282] Vij Krishan, *Textbook of Forensic Medicine and Toxicology*, pub. Elsevier, 2011, p. 180.

[283] M. P. Jambure, R.M. Tandle, "Electrocution Method to Conceal Homicide a Rare Case Report," *Journal of Indian Academy of Forensic Medicine*, 2012, Volume 34, Issue 1, p.92.

CHAPTER 16

Merton Was a Force for Peace and Truth

All Michael Mott really had to argue against murder was that there was no suspect with a motive for the crime. In making that argument, Mott sells Merton short. Merton was a man with a large and influential audience who was confronting the evil he called "The Unspeakable," and, whether he realized it or not, this fact had to have placed him in great danger.

Merton's influence might not have been as great as Robert F. Kennedy's and Martin Luther King's, both Vietnam War opponents assassinated in 1968, but it was considerable. He corresponded with a large number of people, and his writings warning about the dangers of nuclear war were powerful. During the short Kennedy administration, one of the people who received his manuscript, *Peace in the Post-Christian Era*, was Bobby Kennedy's wife, Ethel. Tellingly, the Abbott General of Merton's order did not permit that manuscript to be published as a book on the claim that it "falsifies the monastic message."[284]

President John F. Kennedy had confronted the CIA when he turned toward peace and accepted defeat at the Bay of Pigs in Cuba.[285] JFK's planned withdrawal of American troops from South Vietnam had further put him at odds with this powerful clandestine organization.[286] As with JFK, Merton's pursuit of peace and truth inevitably brought him into confrontation with those who are the enemy of truth.

Paradoxically, etched into the wall of the main lobby of the CIA headquarters building is the Bible verse, "And ye shall know the truth and the truth shall set you free." (John 8:32)

The CIA is better understood by another verse from John's Gospel, "Everyone who practices evil hates the light; he does not come near it for fear his deeds will be exposed." (John 3:20)

In an address to the American Newspaper Publishers Association President John F. Kennedy said:

> The very word "secrecy" is repugnant in a free and open society; and we are as a people inherently and

---

[284] Thomas Merton, *Peace in the Post-Christian Era*, Orbis Books, 2004, pp. ix-x.

[285] James W. Douglass, *JFK and the Unspeakable*, Touchstone 2008, p. 14.

[286] Ibid., p. 195.

historically opposed to secret societies, to secret oaths, and to secret proceedings.[287]

After the Bay of Pigs disaster, Kennedy had told a high administration official, as reported by *The New York Times*, that he wanted "to splinter the CIA in a thousand pieces and scatter it to the winds."[288]

Merton understood that the enemies of truth used the news media to encourage wars and keep people in darkness. The knowledge that the CIA has relationships with the news media that forms public opinion is as big a key to understanding why the CIA would have wanted to kill Merton as it is to understanding the effectiveness of the cover-up of his murder.

The report of the U.S. Senate Select Committee on Intelligence Activities stated:

> Although the variety of the CIA relationships with the U.S. media makes a systematic breakdown of them almost impossible, former CIA Director Colby has distinguished among four types of relationships.

---

[287] President John F. Kennedy, address before the American Newspaper Publishers Association, Waldorf-Astoria Hotel, New York City, April 27, 1961, https://www.jfklibrary.org/Research/Research-Aids/JFK-Speeches/American-Newspaper-Publishers-Association_19610427.aspx

[288] Tom Wicker, John W. Finney, Max Frankel, E. W. Kenworth, "The C.I.A.: Maker of Policy, or Tool?", *New York Times*, April 25, 1966, p. 20.

These are:

(1) Staff and general circulation, U.S. news organizations;

(2) Staff of small, or limited circulation, U.S. publications;

(3) Free-lance, stringers, propaganda writers, and employees of U.S. publishing houses;

(4) Journalists with whom CIA maintains unpaid, occasional, covert contact.[289]

The CIA's first chief of political warfare, Frank Wisner, called his operation the "Mighty Wurlitzer" with the ability to play any propaganda tune.[290]

Deborah Davis wrote about Wisner's operation in her biography of Katharine Graham, *Katharine the Great: Katharine Graham and the Washington Post*.[291] Davis wrote that Wisner "owned" four to six hundred leading journalists at the *New York Times, Newsweek, CBS* and other respected news outlets. Davis said all of this was according to a former CIA employee who worked with the Mockingbird operation.

---

[289] Foreign and Military Intelligence, Senate Select Committee to study government operations with respect to Intelligence Activities, Final Report, Vol 1, 1976, p. 195.

[290] Hugh Wilford, *The Mighty Wurlitzer: How the CIA Played America*, Harvard University Press, 2008.

[291] Ironically, the press coverage that was given to the powerful publisher's death, supposedly from an accidental fall, was remarkably similar to that given to Merton's, strongly suggesting that she, too, was the victim of a "secret assassination." See David Martin, "Was Katharine Graham Killed for 9/11?" http://www.dcdave.com/article5/120921.htm

Journalists had code names, field supervisors, and a field office. Journalists, stringers, and some thinking they were just patriots helping the agency were all considered operatives.[292]

Secret assassinations by the CIA succeed with a controlled and compliant press. Merton's killers would have had to be certain that the press and the abbey leadership would do nothing to expose the assassination. Accordingly, from the beginning, the press misstated the facts about Merton's death. They also ignored the official Thai reports and the evidence of murder. Abbot Flavian, Brother Patrick, and the journalists who had seen the police report and Say's photograph of Merton's body remained silent.

Considering the CIA's heavy hand in the media, we should not be surprised that *The Washington Post,* in its review of Mott's Merton biography, should call the murder of Merton improbable and a bizarre theory. Nor should we find it unusual that the *Tennessee Register,* Catholic News Service and *Louisville Courier-Journal* should plant false stories about Merton's death and publicize the defense of the CIA by Brother Patrick.

Before Deborah Davis' biography of Katharine Graham described the CIA's program, Operation Mockingbird, Merton already understood how the news media operated.

It is a rare individual who is able to pose a threat to the CIA. Men may possess the damaging truth, but they rarely

---

[292] Deborah Davis, *Katharine the Great: Katharine Graham and the Washington Post*, Harcourt Brace Javanovich, 1979 p.130.

have the power to communicate it that Merton did. Merton was an exceptional and influential writer able to reach a large audience. The powerful opinion molders could not have been pleased that Merton was challenging their message. As Paul Goodman astutely observed, in the United States you can say anything as long as it does not have any effect.[293]

Living in a monastery, Merton did not read a daily newspaper or watch television. He did, as we have noted, though, correspond with important people, and he understood what was going on in the world outside the monastery. Merton was writing things that challenged the integrity of the news media at the same time that the public was given to believe that the CBS News anchor, Walter Cronkite, was the "most trusted man in America."

In 1962, Merton characterized world politics as a sort of gang warfare that employed police, newspapers, lawyers, and even clergymen in their armies.[294] In 1966, he wrote that the propagandists in the press make up our minds for us in terms that are strikingly similar to the first verse of David Martin's poem, "The News." [295]

> The keepers of the knowledge gate
> Demark the bounds of the debate

---

[293] Paul Goodman, Social Anarchism, 1986, Read more at http://www.notable-quotes.com/g/goodman_paul.html

[294] Thomas Merton, Letter to Ernesto Cardenal, Nov. 17, 1962, The Courage for Truth, Merton Legacy Trust 1993, p. 138.

[295] Thomas Merton, *Conjectures of a Guilty Bystander*, op. cit., p. 216.

And manufacture an illusion
That we've reached our own conclusion.[296]

In 1968, the year of his death, Merton decried the way in which the powerful used deception as an everyday tool and, in the process, even managed to convince themselves that the false history that they had created was true.[297]

Merton's peace activities alone probably would not have targeted him for assassination. The combination of being a moral authority and critical of the news media in a way that was far ahead of his time made Merton a genuine threat. More than anything else, it was Merton's love of the truth that brought him into a confrontation with powerful enemies.

Merton saw clearly that devotion to truth could not help but bring a person into conflict with sinister special interests. The effectiveness of the truth-seeker would, of course, be greater to the extent that he could rally others to his cause, but ultimately, he said, the truth seeker's strength lay in trust in God.[298]

Merton was particularly powerful because of his poverty. Merton had said that poverty, like faith in God itself, is our strength. Men are often impeded from telling the truth when they fear losing their job, property, or even the approval of

---

[296] David Martin, "The News," http://dcdave.com/poet15/171027.htm

[297] Thomas Merton, *Faith and Violence,* University of Notre Dame Press, 1968, p. 250.

[298] Thomas Merton, Letter to Ernesto Cardenal, op. cit., p. 159.

others. A truly detached man has no fear, not even of losing his life.

Merton's love of God and his fellow man placed him on the path to become a saint. In his autobiography, Merton said his friend Robert Lax told him that the only thing necessary to be a saint was to want to be a saint.[299] Merton's ultimate strength was in the Lord, so he was unafraid of the Evil One and those who dwell in darkness. His enemies might put him to death, but this would only serve to bring him to his ultimate end with God.

Jim Knight, a lifelong friend of Merton, said that he had many enemies including the CIA, FBI, and even some powerful enemies within the Church, even within his own monastery.[300] In a letter to friends the day Merton was buried, Fr. Matthew Kelty, O.C.S.O., wrote that Merton had been a problem to many, even at the abbey. Kelty said that Merton knew all that was going on and that he was above things trivial and petty. He said there was a tenderness and gentleness in Merton and at the same time courage and strength. Merton loved the monastery but not it's foolishness and faults. Kelty said Merton would argue with the abbot but was always obedient.[301]

---

[299] Thomas Merton, *The Seven Storey Mountain*, Harcourt, 1948, p. 260.

[300] William James Knight, "The Thomas Merton We Knew," http://www.therealmerton.com/tommie5.html

[301] Matthew Kelty letter to friends, Abbey at Gethsemani, December 17, 1968, Mott Collection.

Merton found fault with the Dallas police after the assassination of President Kennedy.[302] Following Merton's death, the Thai police were comparable to the Dallas police, and then his own monastery didn't bother to learn the cause of his death. The return of Merton's body to the Gethsemani was reminiscent of the return of Jesus to his native town of Nazareth. "They found him altogether too much for them. Jesus said to them, 'No prophet is without honor except in his native place, indeed in his own house.'" (Mt 14:57) The abbey community chose to remain ignorant of the truth about Merton's death by not requesting an autopsy. Consequent ignorance, called "ignorance of evil choice" by St. Thomas Aquinas, happens when "one does not take the trouble to acquire the knowledge which one ought to have."[303]

Looking at the crucial role played by Abbot Flavian and Brother Patrick in preventing the facts of Merton's death from being known and in their promotion of a false alternative narrative, one is forced to conclude that a strong, sinister motivational force had to be at work. What power could possibly have been so strong as to assure the killers in advance that they would have the complete cooperation of the abbey leadership in covering up Merton's brazen murder?

The man who presided over the conference at which Merton died, Archbishop Rembert Weakland, was not

---

[302] Thomas Merton, *Seeds of Destruction*, Farrar, Strauss, and Giroux, 1964, p. 315.

[303] Thomas Aquinas, *Summa Theologica*, I-II, Q.6, a.8.

connected to the Gethsemani Abbey, and, as we have seen, he has hardly played as big a role in the cover-up as others have, but, at this point, some details about his life after that fateful day in Thailand might be germane. In 2009 the Milwaukee *Journal Sentinel* reported that Weakland had shredded reports of sexual abuse by priests and that Weakland had admitted allowing priests guilty of child sex abuse to continue as priests, without warning parishioners or alerting police.[304] In his autobiography, Weakland stated that in the early years he did not think child sexual abuse was a crime.[305] Weakland would later apologize for calling those who reported sexual abuse by priests, "squealers."[306]

Archbishop Weakland retired in 2002 at the mandatory age of 75, and only then did it become known that he had paid $450,000 of diocesan funds in 1998 to Paul J. Marcoux, who had accused him of date rape years earlier.[307] It appears

---

[304] Bruce Vielmetti, "Weakland Shredded Copies of Sex Abuse Reports, Documents Say," *Milwaukee Journal Sentinel*, Dec. 3, 2009; Rachel Zoll, "Archbishop Rembert Weakland, Former Catholic Bishop of Milwaukee, Says He's Gay" AP, *The Huffington Post,* Jun. 12, 2009.

[305] Annysa Johnson, "Weakland Says He Didn't Know Priests' Abuse Was Crime," *Milwaukee Journal Sentinel*, May 15, 2009.

[306] Dave Umhoefer, "Scandal Casts New Light on Weakland's Statements", *Milwaukee Journal Sentinel*, May 26, 2002.

[307] Laurie Goodstein, "Ex-Archbishop Speaks About Catholic Church and Homosexuality," *New York Times*, May 15, 2009, p. A14.

Marcoux extorted the diocesan money in exchange for his silence.

Were there things that the killers of Merton knew about their cooperators at the Abbey of Gethsemani that made them controllable. Can anyone think of a better explanation for the latter's behavior?

CHAPTER 17

The Press in Full Cover-up Mode

It can hardly be repeated enough that in a nominally free and open society, cover-ups of murder by the state depend upon a corrupt and compliant press. Over 50 years after the assassination of President John F. Kennedy, the American press still reports that Oswald killed Kennedy, just as they did from the beginning, prior to any investigation. The press, one may be assured, will continue to call Thomas Merton's death an accident, no matter how much evidence we or anyone else might marshal that points inexorably to homicide.

The first American news story about Merton's death came from the Associated Press reporter John T. Wheeler. He covered the war in Vietnam and the rest of Indochina. Wheeler may be regarded as part of the American war effort. His role as the AP gatekeeper of information was twofold. He publicized stories that were authorized and suppressed stories that were not. Stories of war crimes committed by Americans, for instance, were not authorized, so Wheeler would doubtless suppress such news. It might as well have been written into his job description.

Wheeler, therefore, duly reported that Merton was electrocuted when he touched a cord with a short in it while moving an electric fan.[308] Wheeler did not reveal his sources, and he did not report that the Thai officials concluded that the death was due to cardiac failure. Wheeler also reported that no one noticed when Merton failed to show up for lunch. Wheeler attributed this completely false statement to an unnamed priest. What is more likely is that he made it up out of whole cloth. Say sat across from Merton at lunch and gave him the key to the cottage when he left with de Grunne.[309] Wheeler could make up any of the story details as long as he stuck with the script that the death was an "accidental electrocution."

Wheeler suppressed news that the police were summoned and only reported that a doctor said Merton's heart failed after the electric shock. This statement was false. The doctor said the exact opposite, that is, heart failure caused Merton to fall into the fan and get shocked. Wheeler made Merton's death appear to be an accident by saying the heart attack resulted from the electric shock.

---

[308] John T. Wheeler, "Thomas Merton Dies in Electrocution Accident," Associated Press, Dec. 11, 1968.

[309] Celestine Say, letter to John Moffitt, July 1, 1969, Moffitt papers.

The AP report by Wheeler reveals the early participation of the news media in the cover-up of Merton's murder, and that in itself is a very suspicious happenstance. From the very beginning the cause of death was reported to be an accident. One can almost believe that the story had been written in anticipation of the completion of the dastardly deed.

Wheeler's role as a journalist also included suppressing information. Wheeler made it difficult for any independent minds to learn anything more about Merton's death. By not mentioning that the police arrived at the scene, he damped any curiosity that there might have been about a police report. By failing to name the doctor or any witnesses, he made it difficult for people to find these valuable sources of information. The language barrier for non-Thai speakers presented an additional obstacle. The venue for the murder was in many ways ideal.

Interestingly, Fr. Jean Leclercq wrote in an article on February 26, 1969, that the Thai newspapers, in contrast to U.S. newspapers that all said that Merton died from accidental electrocution, were unanimous in reporting that he had died of a heart attack, which was in conformity to the Thai police report.[310]

---

[310] Jean Leclercq, "Final Memories of Thomas Merton,' Gethsemani, February 26, 1969, published in French, Vol. 9 (1969) of *Bulletin of AIM*, a translation by William Skudiarek, published by *Monastic Interreligious Dialogue* sponsored by North American Benedictine and Cistercian Monasteries, July 2008.

The *New York Times*, for its part, reported that Merton was shocked when a fan toppled on top of him in his room.[311] *Time* magazine said only that Merton had been electrocuted when he evidently touched an exposed wire trying to move a fan.[312] None of the news reports mentioned the bleeding head wound. People might expect burns to be associated with electrocution, but they might have had bothersome suspicions had they been told about a bleeding head wound, so the press, led by Wheeler, left out that inconvenient detail. Almost fifty years later hardly anyone knows about these additional wounds.

The initial reports by the news media about Merton's death were also the last reports by the press for a very long time. Journalists did not bother to ask for any official documents, a police report, or inquire about any eyewitnesses. No one even asked about an autopsy, and no one reported that there was no autopsy. It was reported to be an accidental death based on anonymous Catholic sources, and that was the end of the contemporary news reporting. In the years that followed there has never been any English language news report about what the police report said or that a police report even existed.

---

https://web.archive.org/web/20081212155450/http://monasticdialog.com/a.php?id=873

[311] Israel Shenker, "Thomas Merton is Dead at 53; Monk Wrote of Search for God," *New York Times*, December 11, 1968, p 1.

[312] *Time*, p. 65, December 20, 1968.

Merton understood the news media, having written once that ninety percent of the news that we see in the newspapers should not really be regarded as news at all and was not a reflection of reality but, rather, was a concoction designed to create a false reality.[313] That is a conclusion that large numbers of Americans are only beginning to arrive at more than half a century later.

We can believe the American press or we can believe Merton's observations about it. If we believe Merton, then we can see clearly from the evidence that we have mustered that the "news" that Merton electrocuted himself is a sort of media-generated pseudo-reality. Merton was telling too much truth about the news media, and in doing so, he became at least as big a threat to the propaganda machine as he was to the war effort.

Saturation is part of propaganda, so official narratives are aimed at several levels. The story mentioned earlier by the Catholic News Service was directed to the Catholic audience. It was designed to dispel any suspicion that people might have had that Merton had been murdered by publicizing a false story that could easily be refuted. The strategy was to first cast suspicion on the CIA using spurious evidence and then to exonerate the CIA.

Griffin and Moffitt, journalists behind the scenes

Two journalists were particularly close to the early cover-up of Merton's death. As we have noted, one of these

---

[313] Thomas Merton, *Faith and Violence*, op.cit., 1968, p. 151.

journalists, John Moffitt, an editor at the magazine *America*, was staying in the room above Merton in the cottage. The monastic conference continued for four more days after Merton's death, and Moffitt, the journalist covering the conference could have interviewed all of the witnesses and the Thai officials. The most significant event at the conference was the death of Thomas Merton, but Moffitt apparently gathered no information about it at the time.

The other journalist active in the early years on the story was John Howard Griffin. Griffin and Moffitt exchanged letters. Griffin agreed with Moffitt to keep their correspondence confidential, though Griffin often open copied his correspondence with Moffitt to Brother Patrick and Abbot Flavian.

Moffitt and Griffin agreed that there were a number of inconsistencies and contradictions, especially between Say and de Grunne.[314] They agreed that there were problems explaining Merton's death, and in a letter to Moffitt, copied to Brother Patrick, Griffin said that he had a responsibility to dispel the suspicions or resolve the contradictions.[315] Griffin worked two weeks every month at the abbey.[316]

According to Griffin, certain materials were to be available only to him as Merton's biographer and to no one else. He told Moffitt that the Merton Legacy Trust and the

---

[314] John Howard Griffin, letter to John Moffitt, August 18, 1969, Moffitt papers.
[315] John Howard Griffin, letter to John Moffitt, August 11, 1969, Columbia University.
[316] John Howard Griffin, *The Hermitage Journals*, Image Books, 1983 p. ix.

abbey were very strict about this. Brother Patrick shared the Thai Police report with Griffin when it arrived at the abbey on August 7, 1969.

On August 18, Griffin wrote to Moffitt telling him that he had the police report and that it included reports by Haas, de Grunne, and Dr. Weist.[317] Griffin is the only known source for the information that these reports were included in the police report. The cover letter with the police report did not mention any attachments.

Griffin also impressed upon Moffitt that he had "several" detailed accounts from Say, who, Griffin said, was "quite definite" about his times. What Griffin told Moffitt based on this Say intelligence was that Merton and de Grunne left from lunch to go to the cottage at 2:10 p.m., that Say returned to the cottage at 2:30 p.m., and that Merton's body was discovered at 3:20-3:30 p.m. Moffitt, however, drew question marks along the margin of his copy of Griffin's letter, clearly indicating that he found those times to be questionable.[318]

Say was, indeed, certain about the times of events, but they were not the times that Griffin relayed to Moffitt. A letter from Say to Griffin states clearly that Merton and de Grunne left for the cottage at about 1:40 p.m. and not at 2:10 p.m.[319] Griffin's mendacious attempt to bring Moffitt around

---

[317] John Howard Griffin, letter to John Moffitt, August 18, 1969, Moffitt papers.
[318] Ibid.
[319] Celestine Say, letter to John Howard Griffin, June 25, 1969, Columbia University.

to a Merton death scenario that was in accord with the Thai police report was later thwarted once and for all when Say wrote directly to Moffitt that Merton and de Grunne may have left for the cottage around 1:30 p.m. In that letter, Say told Moffitt that Merton had died at about two o'clock.[320]

Moffitt was so little deceived by Griffin that, as we noted earlier, he later convinced Brother Patrick to change the time of death to 2:00 p.m. in the draft of his postscript for *The Asian Journal of Thomas Merton*. Moffitt told Brother Patrick that the times he had been given by Say did not agree with the times that Griffin had told him that Say was "quite definite" about.[321]

In October Abbot Flavian would eventually share the police report and the reports of Haas and Dr. Weist with Moffitt on the recommendation of Griffin.[322] Say signed a statement for the police, but its whereabouts is unknown.

Griffin told Moffitt that reports from forensic medical experts were not yet in.[323] Later Griffin mentioned his desire to discuss some things with the forensic medical men.[324] If there were ever any reports from specialists in forensic medicine, one must wonder why they have never been made

---

[320] Celestine Say, letter to John Moffitt, December 11, 1969, Moffitt papers.
[321] John Moffitt, letter to Brother Patrick Hart, February 8, 1970, Moffitt papers.
[322] John Howard Griffin, letter to John Moffitt, October 24, 1969, Moffitt papers.
[323] John Howard Griffin, letter to John Moffitt, August 11, 1969, Columbia University.
[324] John Howard Griffin, letter to John Moffitt, August 18, 1969, Moffitt papers.

available if they support the accidental electrocution narrative. Furthermore, it is difficult to imagine what these forensic medical reports could be in the absence of an autopsy.

Moffitt in his correspondence made it clear that he did not want to write anything that he did not think was true. What might appear to have been a matter of scruples could well have been simply a matter of tactics on the part of the crafty journalist. One can be caught in a blatant lie. His "scruples" did not prevent him from going along quietly with lies told by others and from concealing evidence. He once wrote to Abbot Flavian about his difficulty in writing about Merton's death because he was not convinced that it was an accident, and he wanted to tell the truth based on the facts. At the same time, he told the abbot he did not wish to state anything that would go against his wishes.[325] At times Griffin, Brother Patrick, and the abbot would speculate about "facts" that Moffitt knew were not supported by the evidence.

Moffitt tried his best to reconcile the witness accounts to conclude Merton's death was either a heart attack or an accident. Moffitt would not entertain the possibility of homicide, at least insofar as one can discern from his letters. He surely knew that that would have been unacceptable to Abbott Flavian, Brother Patrick, Griffin and others.

Griffin seemed to enjoy having access to the witness accounts and official reports and keeping everything secret. He once told Moffitt that he had received and read his

---

[325] John Moffitt, letter to Abbot Flavian, December 11, 1969, Moffitt papers.

confidential letter and then burned it.[326] One may well surmise that letters would not need to be burned if Merton's death had been a mere accident.

In November of 1969, Moffitt told Griffin that he was still confused by the contradictory evidence. Moffitt had endless theories and once speculated that Merton may have had diabetes, felt faint, and grabbed the fan.[327] Eventually, in 1970, Moffitt decided that no one could decide what caused Merton's fall, but regardless of why he fell, he did not think anyone could prove that Merton did not pull the fan onto himself.

Although Moffitt had seen the death scene photograph taken by Say, he was willing to accept that Merton fell into an unlikely position with the fan on top of him. Moffitt ignored what the photo showed and what the eyewitnesses saw. Moffitt as an editor at *America* could have reported what the photo showed and the inconsistencies that did not point to an accident, but he suppressed this information. In the final analysis, John Moffitt may be described as the Hamlet of the Thomas Merton tragedy ("To be, or not to be..."). Perhaps someone would consider doing a truthful play about Merton's murder and its cover-up with Moffitt as the principal protagonist. That would have real dramatic potential.

---

[326] John Howard Griffin, letter to John Moffitt, November 5, 1969, Moffitt papers.
[327] John Moffitt, letter to John Howard Griffin, November 25, 1969, Moffitt papers.

The journalists Griffin and Moffitt both recognized the importance of Say's original negatives. They agreed the photograph must be kept secret and never shown. This conspiracy of silence could only have been because they knew full well that the photographs undermined the accidental electrocution story.

CHAPTER 18

Penn Jones: Covert Agent?

In the late spring of 1969 Penn Jones traveled to Bangkok, purportedly to investigate Merton's death. Griffin wrote to Moffitt from Gethsemani to inform him that Jones had photographed the room where Merton had died, and a Hitachi fan was there, just like the one that was lying across Merton in the photograph taken by Say.[328] Jones also traveled to the Philippines where he met with Dom Bernardo Perez and Fr. Celestine Say. As stated previously, Say wrote that Jones implied to him that he suspected that there was a strong possibility that Merton had been murdered and that it could be related to the assassinations of Martin Luther King and Kennedy.[329]

Griffin and Jones were close friends who lived only 12 miles apart in Texas. Jones owned a small newspaper in Midlothian, Texas. He was a professional journalist, best

---

[328] John Howard Griffin, letter to John Moffitt, December 5, 1969, Moffitt papers.
[329] Celestine Say, letter to John Moffitt, July 1, 1969, Moffitt papers.

known as a pioneer John F. Kennedy assassination "conspiracy theorist." Jones wrote *Forgive My Grief*, a four volume critical review of the Warren Commission Report on the Assassination of President John F. Kennedy. Griffin wrote the preface of Volume One in 1966.

Jones also co-edited *The Continuing Inquiry* newsletter with Gary Mack, the curator of the Sixth Floor Museum at Dealey Plaza. The museum, as the name implies, is on the sixth floor of the former Texas School Book Depository where Lee Harvey Oswald is said to have been positioned when he shot President John F. Kennedy on November 22, 1963, according to the Warren Commission Report and its virtually unanimous advocates in the press,

Griffin had been a contributor to *The Continuing Inquiry*, and he once wrote about the FBI's influence over Catholic Church leaders, Cardinal Spellman of New York in particular.[330]

James W. Douglass, author of *JFK and the Unspeakable*, mentioned the Penn Jones investigation of Merton's death in a keynote address to the International Thomas Merton Society meeting on June 13, 1997. Douglass said that he had posed the question of Merton's death to Roberto Bonazzi, the biographer of John Howard Griffin and also a friend of Penn Jones. Bonazzi responded that Jones had gone to Bangkok

---

[330] John Howard Griffin, "J. Edgar Hoover's Interference with Church Leaders Revealed in Reports," *The Continuing Inquiry*, January 22, 1977.

and investigated Merton's death, and he had found no evidence of murder.[331]

We asked Bonazzi by email about this Jones investigation of Merton's death. Bonazzi told us that Griffin believed that when Jones went to Bangkok and investigated Merton's death and came up with nothing, that had settled the matter that the death was an accident. But after Jones returned from Thailand, he apparently wrote nothing at all about Merton's death.[332] Bonazzi knew of nothing that Jones had written on the subject, and we have been unable to find anything, either.

Douglass may have been naïve to accept the second-hand word of Jones. The Jones investigation of Merton's death raises many questions. If Griffin thought it proved Merton's death was an accident, how so?

Who paid for Jones's trip to Asia? It was very expensive in 1969 to fly to Thailand and the Philippines. What could Jones possibly have hoped to find by traveling to Thailand and visiting Merton's room six months later?

If Jones had obtained the official death certificate and doctor's certificate while he was in Thailand, he might have accomplished something. He could have learned, for instance, that these documents falsely stated that Merton's body was taken to the hospital for an autopsy in accordance with the law. But those documents had been given to Weakland and mailed to Abbot Flavian, so Jones did not have to travel to

---

[331] James W. Douglass, "Compassion and the Unspeakable," *The Merton Annual*, Vol. 11, 1998, p. 82.

[332] Roberto Bonazzi, email to HughTurley, August 12, 2017.

Thailand to obtain them. Jones might have obtained the original Thai police report and investigative records, but there is no indication that he did. It looks, rather, as if the expert JFK assassination researcher failed to obtain even the most basic official Thai documents on Merton's death. If Jones, the journalist, interviewed any witnesses other than Say, he said nothing about it.

Jones told Say that he strongly suspected Merton was murdered. Then Jones told Griffin that he found no evidence of murder. What changed his mind? There is something very peculiar about Jones traveling all the way to the Philippines for apparently no other purpose than to tell Say that he suspected that there was a good possibility Merton had been murdered.

It looks very much like Jones's primary purpose in traveling to Asia was not to nose around the crime scene but, rather, to learn whether Say represented any sort of a threat to the cover-up. Griffin told Moffitt that Say had given more information to his investigator than he did to either of them in his letters. Considering how much Say revealed in his letters this is an intriguing statement. And for some reason Griffin didn't tell Moffitt the name of his investigator.[333]

In a later letter, Griffin wrote to Moffitt that Say had spoken to his investigator.[334] We know from Say that Jones

---

[333] John Howard Griffin, letter to John Moffitt, November 5, 1969, Moffitt papers.

[334] John Howard Griffin, letter to John Moffitt, November 26, 1969, Moffitt papers.

visited him in the Philippines. Griffin said only that "his investigator" visited Say in the Philippines.[335] Jones reported to Griffin that he had seen a Hitachi fan in the room where Merton died. Jones and the investigator both reported to Griffin, so there is hardly any doubt that they are the same person. Nailing the matter down further, in his short note to Moffitt in which he related from his investigator the fact that, contrary to the assertion of Fr. de Grunne, the Hitachi fans were all still in place at the Thai retreat center, Griffin revealed that Jones was that investigator.[336] He just never said that this was the same person who interviewed Say in the Philippines.

It is interesting that Jones would tell Say that he believed that Merton was assassinated since Jones was working for Griffin. Griffin was always quick to reject the possibility of assassination. It looks very much like Jones was trying to draw Say out to confide in him any opinion or knowledge that he might have that could cause trouble for the cover-up.

The existence of agents who offer false opposition to nefarious or odious actions by the government is hardly an unknown phenomenon. Penetrating the leadership of an enemy is part of the CIA's admitted tradecraft. If the enemy happens to be American citizens who suspect the CIA of domestic skulduggery, it follows that they would use the

---

[335] John Howard Griffin, letter to John Moffitt, November 5, 1969, Moffitt papers.

[336] John Howard Griffin, letter to John Moffitt, December 5, 1969, Moffitt papers.

technique on them, as well. From the JFK assassination to 9/11 to the case of a number of the highest profile alternative media government critics, suspicions of such supposed fake opposition abounds.

The experience of both authors with one such person in the Vincent Foster case carries us beyond mere suspicion. We speak of the former reporter for the *New York Post*, the *Pittsburgh Tribune Review* and current editor of *Newsmax*, Christopher Ruddy. Ruddy gained prominence as virtually the only reporter in the country to look into the Foster death critically.

Both David Martin and Hugh Turley, the latter in particular, gave a great deal of their time in assisting Ruddy when he came to the Washington, DC, area. He almost always stayed at Turley's house, and since he never rented a car, Turley would always pick him up at Washington's National Airport when he flew in from New York on the Delta Shuttle and drive him around for his appointments.

Ruddy was also responsible for Martin beginning work on what became the six-part online article, "America's Dreyfus Affair, the Case of the Death of Vincent Foster," after Martin had told Ruddy of some similarities that he had seen in the two cases. At the time, the mainstream media dismissed Ruddy as a wild-eyed conspiracy theorist. He was even a guest on CBS's 60 Minutes where, to the average viewer, he appeared to be humiliated by Mike Wallace.

Now he has disavowed his previous hard-hitting work, leaving a lot of explaining to do, like all of the evidence of foul play that he presented in his book, *The Strange Death of*

Vincent Foster. But his newfound "respectability" has served him well. As a big contributor to the Clinton Foundation, he has become very close to this power couple that at one time everyone thought he was out to get. He is also eagerly sought out for interviews by the mainstream press to offer his insights and wisdom on major affairs of the day. His opinions are particularly valued because he is a friend of fellow New York native and West Palm Beach, Florida, resident, President Donald Trump, and is thought to be an informal adviser.

What could be responsible for Ruddy's transformation? Actually, it is very clear that he is the same Christopher Ruddy that he always was. As an independent truth seeker he was just playing a role. Some things he accomplished in that role were to monopolize and personify the opposition to the government and the mainstream press, to discover what the genuine independent truth seekers were up to, and to determine where those perpetuating the cover-up might encounter problems that needed to be addressed.[337]

Penn Jones, Jr., went through a similar apparent "mellowing" process, from being one of the first journalists to dig up evidence that appeared to contradict the Warren Commission's two-lone-crazed-gunmen (Lee Harvey Oswald and Jack Ruby) conclusion to working with Gary Mack at the Sixth Floor Museum. As far as transformations go, Mack's was the more Ruddy-like of the two. A Dallas television

---

[337] David Martin, "Double Agent Ruddy Reaching for Media Pinnacle." http://www.dcdave.com/article5/140314.htm

journalist, Mack started out as a "conspiracy theorist" in the JFK assassination case, but by the time he died in 2015 at the age of 68, he had come around so far to the side of the government that he merited a glowing obituary in *The New York Times*.

Jones never went quite so far as Mack, and we might be accused of tarring him with guilt by association. After all, we once worked closely with Christopher Ruddy. But as soon as we figured out what Ruddy was about, we put as much distance between him and ourselves as possible. Jones, on the other hand, got closer to Mack after Mack had really dropped all pretense of being an independent seeker of truth in the JFK case. Also, like John Howard Griffin and Christopher Ruddy, and unlike the current authors, they were both professional American journalists.

Returning to Jones's early 1969 Asian odyssey, if there were precipitating events causing Jones's handler Griffin to send him off to the Philippines, they might have begun with the previously mentioned article published in the Philippines based on the accounts of Say and Fr. Bernardo Perez, O.S.B. That article raised doubts about the Thai police conclusion of death due to heart failure, because there had been no autopsy and Merton had no history of a heart condition.[338] Then Say sent that alarming March 1969 letter to Abbot Flavian with the photograph he took and asking about the autopsy results. The following month Perez wrote a long article for the

---

[338] Abraham C. Florendo, "The Final Ascent on the Seven Storey Mountain," *Mirror*, Jan. 18, 1969, pp. 10-11, the Merton Center.

Philippine Free Press that called Merton's death "absurd" if it was indeed caused by electrocution.[339] These events surely would have made Griffin curious to learn if Say and Perez suspected Merton had been murdered.

If there were reasons for Say and Perez to be suspicious they needed to be addressed. As Griffin told Moffitt, he had a responsibility to dispel the suspicions or resolve the contradictions. [340] Jones would report back to Griffin, probably much to Griffin's relief, that Say and Perez did not suspect murder.

Say informed Moffitt about the visit from Jones and told him it just seemed too far-fetched that Merton was murdered and that it was connected to the Kennedy and King assassinations. Say told Moffitt that he believed that Merton's death was caused by a heart attack or electrocution.[341]

Say only asked about the autopsy because he wanted to know if there was any clarification of whether the death was the result of a heart attack or of electrocution. One monk had told Say that he "practically killed [Merton] for not coming to his rescue earlier."[342] Say felt regret that he had not been

---

[339] Bernardo Perez, O.S.B., "The Death of a Monk," *Philippines Free Press*, April 2, 1969, p.12.

[340] John Howard Griffin, letter to John Moffitt, August 11, 1969, Columbia University.

[341] Celestine Say, letter to John Moffitt, July 1, 1969, Moffitt papers.

[342] Celestine Say, letter to Flavian Burns, Mar. 18, 1969, the Merton Center.

able to save Merton. If he had known for certain that Merton had died of a heart attack, it might have eased his conscience.

Say probably never imagined that Merton was already dead when Say got to the cottage and that the crime scene had been quickly and neatly arranged. It had apparently not occurred to him that an autopsy might have found additional wounds not consistent with an accident or a heart attack. Perhaps it was fortunate that Say was not suspicious. If Say had suspected that Merton was murdered it might have been unwise—even dangerous—to share his suspicions with Jones.

As noted, we have found no evidence that Jones ever did anything in the wake of Merton's death that is worthy of being called any sort of an investigation. There is only the unwarranted inference made by Roberto Bonazzi and second hand by James Douglass that if Jones, the JFK researcher, found no evidence of murder that alone "proves" that Merton's death was an accident.

Few people ever suspect journalists would act as agents to cover up state-sponsored secret assassinations. One of the few people who was astute enough in 1968 to have suspected such things would have been Thomas Merton.

CHAPTER 19

Pope Francis and Thomas Merton

On September 24, 2015, Pope Francis became the first pope to address a joint session of the U.S. Congress. He singled out four Americans to mention as model citizens, Abraham Lincoln, Dorothy Day, Martin Luther King, and Thomas Merton.

Three of them were advocates for peace. Lincoln, by contrast, embarked upon a war of choice to bring the residents of seceding states back into the Union, a war that would become the nation's deadliest. Lincoln's contemporary, Pope Pius IX, hardly shared Pope Francis' admiration for the unreligious president. Although the Vatican officially favored the Union cause, Pope Pius IX was deeply disturbed by the carnage of the war. Lincoln, however, rejected the pope's efforts to mediate an end to it. The pope was also concerned over the Union's cynical use of desperate

Irish Catholic immigrants as virtual cannon fodder in the Union army.[343]

Speaking to the U.S. Congress, Pope Francis said, "Merton was above all a man of prayer, a thinker who challenged the certitudes of his time." Merton certainly would have challenged the certitude of the 9/11 narrative that launched the endless Global War on Terror, accompanied by the loss at home of civil liberties and privacy. Not so for Pope Francis. The day following his address to Congress, he visited the 9/11 memorial in New York. The pope led an interfaith prayer service saying, "O God of love, compassion, and healing, look on us, people of many different faiths and religious traditions, who gather today on this hallowed ground..." Catholics ought to ask in what sense the 9/11 memorial is "hallowed."

Belief in the official 9/11 narrative was elevated to religious status with the pope's blessing. The Catholic News Service reported that a widow whose husband died in the south tower called the memorial a "sacred and hallowed space," made even more symbolic by the blessing of the

---

[343] "American Civil War, Papal Stance Toward." New Catholic Encyclopedia Supplement 2010, edited by Robert L. Fastiggi, vol. 1, Gale, 2010, pp. 38-42. World History in Context, link.galegroup.com/apps/doc/CX1388100038/WHIC?u=catholiccenhs&xid=f755aa97. Accessed 13 Nov. 2017.

pope.[344] On the tenth anniversary the *National Catholic Reporter* wrote that the 9/11 site was "forever sacred" and had "religious and spiritual qualities."[345]

Pope Francis was correct in saying that Merton "challenged the certitudes of his time." Merton questioned the truth of the news reports immediately following the assassination of President John F. Kennedy. Modern churchmen, including Pope Francis, willfully reject objective facts and march in step with the news media.

Before Pope Francis spoke to the Congress, he visited St. Matthew's Cathedral in Washington, D.C. and spoke to a gathering of bishops. The pontiff was standing on the very spot in the cathedral where these words are inscribed in the floor, "Here rested the remains of President Kennedy at the Requiem Mass, Nov. 25, 1963, before their removal to Arlington where they lie in expectation of a heavenly resurrection." Incredibly, the pope stood on that spot and never mentioned John F. Kennedy, America's only Catholic president.

Visiting the nearby Arlington graves of the assassinated Catholics John and Robert Kennedy might have placed the pontiff in the awkward position of endorsing the official assassination stories that many Americans no longer believe,

---

[344] Carol Zimmermann, "Pope's Ground Zero Visit Was Somber Moment for 9/11 Survivors, Relatives," Catholic News Service, September 26, 2015.

[345] Eugene Cullen Kennedy, "9/11 Site, Sacred in Itself," *National Catholic Reporter*, September 9, 2011.

so he gave those a pass. Questioning official truth was not an option, so Pope Francis avoided any mention of the assassinated Catholic president.

Modern churchmen have accepted the popular story of Merton's accidental death that virtually originated with the news media and has been spread by them for half a century. The same news media, dominated by the traditional enemies of the Church, elevate Pope Francis, whose favorite painting is said to be Marc Chagall's well-nigh blasphemous, "White Crucifixion," with flattering press coverage. Thomas Merton knew that the news media in his day were generally opposed to truth and reality, and there is no indication that they have changed.

CHAPTER 20

The Logical Explanation

There have been theories presented that attempt to explain how a fan came to be on top of Merton's dead body. Dr. Nakvachara said, "the dead priest fainted" and pulled the fan on top of himself. Mother Pia speculated that Merton fainted and damaged the fan, dragging it onto himself. De Grunne said the fan killed Merton and nothing else. Abbot Flavian theorized that Merton undressed, bathed, tried to move the fan with a defective cord, and there were no fuses. Brother Patrick said Merton took a shower, then turned the fan on, or moved it, collapsed and the fan "tumbled" on top of him.

Moffitt and Mott suggested that Merton might have been stuck to the fan. Moffitt also speculated that Merton "disarranged" the wires in the fan as it fell. Mott also theorized that Merton may have been naked when he came out of a shower and his feet may have still been wet when he slipped and pulled the fan toward himself for support.

No actual evidence supports any of these theories.

The eyewitnesses Dr. Weist, Haas, Say, and Donovan were puzzled by what they saw and they did not know how the fan landed on Merton. Donovan did not think Merton's hands could be in the position as they were found if he had pulled the fan onto himself.

For anyone arguing accidental electrocution, how the electrified fan came to be top of Merton is a mystery. How the fan became electrified is another mystery. The solution by the Thai officials was simply to declare that Merton suffered acute cardiac failure at the same instant he was next to a Hitachi fan that, by chance, happened to be lethally wired, and, by chance, he pulled the fan on top of himself as he died. Not surprisingly, as we have seen, the key witnesses did not believe this very unlikely scenario. Furthermore, even with all their mental gymnastics, the Thai police were left with the very loose end of how and when the defective wiring came to be installed in the fan.

Speculation on how the fan came to be on top of Merton should be based on real possibilities and not impossibilities, a dead priest fainting, a tumbling fan, or a wet and naked Merton slipping and pulling the fan onto himself. The photographic evidence from Say supports Donovan's suspicion that Merton did not place the fan on himself. Without any evidence that Merton placed the fan on himself, an alternative hypothesis is needed.

If Merton did not place the fan on himself, someone else placed the fan on top of Merton to stage an "accident."

Another big loose end that the Thai police and Dr. Nakvachara failed to tie up was the bleeding wound on the back of Merton's head. They dealt with that problem by simply ignoring it. Had there been an autopsy the question of any wounds that were not consistent with the police theory of how Merton died would have to have been addressed. But then the police and the Thai doctor simply wrote falsely that there was an autopsy, and that was that.

Dr. Weist speculated that the head wound may have been caused by the fall, but in that case there would have to have been a cut, and there was nothing near Merton's head but the level floor, which is not likely to have caused such a cut. Is it not far more likely that the head wound brought Merton to the floor? A professional assassin, like those in the CIA Phoenix Program, could subdue a subject in seconds, and the bleeding head wound on the back of Merton's head could well have been from a blow to the head, or, as we speculated previously, by a bullet. In favor of the blow to the head, we are reminded that they struck Frank Olson with a hammer before they threw him out of a 10th floor window. Leon Trotsky was killed in a similar manner by an assassin wielding an ice axe.

We might be reminded that the CIA assassination manual suggests using among other things a blow "to the lower, rear portion of the skull," perhaps with an everyday implement such as a "hammer, axe, wrench, screwdriver, fire poker, kitchen knife, lamp stand, or anything hard, heavy and handy." The manual adds that "even a rock or heavy stick will do."[346]

To make it appear that Merton was electrocuted, the electrified fan was laid across him. The perfect time for the attack would have been when he removed his habit, to avoid having to take it off him after he had been immobilized.

It was typical during the hot weather in Thailand for monks to remove their habits before lying down to rest. When Fr. Say arrived at the cottage, the first thing he did was to remove his habit before going to brush his teeth. Merton would hang his habit on a clothes stand to dry. The clothes stand in Merton's room was in the corner, so he would have faced the corner with his back to an assassin. There is evidence that the room may have been arranged with this in mind. Fr. Say reported that someone had entered the cottage and rearranged Merton's room. Merton told Say that he thought it might have been a maid. We do not know exactly how it was rearranged, but it is suspicious that only Merton's room was rearranged and not Say's room.

The evidence shows that Merton was found at the clothes stand where his habit was hanging when he was killed. His body was found lying at a 45-degree angle to the corner of the room, with the top of his head at the clothes stand, and his feet 40 inches from the foot of the bed. Dr. Weist, as we have seen, drew the position of Merton's body. Although she

---

[346] Operation PBSuccess, CIA, A study of assassination, online at George Washington University,
 http://nsarchive.gwu.edu/NSAEBB/NSAEBB4/ciaguat2.html

did not draw the clothes stand in the corner, Say's photographs show that Merton was found with his head in the corner of the room in front of the clothes stand. Dr. Weist's drawing was a close representation.

The immediate removal of the plants outside the windows of Merton's cottage is also suspicious. A professional assassin could have lurked outside Merton's window among those plants. He would not have aroused suspicion if disguised as a gardener tending the plants on the 100-acre property. As Merton pulled his habit over his head, the assassin could have struck and then quickly placed the fan on him. Then he could have left the room and locked the door from the outside in the same way that the witnesses would later unlock it. He could have exited a bathroom window, which was not of the louvered type. Alternatively, and more simply, he might well have gone upstairs and remained there with de Grunne until the coast was clear.

There is a precedent for plants being removed after an assassination. Officially Martin Luther King Jr. was shot by James Earl Ray from the second-floor bathroom window at the rear of a rooming house. "At least two eyewitness accounts placed the origin of the shot in a clump of bushes beneath the windows of the rooming house, not the bathroom window."[347] One witness saw a man run from the bushes to a waiting Memphis police car. The following day,

---

[347] "Investigation of the Assassination of Martin Luther King, Jr." Select Committee on Assassinations of the House of Representatives, Volume XI, p. 4.

Memphis Police Inspector Sam Evans asked Maynard Stiles, the city public works administrator, to cut down and remove all the bushes at the back of the rooming house.[348] The evidence of where witnesses say they saw the shots fired was destroyed.

The crime cannot be reconstructed when the crime scene has been destroyed. A crime scene is usually secured and preserved for an investigation. The King family does not accept the official story that James Earl Ray assassinated King. The King family believes there was a cover-up and removing the bushes from the back of the rooming house was part of the cover-up from the beginning.[349]

An interpreter told Say that the plants were removed near the cottage because Thais are afraid of ghosts. "When a person dies in a house, the building is unsalable," Say was told, "No Thai person in his right mind would dare purchase the house or live in it."[350] Is it true that if a person dies in a house in Thailand the house cannot be sold? Or did the Thai police, like the Memphis police, ask that the plants be removed?

---

[348] Transcript Coretta Scott King, et al. Vs. Lloyd Jowers, et al. defendants, excerpt of proceedings, In the Circuit Court of Shelby County, Tennessee for the 13th Judicial District at Memphis, Dec. 8, 1999.

[349] The King Center, http://www.thekingcenter.org/civil-case-king-family-versus-jowers.

[350] Celestine Say, letter to Flavian Burns, Mar. 18, 1969, the Merton Center.

The performance of the news media is a strong indication that Merton was murdered. The initial reports from anonymous sources that the death was an accident point to complicity with the staged crime scene. The accident story was likely prepared before the assassination, because the official conclusion was ignored. The press knew what the result would be before witnesses were interviewed, before the fan was analyzed, and without any autopsy. The press concealed the fact that eyewitnesses saw a bleeding head wound and said nothing about the strange position of Merton's body. The press failed to report on the falsification of documents about an autopsy that was never performed. In fact, they didn't even report that there wasn't any autopsy. Later, the press conspired in the planting of the false story that Merton showered and caused his accidental death.

The circumstances of Merton's "accident" are so curious as to be hardly believable. In that regard, they remind us that Merton wrote in November of 1963 that the notion that the nightclub owner Jack Ruby shot Lee Harvey Oswald out of some sort of patriotic impulsiveness was very difficult to believe.[351]

If Merton thought the story of the murder of Oswald was hard to believe, what would he have thought about the stories told about his own death?

---

[351] Thomas Merton, *Conjectures of a Guilty Bystander*, op. cit., p. 314-315.

CHAPTER 21

The Forbidden Photos and the Six Trappists Again

The photographs taken by Say are the best available evidence of the actual scene of Merton's death. We commissioned pencil drawings to be made of the photographs by a professional courtroom artist for the United States Supreme Court. The drawings were an accurate and respectful representation of the photographs showing exactly how eyewitnesses found Merton's body before the scene was disturbed. The reason the monks took the photographs, as we have emphasized, was to document exactly how they found the body. As we have seen, people whom they would hardly have ever suspected have consistently done their best to suppress those images.

The photographs are an essential resource to anyone interested in knowing the truth about how Merton was killed. The photos are, at the same time, a danger to expose those who have spread false information about Merton's death.

We wrote to the current abbot of Gethsemani, Fr. Elias Dietz, to request permission to publish these drawings—not the actual photographs—so readers could see exactly how Merton's body was found, which is not at all how people might imagine it was found, based on the widely published misinformation. Fr. Say had sent the original negatives to the abbey as a gift.[352] Since the photographs, even the ones sent with Griffin's papers to Columbia, are technically the property of the abbey, we lack the legal right to display them, or as we have been counseled, even an artist's rendering of them, without the abbey's consent.

Abbot Dietz responded that after consulting with several monks at the Abbey of Gethsemani, he thought that it would not be appropriate to print these images, even as drawings, and denied us permission to do so.[353]

Though Abbot Dietz spoke of several monks, there can be little doubt that the most influential among them in matters such as this would have to have been Brother Patrick Hart. He is the key surviving monk at the abbey with a direct interest in Thomas Merton's death, and, as we have seen, his interest has been, along with the late Abbot Flavian Burns, to prevent the actual facts about Merton's death from coming to light. He was on the scene when Abbot Flavian made the key decisions that precluded any possibility of the precise cause of Merton's death from becoming known. He conspired with the abbot and with the first authorized Merton biographer,

---

[352] Celestine Say, letter to John Howard Griffin, June 25, 1969, Columbia University.
[353] Abbot Elias Dietz, letter to Hugh Turley, September 2, 2017.

John Howard Griffin, to withhold from the public all of the information that they had received from Thailand, most importantly, that the Thai authorities had concluded that heart failure had caused Merton to fall into a defective fan and that they had reached that conclusion in the absence of an autopsy.

It is unlikely that Abbot Dietz and the other monks at Gethsemani even know that Brother Patrick, in obvious furtherance of the accidental-electrocution thesis, invented the story that Merton had taken a shower and that he most unforgivably cut out the words, "in his pajamas," from the supposed letter received from "the six Trappists" at the Thai conference, describing how Merton's body was found (more about that letter later).

Abbot Dietz said it should be enough for the purpose of our book to mention the photos exist and perhaps describe them. We have done our best to describe these images, but they really speak best for themselves, and other people with different perspectives may see things that we may have missed.

The abbot told us that anyone with a need or desire to see these images could obtain them, as we did, from the library. Ordering digitized copies of the photographs from the Rare Book and Manuscript Library in the Butler Library at Columbia University in New York City will cost each person $36. The photographs have been suppressed for almost 50 years, but this may finally be coming to an end, as more people are able to obtain them and share them.

The abbot offered two reasons for denying publication of the drawings. His first reason was that it was Thomas Merton's wish not to be the subject of films or dramatizations, and publishing these photos, in the abbot's view, is in this category. We did not ask to publish the photos, but only drawings of the images, and the photos or drawings are not a motion picture film or dramatization. The images are precise drawings of the scene exactly as Merton's body was found.

As we have noted, Merton's death has already been presented dramatically in the play, *Under the Sign of the Waterbearer: A Life of Thomas Merton* by James T. Baker. It appears that Merton's wishes concerning dramatization are immaterial as long as the story follows the authorized narrative that Merton was wet from bathing and electrocuted himself. Merton's wishes notwithstanding, a copy of Baker's dramatization with its phony story about Merton bathing in a tub is on the shelf at the Merton Center at Bellarmine University. If Merton did not wish to be the subject of a dramatization, he might well have had in mind those who would dramatize his death inaccurately and cover up the truth.

Abbot Dietz wrote that the second reason that we not publish the images was the more important one. The abbot said that Merton's death is essentially a family affair, and the sensibilities of Merton's community are the most important thing.

But could those sensibilities be more important even than the truth about Merton's death? Abbot Dietz now carries the mantle of a monastic leadership that has concealed the truth about Merton's death at seemingly every opportunity. There is no good reason why this concealment should continue, however.

We might also be reminded that Abbot Dietz is propounding a thoroughly modern notion that really doesn't have anything to do with the Christian religion. Scripture doesn't place any importance on people's "sensibilities." The truth about how the great Thomas Merton died is far more important, and the sketches that the abbot would not let the public see bear heavily upon that question.

Abbot Dietz is on as shaky ground from the perspective of modern jurisprudence as he is from ancient Scripture. From his cloister in Kentucky, he would take us back to early 12th century England, before the issuance by King Henry II of the Assize of Clarendon, when crime was considered to be primarily a matter of concern only to the perpetrator and the victim and his family. Since that time, we have regarded criminal actions as crimes against society. Even more is that the case with an important public figure like Merton. When a Thomas Merton is killed, no less than the Kennedys or King or James Forrestal, it is not just the immediate family that suffers but also society as a whole. The sensibilities of a few monks are really beside the point.

Furthermore, it is reasonable to expect that the families of murder victims would want the truth to be known. The families of Tommy Burkett, Frank Olson, Kenneth Trentadue, James Sabow, and Martin Luther King have all fought for the truth about the murder of their loved one. These courageous families have struggled against powerful evil forces to find and to tell the truth.

Sometimes a victim's family, for whatever reason, is unwilling to step up and testify to the truth. Vincent Foster's own sister has taken the side of the government and press and argued that her brother killed himself. The behavior of a few key people at the Abbey of Gethsemani, unfortunately, has been distressingly similar.

Efforts have been made by those key people to spread the blame around. Brother Patrick, recall, told the *Louisville Courier-Journal* in 1980 that the "monks at Gethsemani" wanted Merton buried at home more than they wanted an autopsy to be performed and that no one at the abbey had any suspicion that the CIA could have had anything to do with Merton's death.

Long before that, just nine days after the death, the abbey, as we have noted, sent out a "Dear Friends" letter accompanying the letter from "The Six Trappists" at the monastic conference that served as a sort of explanation for what had happened. Abbot Flavian Burns did not sign this cover letter, as one might expect. Rather, the letter closed, "Gratefully yours in Christ, *The Monks of Gethsemani.*" Unlike the body of the letter, the closing was italicized.

The closing was strangely similar to the one on the wholly unsatisfactory "explanatory" letter that it accompanied. That one closed this way: "Your brothers and sisters in Christ, *(Signed by the six Trappist delegates at the Conference)."*

How odd! Again, the italics are in the original version, or at least that's how the document that we received from the

Merton Center appears. Surely this could not be how those Trappists actually closed their letter, could it? Would they not have each affixed their signatures, followed by "O.C.S.O." as is customary?

To get to the bottom of things, we first contacted the Merton Center to request a copy of the original signed letter. Dr. Paul Pearson thought a signed copy would be among the abbot's papers in the monastery archives so we wrote to Abbot Dietz. After getting no reply for a couple of weeks, we reached him by telephone, and he told us that he had passed along the request to their archivist, Brother Lawrence Morey, and he had Brother Lawrence give us a call. Brother Lawrence, who has been at the Gethsemani Abbey for fourteen years, told us that any such letter would have long since been sent to the Merton Center and that he had never seen the letter among their records.

At this point, we are forced to take a cold, hard look at that letter to Abbot Flavian that begins with a promise that the "undersigned" will provide the information that they know the monks at Gethsemani "would all be anxious to know" and then proceeds to deliver no such thing.

Since neither the abbey nor the Merton Center has any such signed letter, there are only two possibilities. This valuable document has either been lost or disposed of by someone or it never existed as a signed letter. Careful examination of what it says and how it has been used strongly suggests to us that the latter is the case.

In the first place, for the supposed creators of the letter to have called themselves "*the* six Trappist delegates at the

Conference" amounts to their telling a lie. They surely would have known that after Merton's death there were seven of them remaining. Why would they tell such a lie? When *The Asian Journal of Thomas Merton* published the letter for the first time in 1973, six actual names were listed after the closing, with Sister Marie de la Croix left out, but in the absence of the original letter, we have no way of knowing if they were the actual originators of the letter. The roster of conference attendees was available, and it would not have been difficult to pick out six Trappists. Sister Marie de la Croix, at that point, was the logical one to leave out because she had published a short synopsis of the mysterious death in which she stated that she expected that an autopsy would be performed, an inconsistency with the six-Trappists document.

The original error of six instead of seven was either inadvertent or it was intentional. If the six Trappists named in the *Asian Journal* actually got together and wrote the letter, the chance that it was inadvertent, as we have explained, is virtually nil. Originally, when we were taking the letter at face value as authentic, we believed that de la Croix had been left out because she did not endorse the letter's contents, but it would have been the height of dishonesty for the others to pretend that she didn't exist by purposely representing themselves as "*the* six Trappist delegates at the Conference," and they simply could not have done it accidently. One of the supposed signatories of the letter, you see, was the Abbess Mother Christiana, of de la Croix's home monastery at Seiboen, Japan. They were the only two Trappistines at the conference. The editors of *The Asian Journal*, not realizing the game that was being played, and feeling the need for actual names, proceeded to supply them five years later.

When the letter was placed on display at the Merton Center website during the 50th anniversary year of Merton's death someone recognized the absurdity of calling the signatories, "the six," so they changed this to call them simply "the Trappist delegates." The letter is almost certainly bogus, and the error in number is likely a bureaucratic blunder, resembling the inadvertent errors that we saw in the fake Haas document. And the resemblance to the Haas document doesn't stop there.

As with the Haas document, the likely intentional errors are more important. The "shout," supposedly heard in this case by "others," some time after Merton had retired to his room has a prominent place just as it does in the Haas document and in the police report. The notion that that was the moment of electrocution and death is thereby planted, and it is a notion that has persisted to the present day. Later writers, as we have seen, have said that the shout was unfortunately ignored, which is likely to have been drawn from this original erroneous story. In the world of disinformation, this is known as the "first impression trick," and we have seen it played over and over, from one lone crazed gunman after another right through the nineteen hijackers with box cutters.

The Haas document has the fan misplaced, with the head of the fan near Merton's head and the base between his legs, while the Trappists' document has it across his chest (the better to deliver a lethal shock?) rather than across his pelvic area where it was actually found. Another similarity of probably minor consequence is that both documents have the fan still running, while other witnesses said that it was not. Though it hardly makes a difference one way or the other, it leaves the impression that these folks must know what they are talking about when they include such minutiae, when, in fact, none of them were witnesses at the scene.

The letter appears to have been used as a template for Brother Patrick's postscript where none of the key people, neither the actual witnesses nor the Thai investigating authorities, are named. The letter names the individuals who later checked Merton's personal belongings and who said Mass the following day. Actual witnesses to the event of Merton's death are called "others," "they", and "the nun." Merton's body "was found" in the passive voice. The unsigned letter left the "Trappists" unnamed just as Brother Patrick did not name the Trappists who identified Merton's body at the mortuary in Kentucky.

Furthermore, we are told nothing about an autopsy, neither that at the time the document was created there had not been one nor if there was any prospect for one. The key word, "autopsy," is simply missing. Rather, the writers presume to "inform" Merton's fellow monks at Gethsemani with a mishmash of conjecture, in the manner of the biographer, Michael Mott. Merton could have had a heart attack and knocked the fan onto himself, they say, but what they don't say is that that was the incredible official conclusion of the Thai authorities. But then they add another note to the journalists' "first impression trick" by saying that he might have simply been electrocuted by the fan, and the fact that he was barefooted on a stone floor likely helped to make the shock lethal.

The writers even go beyond the unsigned Haas document, the unsigned police report, and the testimony of all the witnesses by introducing the possibility that Merton might have taken a shower. That is what Brother Patrick seized upon in 1973 when he turned the idle, unfounded conjecture into concrete fact, over the objection of John Moffitt.

The document does tell us that the back of Merton's head was "bleeding slightly," but they dilute that vital bit of information and distract us by saying before that that there were cuts on his right side and arm, cuts that nobody else, not even the examining physician, Dr. Edeltrud Weist, seemed to have noticed.

We also learned from Brother Lawrence that the Thai doctor's report, the death certificate, and the U.S. Embassy's Report on the Death of an American Citizen, which we know were sent to the abbey, are not there anymore, either. Neither were they at the Thomas Merton Center until we sent them the copies that we had found. One might argue, then, that like these documents, the original signed letter from those six Trappists was simply either lost or destroyed. But one can easily see why those documents, which all say that Merton died of heart failure, might have been disposed of. They undermine the approved story of death by faulty-fan electrocution. Because it was one of the foundation pieces of the approved story, one would think that those promoting that story would surely have held onto the signed letter from six Trappist attendees of the Thai monastic conference if, in fact, it ever existed.

The most compelling argument of all that, like the Haas statement, the six-Trappists letter is a fake document is that it fortifies the "first impression" that the cause of Merton's death is simply an unknowable mystery. You may believe what you want to believe, the letter says in so many words, but, in the meantime, you might as well go with the media's "first impression trick" of accidental electrocution.

The two photographs of Merton's body taken by Father Celestine Say are of surpassing importance because they recreate the real first impression of the actual witnesses at the scene, not the ginned-up first, and so far, lasting impression that was foisted upon the public. Yes, those three witnesses were mystified by what they saw, but they fully expected that, at the very least, an autopsy would be performed to help solve the mystery.

Conclusion

Contrary to the common view, there is really no mystery about how Merton died. The best evidence indicates beyond any serious doubt that Merton was murdered. It's a simple fact that the average person is far more likely to be murdered than to be killed by an electric fan, and Merton was no average person. The story that a fan killed Merton is so preposterous that a series of fantastic stories have had to be invented to make it believable.

The murder of Merton inevitably raises two questions. Who did it and why? Solving the crime completely to learn the identity of the killer(s) without all the powers of the state at our disposal will remain beyond our capacity, but formally uninvestigated homicides are still homicides.

We *can* point a finger at the most likely suspect in Merton's murder cover-up, Brother Patrick Hart notwithstanding, and that is the CIA. The CIA had the motive and they had the means. When Penn Jones and others would make a connection between Merton's death and that of the Kennedy brothers and Martin Luther King they were not just blowing smoke. All four of those people were obstacles to the CIA's war ambitions in Southeast Asia, a war that was raging right next door to the scene of Merton's death. The difference between Merton and the others is that he represented a much less obvious obstacle to their ambitions, but the danger that they perceived in him was no less real. He was more like the burr under the saddle or the pebble in the shoe. The danger that Merton represented might not have been perceived by the general public—a fact that was capitalized upon by the biographer Mott when he dismissed the possibility of murder for absence of a motive—but it had to have been acutely felt by the pernicious powers in charge of policy. He was completely independent and thoroughly incorruptible, and they knew that he was reaching a large and influential audience. One might well imagine how much greater influence he might have had if he had lived out a natural life. The only way to shut him up was to kill him.

Concerning the means, we have seen from examination of the CIA's manual for assassinations that the manner in which the killing was accomplished is well within their capabilities. We have also seen that the CIA had a long, corrupt relationship with the police of Thailand, so they could anticipate full cooperation from the people who would be officially responsible for the investigation, and we have seen how corruptly they handled that responsibility. The CIA had made Vietnam a killing field of assassinations right next door with its Phoenix Program. What was one more assassination to them, especially when it was directed, in their eyes, toward the same objective, the successful prosecution of the war?

The role played in the cover-up by the U.S. Embassy and the U.S. military in Thailand also betrays the fine hand of the CIA at work. Working in conjunction with one another, they were quick to take control of Merton's body and to spirit it out of the country, making sure not only that the Thais did not perform an autopsy, but that one was not done at the U.S. Army hospital, either. The embassy was the source of that unsigned and undated police report with all the wildly misspelled names of witnesses. For all we know, operatives at the embassy could have been responsible for the misspellings, making the witnesses hard to track down.

The embassy also supplied the "statement" of the witness, Odo Haas, which we have concluded could not be authentic. The CIA was, in all likelihood, also the originator of the phony six-Trappists letter. Brother Patrick Hart could easily enough cut out the "in his pajamas" passage in that letter when it suited his purposes, but the crafting of the entire letter would likely have been beyond his capacity or inclination. The fabrication of documents, on the other hand, is little more than a routine part of the CIA's or any spy organization's bag of tricks.

We were also told by Archbishop Weakland that he had heard about that supposed Thai law that required anyone who is autopsied in Thailand be buried in Thailand, and, to the best of his recollection, the U.S. Embassy was the source of that information. The CIA has long penetrated the U.S. military officer corps and diplomatic corps, and that would especially have been the case in Thailand in 1968.

Perhaps the strongest evidence of all in support of the conclusion that this was a CIA hit is to be found in the performance of the heavily CIA-controlled American news media. From the beginning, they called the death an accidental electrocution, caused by a faulty fan, and they have never wavered from that story. In the process, they have suppressed the news of the official findings by the Thai police and medical authorities, and they have done not one iota of independent investigation, that is, not any that they have chosen to share with the public. In that regard, their behavior has been exactly as it has been in the wake of the deaths of the Kennedy brothers, Martin Luther King, Vincent Foster, and countless other major outrages before and since.

Since John Howard Griffin, Penn Jones, and Michael Mott were all professional journalists we may place them in this last category of CIA accomplices. Mott was a British journalist, now resident in the United States, but the U.S.-British intelligence/journalist connection represents a more or less smooth continuum. But it was the abbey leadership that ostensibly chose Griffin and then Mott to write Merton's biography with its intentionally deceptive section on his death. The abbey leadership was also ultimately responsible for no autopsy being performed, and they even supplied some cover-up lies of their own, such as that Merton was wet from a shower when he touched the deadly fan. The best explanation that we can come up with for their indefensible behavior is that they must have been subject to coercion of some nefarious sort, and that is another reason to suspect the hand of the CIA at work.

We also must explain the extraordinarily suspicious behavior of the Belgian priest, Fr. François de Grunne. Abbott Flavian Burns, Brother Patrick Hart, and the three journalists might have been instrumental in perpetrating the cover-up, but de Grunne is the one person in the drama who looks very much like a participant in the crime itself. Proper police investigators would have certainly treated him as a suspect, at least as an accomplice to the crime.

What could have made him do it? We might be able to make at least a good guess about that if we could learn anything about his life after he went back home to his abbey in Belgium, but he seems to have fallen off the face of the earth. The fact that his abbey will not even respond to our questions about him might well be telling. We have to suspect strongly that there was some scandal in his life that made him vulnerable to blackmail. His behavior was so very odd, so creepy, in fact, that it is hardly beyond the realm of possibility that he even could have been a subject of the mind-control program, dubbed MKUltra by the CIA, that possibly cost the conscience-smitten Frank Olson his life.

Reflecting upon Thomas Merton's life, and especially upon his death, now that we have penetrated the dense smoke screen around it, we see a man who was truly chosen by God for his task.

If you belonged to the world, the world would love you as its own; the reason it hates you is that you do not belong to the world, because my choice of you has drawn you out of the world. (John 15:19)

Merton chose to live apart from the world in a monastery. His love of his neighbor brought him back into the world to testify to the truth about our reality. At a time when virtually everyone in the country was accepting the solemn assurances of journalists like Walter Cronkite as the gospel truth, one week after the assassination of President Kennedy, Merton was already questioning. The widespread acceptance of the official version of events he saw as more of a psychological matter than anything else. People simply wanted things put to rest so they could get on with their lives and were willing to accept whatever they were told, regardless of how poorly the explanation addressed the many complexities of the matter.[354]

Merton said we should know our real history and not history that has been corrupted by propaganda. Merton, the Catholic intellectual has been replaced by George Weigel, the Catholic intellectual who claimed that the U.S. attack on Iraq was a "just war," in accordance with the teachings of St. Augustine. On the 50th anniversary of the assassination of JFK, Weigel wrote about his visit to the Texas School Book Depository at Dealey Plaza in Dallas. That would have placed him at the Sixth Floor Museum of Gary Mack and Penn Jones.

> Standing at the window from which the shots that changed American history were fired, I quickly decided that a trained marksman could have easily done, by himself, what the Warren Commission concluded he had done.[355]

Weigel is satisfied with the world's story about the murder of America's only Catholic president and his syndicated columns are published in diocesan newspapers. The death of Thomas Merton is much graver than people care

---

[354] Thomas Merton, *Conjectures of a Guilty Bystander*, op. cit., p. 315.
[355] George Weigel, "JFK After 50 Years," *First Things*, November 20, 2013.

to know. Men cower from great evil and so Merton's death has been "settled" as an accident. All have agreed on that answer. Is it good enough?

Weigel holds a title befitting his worldly prominence, as a distinguished Senior Fellow of the Ethics and Public Policy Center in Washington D.C. Weigel once speculated, amazingly enough, that if Merton had lived he might have become the first Catholic neoconservative.[356] Weigel would have us think that Merton would have been a believer in the official 9/11 story and the endless war on terror.

If Merton had been openly assassinated it would have been evidence of his goodness. To deny him this honor Merton's enemies concealed his assassination and made it appear to be an accident.[357] When Merton died one monk at Gethsemani said he was an extraordinary man and called him a living witness to God.[358] Jesus said:

> You shall love the Lord your God, with all your heart, with all your soul, and with all your mind. This is the greatest and the first commandment. The second is like it: You

---

[356] George Weigel, "Among the 'Progressed'," *First Things*, August 24, 2011.

[357] This subterfuge clearly had the desired effect on Paul Hourihan, author of the novel, *The Death of Thomas Merton*. In an interview at Amazon.com, he offers as his first reason for concluding that Merton was not truly a holy man the banal nature of his death, which he says could happen to anybody. More even than the many Merton scholars cited in this work, Hourihan badly wants to be taken seriously, but he makes it difficult. https://tinyurl.com/ycxc67t5

[358] Matthew Kelty letter to friends, Abbey at Gethsemani, December 17, 1968, Mott Collection.

shall love your neighbor as yourself. The whole law and the prophets depend on these two commandments. (Matthew 22: 37-40)

At the final judgment men will be measured by how they keep these two commandments. Undeniably, Merton was a man who loved God and his neighbor, and he was willing to give his life to testify to the truth. Merton's killers recognized his holiness and this motivated them to keep his murder a secret. Men call the death of Thomas Merton an accident, but they have not changed what it is. God knows how his servant Thomas Merton died.

The first law of history is not to dare to utter falsehood; the second, not to fear to tell the truth.
–Pope Leo XIII, public letter, 1883

Appendix 1

Seventeen Techniques for Truth Suppression

Strong, credible allegations of high-level criminal activity can bring down a government. When the government lacks an effective, fact-based defense, other techniques must be employed. The success of these techniques depends heavily upon a cooperative, compliant press and a mere token opposition party.

1. Dummy up. If it's not reported, if it's not news, it didn't happen.
2. Wax indignant. This is also known as the "How dare you?" gambit.
3. Characterize the charges as "rumors" or, better yet, "wild rumors." If, in spite of the news blackout, the public is still able to learn about the suspicious facts, it can only be through "rumors." (If they tend to believe the "rumors" it must be because they are simply "paranoid" or "hysterical.")

4. Knock down straw men. Deal only with the weakest aspects of the weakest charges. Even better, create your own straw men. Make up wild rumors (or plant false stories) and give them lead play when you appear to debunk all the charges, real and fanciful alike.
5. Call the skeptics names like "conspiracy theorist," "nutcase," "ranter," "kook," "crackpot," and, of course, "rumor monger." Be sure, too, to use heavily loaded verbs and adjectives when characterizing their charges and defending the "more reasonable" government and its defenders. You must then carefully avoid fair and open debate with any of the people you have thus maligned. For insurance, set up your own "skeptics" to shoot down.
6. Impugn motives. Attempt to marginalize the critics by suggesting strongly that they are not really interested in the truth but are simply pursuing a partisan political agenda or are out to make money (compared to over-compensated adherents to the government line who, presumably, are not).
7. Invoke authority. Here the controlled press and the sham opposition can be very useful.
8. Dismiss the charges as "old news."
9. Come half-clean. This is also known as "confession and avoidance" or "taking the limited hangout route." This way, you create the impression of candor and honesty while you admit only to relatively harmless, less-than-criminal "mistakes."

This stratagem often requires the embrace of a fallback position quite different from the one originally taken. With effective damage control, the fall-back position need only be peddled by stooge skeptics to carefully limited markets.

10. Characterize the crimes as impossibly complex and the truth as ultimately unknowable.
11. Reason backward, using the deductive method with a vengeance. With thoroughly rigorous deduction, troublesome evidence is irrelevant. E.g. We have a completely free press. If evidence exists that the Vince Foster "suicide" note was forged, they would have reported it. They haven't reported it so there is no such evidence. Another variation on this theme involves the likelihood of a conspiracy leaker and a press who would report the leak.
12. Require the skeptics to solve the crime completely. E.g. If Foster was murdered, who did it and why?
13. Change the subject. This technique includes creating and/or publicizing distractions.
14. Lightly report incriminating facts, and then make nothing of them. This is sometimes referred to as "bump and run" reporting.
15. Baldly and brazenly lie. A favorite way of doing this is to attribute the "facts" furnished the public to a plausible-sounding, but anonymous, source.
16. Expanding further on numbers 4 and 5, have your own stooges "expose" scandals and champion popular causes. Their job is to pre-empt real

opponents and to play 99-yard football. A variation is to pay rich people for the job who will pretend to spend their own money.

17. Flood the Internet with agents. This is the answer to the question, "What could possibly motivate a person to spend hour upon hour on Internet news groups defending the government and/or the press and harassing genuine critics?" Don t the authorities have defenders enough in all the newspapers, magazines, radio, and television? One would think refusing to print critical letters and screening out serious callers or dumping them from radio talk shows would be control enough, but, obviously it is not.

David Martin
Dec. 28, 1999
Online http://www.dcdave.com/article3/991228.html

Appendix 2

Exhibits

View exhibits at: themartyrdomofthomasmerton.com
1. Drawing of Merton's cottage
2. Thai Doctor's Certificate
3. Doctor's Certificate (English translation with Consular Officer comment)
4. Doctor's Certificate (English translation)
5. Thai Death Certificate (front) Death Certificate (reverse)
6. Death Certificate (English translation front only)
7. Death Certificate (English translation front and reverse)
8. Report of Death of American Citizen by American Foreign Service
9. Thai Police Report cover letter from U.S. Embassy
10. Thai Police Report (three pages)
11. Report of Dr. Edeltrud Weist (two pages)
12. Letter from Father Celestine Say to Abbott Flavian Burns (two pages)
13. Letter from Fr. Say to John Howard Griffin (three pages)
14. Letter from Fr. Say to John Moffitt (two pages)

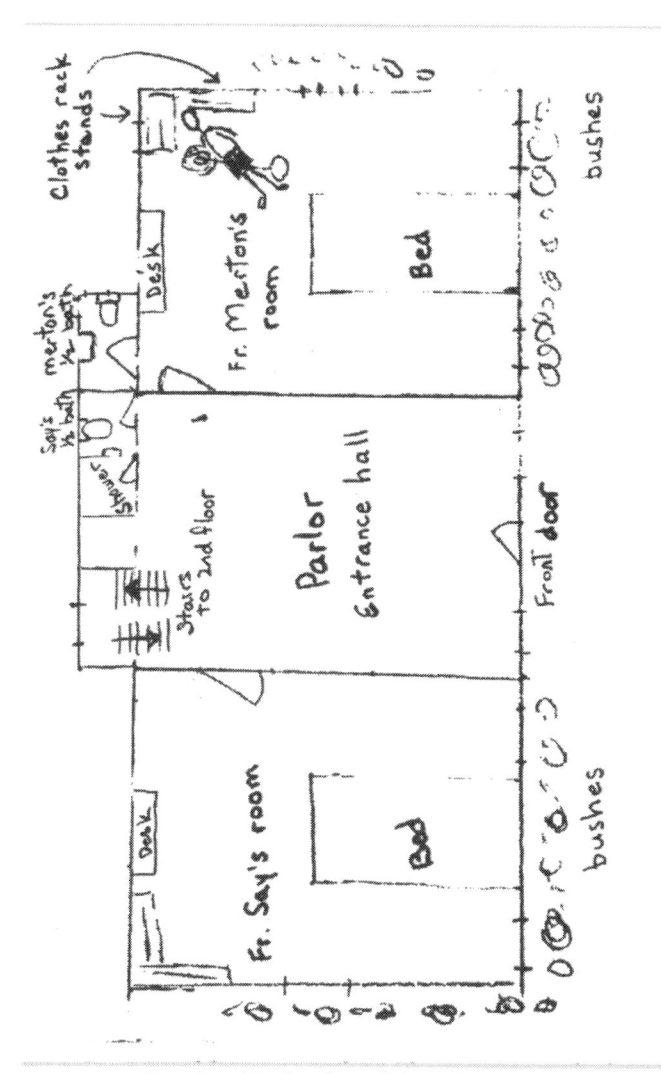

Drawing of the first floor of Merton's cottage
Exhibit 1

Doctor's Certificate (cause of death)
Exhibit 2

Doctor's Certificate
(Cause of Death)

Samutprakarn Hospital
December 10, 1968

I, Dr. Laksana Nakvachara, First Class Practitioner in Medicine, Medical License No. V. 665, after investigation of the remains of R. P. Thomas Merton of Gethsemane Abbey, U.S.A. who died at the Convalescent Home of Sawangkanivas, Taiban Sub-District, Muang District, Samutprakarn Province, state that death was caused as a result of fainting - due to acute cardiac failure and electric shock due to accidental falling against the electric fan to the floor.

(Signed) Laksana Nakvachara
(Dr. Laksana Nakvachara)

Title: Director of Samutprakarn Hospitals

*Remarks: The patient died outside Samutprakarn Hospital. The remains were brought to the Hospital for the purpose of a post-mortem by medical doctors and investigation authority as prescribed by law.

* (CONSULAR OFFICER'S NOTE - NOT A PART OF TRANSLATION): As will be noted from the copy of the original form, the comments under remarks are pre-printed on the form. In this case the remarks are not applicable even though correction was not made. The remains of Father Merton were released to the consular officer following post-mortem examination by Thai medical and investigating authorities at the place of death.

Doctor's Certificate with Consular Officer comment
Exhibit 3

Doctor's Certificate (English translation)
Exhibit 4

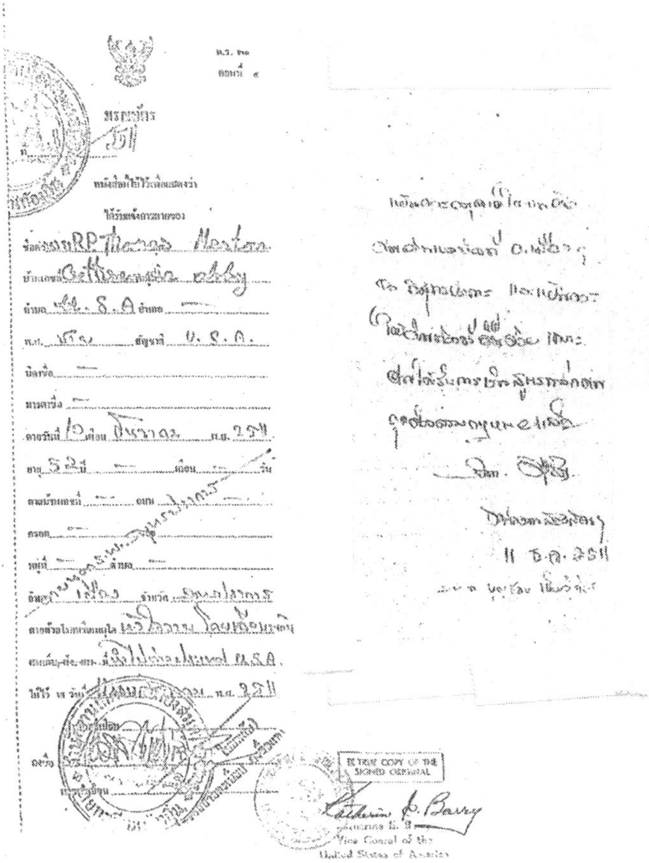
มรณบัตร

RP Thomas Merton

Gethsemani abbey

U.S.A.

IS TRUE COPY OF THE SIGNED ORIGINAL

Catherine P. Barry

Vice Consul of the United States of America

Death Certificate (front and reverse)
Exhibit 5

TRANSLATION

Civil Registration No. 20
Part A

G A R U D A
(Official Seal)

Death Certificate

No. 308/2511

This is to certify that this office has received the report of death of:

First Name: R.P. Thomas   Last Name: Merton of Gethsemane Abbey U.S.A.
House No. -   Village No. -   Sub-District: -
District: -   Sex: Male   Nationality: American
Father's Name: -
Mother's Name: -
Date of Death: 10th day Month: December B.E. 2511 (A.D. 1968)
Age: 52 Years - Months - Days
Place of Death: House No. Outside of Samutprakarn Hospital Road: Lane:
Soi: -   Village No.   Sub-District:
District: Phang   Province: Samutprakarn
Cause of Death: Sudden heart failure
The Remains to be shipped to the United States of America

Given on this 11th day of December B.E. 2511 (A.D. 1969)

Registration Office of Samutprakarn Municipality

(Signature) Tawil Chuiglab
Assistant Registrar

Death Certificate English translation
Exhibit 6

288

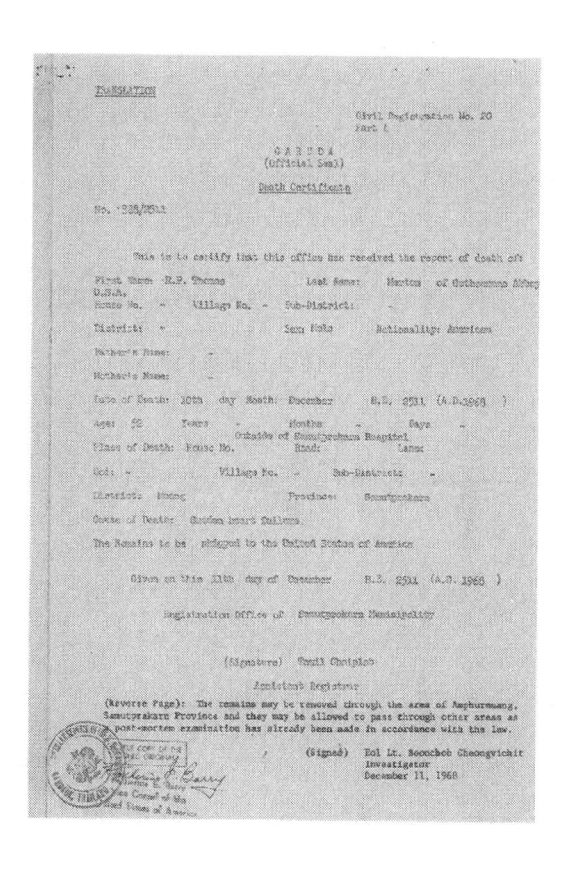

Death Certificate (English translation front and reverse)
Exhibit 7

Form FS-191

AMERICAN FOREIGN SERVICE
REPORT OF THE DEATH OF AN AMERICAN CITIZEN
American Embassy
Bangkok, Thailand, December 13, 1968
(Place and date)

Name in full __Thomas James MERTON__ Occupation __Trappist Monk__

Native or naturalized __DOB: January 13, 1915; POB: France__ Last known address
in the United States __Abbey of Gethsemane, Trappist, Kentucky__

Date of death __December 10   1500 hrs (approx.) 1968__ Age __53__
                 (Month)   (Day)   (Hour) (Minute)   (Year)   (As nearly as can be ascertained)

Place of death __Convalescent Home, Sawangkaniwas, Samutprakarn, Thailand__
                   (Number and street or [Hospital or hotel])   (City)   (Country)

Cause of death __Sudden Heart Failure (according to official Death Certificate)__
                                    (Include authority for statement)

Disposition of the remains __Embalmed and shipped to Greenwell Funeral Home, Main Street, New Haven, Kentucky__

Local law as to disinterring remains __Not applicable__

Disposition of the effects __In possession of American Embassy, Bangkok, Thailand__

Person or official responsible for custody of effects and accounting therefor __In custody of undersigned,__
Informed by telegram: as Consular Officer

NAME	ADDRESS	RELATIONSHIP	DATE SENT
Right Rev. Flavian Burns	Abbey of Gethsemane, Trappist, Kentucky	Father Superior & Executor	Dec. 10, 1968

Copy of this report sent to:

NAME	ADDRESS	RELATIONSHIP	DATE SENT
Rt. Rev. Flavian Burns	(as above)	Father Superior & Executor	Dec. 17, 1968

Traveling or residing abroad with relatives or friends as follows:

NAME	ADDRESS	RELATIONSHIP
Father Merton was attending a Congress of Roman Catholic Monks which was coordinated by Abbot Primate WEAKLAND of Rome, Italy, and was being held at Sawangkaniwas, Samutprakarn, Thailand

Other known relatives (not given above):

NAME	ADDRESS	RELATIONSHIP
Not Known		

This information and data concerning an inventory of the effects, accounts, etc., have been placed under __RUBZX__ in the correspondence of this office.
FS-9
Remarks: __PPT No. J. 1083644 issued at Washington August 1, 1968 cancelled and destroyed. Death officially recorded (No. 388/2511) Dec. 11, 1968 at Office of Civil Registrar (Nai Amphur) Muang District, Samutprakarn Province, Thailand__

(Continue on reverse if necessary.)

Katherine E. Barry
(Signature as at signed)

[SEAL]
No fee prescribed.   __Vice Consul__ .... of the United States of America.

Report of Death of American Citizen
Exhibit 8

EMBASSY OF THE
UNITED STATES OF AMERICA
Bangkok, Thailand

July 30, 1969

Right Reverend Flavian Burns
Abbey of Gethsemane
Gethsemane, Kentucky

Dear Father Burns:

Transmitted herewith is a translation of the concluding report of the Police Investigation into the circumstances surrounding the death of Father Thomas Merton. The translation was made by a local employee on the Embassy staff.

If you have any further questions, please do not hesitate to write.

Sincerely yours,

Joseph C. Snyder, III
American Vice Consul

Police Report cover letter from U.S. Embassy
Exhibit 9

Subject: The conclusion of police investigation report on the death of Reverend Thomas Merton, an American. The incident occurred on December 10, 1968, at about 2:00 P.M., at Tai Ban District, Muang County, Samut Prakarn Province. Pol. Lt. Boonchop POOMVICHIT was the officer in charge; Samut Prakarn Police Station.

According to the memorandum of Pol. Lt. Boonchop POOMVICHIT, the Investigating Police Officer in charge, it was shown that after having been informed of the incident and reporting to the supervisor, he then went to the scene for investigation. It was found that the body was lying down on the floor headed to the North East and there was a stand fan resting on the body; urine had flowed onto the floor. There was a burn on the skin where it had contacted the metal part of the fan. Dr. Luksana NARKVACHARA, the Director, Samut Prakarn Hospital, was the doctor collaborating in the investigation.

After the investigation of the appropriate witnesses had been completed, the body was turned over to Reverend George S. Weakland for funeral rites. The stand fan was confiscated for further investigation and sent for examination to the Scientific Crime Detection Laboratory, Police Department.

The conclusion of this case of which the investigation has been completed, reflected that on December 7, 1968, there were 70 Roman Catholic Clergymen from many countries attending a conference at Swang Nivas Resting Place, Thailand. All the clergymen came to stay in the hostel at Swang Nivas. The chairman of that conference was Reverend George S. Weakland, a high ranking monk of the Benedictine Order from Rome, Italy; the conference started on December 9, 1968, at 9:00 A.M.; the Patriarch (Bishop?) of Thailand presiding as the chairman for the opening ceremony. On December 10, 1968, at 10:45 A.M., the usual meeting began and Reverend Thomas Merton was the speaker who gave a talk until 11:45 A.M. Then there was a break for lunch until 2:00 P.M., after which they separated to go to their lodgings for rest. The meeting was to be resumed at 4:00 P.M., the same day. Reverend Thomas Merton went to his room accompanied by Reverend De Grunne from Belgium. Then they separated to their own rooms. At 3:00 P.M., on the same day, De Grunne who stayed in an upper room over the scene, while walking into the bathroom, heard a loud noise coming from the lower story which sounded like a heavy object falling onto the floor. Reverend De Grunne rushed to ask Reverend Selistonse, from the Philippines, whose room was adjacent to Reverend Thomas Merton's room, whether he had heard any strange noise. Reverend Selistonse said he had not heard any unusual noise. Then Reverend De Grunne went up to his room to dress, which took about 20 minutes. He left his room to go down to the lower story to Reverend Thomas Merton's room to get the key to use when Reverend De Grunne came back from outside the compound.

When Reverend De Grunne reached the door of Reverend Thomas Merton's room, he called but got no answer. So he looked through the glass louvers into the room. He saw Reverend Thomas Merton lying on the cement floor with a

Police Report
Exhibit 10 (page 1)

292

stand fan resting on his body. Reverend De Grunne suspected that Reverend Thomas Merton might be in danger, so he attempted to push the door open to see what had happened, but he could not push the door open because it was bolted from the inside. Reverend De Grunne called for Reverend Solistonse, a witness, staying in the adjacent room, to come to the scene, and at that time Reverend O.O. Hars, from Korea, a witness, also came to the scene. They helped to push the glass louvers of the room apart to reach the inside door bolt and open it.

They got into the room to help Reverend Thomas Merton. When Reverend O.O. Hars touched the fan which rested on Reverend Merton, he was seen to jerk away. This was caused by an electrical shock from the fan's stand. Simultaneously, there was a flash at the metal part of the fan where it contacted the body of Reverend Thomas Merton and there was a smell of burning skin. Reverend Soliatonse pulled the fan's cord from the socket and the fan stopped running.

Later there were many other clergymen and persons who came to the scene, such as Miss Anam TONGCHAREON, a nurse working there, and Nun Arden Tross Wise from Korea, witnesses who had a knowledge of nursing. These witnesses made a pulse check and also opened Reverend Thomas Merton's eyes to flash into them with a touch light. They found that Reverend Thomas Merton was dead.

Later, Reverend George S. Weakland, Chairman of the conference, came to the scene and asked the doctor at Samut Prakarn Hospital to come for a medical examination of the body. Dr. Luksana NARKVACHARA, Director, Samut Prakarn Hospital, reported the incident to Pol. Lt. Boonchop PORNVICHIT, the Investigating Officer, who went to investigate to make an examination map, and to take photographs for the file of the investigation.

After completion of the investigation, the body was turned over to Reverend George S. Weakland, Chairman of the conference, for funeral rites.

Since no-one saw Reverend Thomas Merton die, someone there assumed that he fainted and collapsed onto the cement floor, colliding with the stand fan as he did so. The wiring of the fan was defective and thus Reverend Thomas Merton received an electrical shock as he lay on the floor with the fan on top of him. It was also found that Reverend Thomas Merton, after having fallen, seemed to be tired and that his face glowed red. It was also known to Nun Arden Tross Wise when the conference was adjourned, that Reverend Thomas Merton had told someone that he was tired.

The Investigating Officer sent the fan for examination and received the report from the examiner, Pol. Maj. Amnuay TUNPRASERT, Chief, Chemical and Physical Section, Scientific Crime Detection Laboratory, Police Department, which showed that the fan had a defective electric cord installed inside its stand. When the cord contacted the metal stand, it caused an electrical leakage throughout the fan. This flow of electricity was strong enough to cause the death of a person if he touched the metal part.

However, the Investigating Officer questioned Dr. Luksana NARKVACHARA, whose views were that Reverend Thomas Merton died because of:

Police Report
Exhibit 10 (page 2)

293

-3-

1. Heart failure,
2. And that the cause mentioned in 1, caused the dead priest to faint and collide with the stand fan located in the room. The fan had fallen onto the body of Reverend Thomas Morton. The head of the dead priest had hit the floor. There was a burn on the body's skin and on the underwear on the right side which was assumed to have been caused by electrical shock from the fan.

Therefore the cause of the death of Reverend Thomas Morton was as mentioned. There were no witnesses who might be suspected of causing the death. There is no reason to suspect criminal causes.

Police Report
Exhibit 10 (page 3)

Report on the first impressions after Rev. F. Thomas Merton's tragic death given by an eyewitness, Sr. Dr. Edeltrud Weist OSB, Dr. med. Specialist of internal medicine, Prioress of the Missionary Benedictine Sisters in Taegu / South-Korea.

"December 10th 1968 just after 4^{00} p.m. I suddenly heard someone saying: 'Father Thomas Merton is lying dead in his room'. Hoping that there was still something to be done I hurried immediately to his room.

Father Th. Merton was lying on the Terrazzo floor, his eyes half-open, no breathing, no pulse, no heartsounds, no light-reaction of the pupils. The face was deep bluish-red and the lower arms and hands showed spots of the same colour. The arms were lying stretched beside the body. The feet were somewhat turned inside like in convulsion. F. Merton was only in shorts. An electric fan of about 150 cm height was lying across his body. The electric cord was pulled out of the plug lying on the floor. A smell of burned flesh was in the air.

As I turned the fan somewhat aside, I realised, that there was a 3rd degree burn, just in the right upper abdominal region, the place where the middle part of the fan with the switchboard had touched the skin. The burnt area of about one hand's breadth was extended to the whole right lower abdomen including the right genital region. The cloth of the shorts covering the burnt area showed no sign of burning itself. The fan itself had lain direct on the skin, above the upper part of the shorts. On the lower region of the right upper arm (or on the upper part of the lower arm) were also signs of stripe like burns.

I only could give the declaration of death, I was convinced that it was due to an electric shock by the fan.

Report of Sr./Dr. Edeltrud Weist

Exhibit 11 (page 1)

However, I could not decide, if this was the first reason, or if F. Merton first fell down (by fainting, dizziness or heart-attack) pulling the fan over himself, or if he first got a shock from the electric fan and then falling down had dragged it along. That he had fallen down was obvious by a bleeding wound on the back of his head.

The location of bed, desk and lying body was like this. →

As I was told later, Abbod Edo Haas OSB of Waekwe / Sankt-Xxxx and Prior Celestine Say OSB of Hamilen/P.I. were the fathers, who had found F. Merton about 4" p.m. lying on the floor. Abbot Edo who had tried to remove the fan, had got also a slight electric shock. So Prior Say had pulled the electric cord out of the plug.

When the police arrived at 6" p.m., the body of F. Merton showed already rigor mortis.

F. Gérard OSB, who had his room on the floor above F. Merton's room, heard a shout about 3" p.m. He went down to look for the source of the shouting. Because after the one shout all remained quiet, F. Gérard again went up to his room. However, this could have been just the time, when F. Merton fell and died.

br. Edeltrud Weist OSB.
Bangkok, Dec. 11. 1968.

Report of Dr. Edeltrud Weist
Exhibit 11 (page 2)

C. Say OSB

PAX   March 18, 1969

Rt. Rev. and dear Abbot Flavian,

Greetings! Taking the opportunity of someone going over to the States, I sent through him some photos I took of Fr. Merton in Bangkok, and a news clipping from one of our dailies. I hope that you would receive the photos in good time and hope that you would excuse some of the inaccuracies mentioned in the news clipping. Fr. Merton is well known to the religious and Catholics here in Manila, who had read his books and one of my hopes in seeing him at Bangkok was to invite him for a talk or two in our abbey and our Benedictine sisters here in Manila. Unfortunately as yet his call from headquarters rather early.

As is stated in the news clipping sent you, I lodged in the same cottage (#11) in the Red Cross resort in Bangkok, with Fr. Merton. In fact there were only two rooms on the ground floor with a tiny parlor separating my room from that of Merton. The screen wire afforded little privacy even with the bed sheets hung as curtains, but I made it a point not to be too curious about the celebrity living next room to me. This is one reason why it didn't occur to me to investigate, when Fr. de Grunne, a Belgian priest who lived upstairs came banging at my bathroom door and told me that he thought he heard someone shouted. He didn't know that I had returned to the cottage that afternoon, and thought it was Merton in the bathroom. Had he turned his head a bit to the right, he could have seen through the room of Merton and seen Merton on the floor. Returning to my room I noticed Merton's bed empty and thought that he might be sleeping on the granolitic floor which was cooler. He had mentioned earlier that the maid took the trouble of clearing all his things from the floor and I thought he preferred the floor to the bed. Bangkok was hot and humid, all through the week that we were there.

That afternoon I couldn't sleep as Fr. de Grunne kept pacing up and down in his room above me. I remembered having heard some sparking sound, and the smell of some burned or dried cider(?). An hour and a half later when Fr. de Grunne came down to go for a swim, I had returned to the bathroom for a shower. Fr. de Grunne again knocked and with a face that seemed to have seen a ghost he asked me: "Do you remember I told you that I heard a short sometime ago? Well come and see, I think something has happened to Merton. He is lying on the floor with the electric fan toppled on top of him." Rushing to the door of Merton he found his door bolted, but could see between two slits of the curtains Merton on the floor. Fr. de Grunne told me he would go and ask for help. When he left I banged on the door and called out to Merton, hoping against hope that he had just knocked himself out in falling backwards. It was then that I saw some sparks in the motor of the fan and the smell of burned flesh made me realized that it was too late, for an hour or so had passed since I remembered having heard sparkling and the smell of something burned. It didn't take long before two abbots came in. Abbot Egbert Donovan of St. Vincent Archabbey, Pa. and Abbot Odo Haas of Korea were returning from the swimming pool when they encountered Fr. de Grunne. About Odo told me later that it was funny the way de Grunne encountered them, first he asked: " and did you have a good swim?" then he continued:" you know that an accident has happened to Fr. Merton. He is lying on the floor with a fan on top of him". The two abbots exploded right into the cottage at that announcement. He started pushing and kicking the door, then abbot Odo happened to push the upper panel of the door and found that it was like a window that opened inwards. He climbed in and unbolted the door. I went in right after him and saw that he went for the fan and rescued from a shock. I unplugged the line. Abbot Egbert told us not to touch anything, as he realized that Merton was beyond help. Abbot Odo turned to me and suggested that I take a picture, but in case the police would ask how we found him, I took two snaps, but since the light was not good inside the room I wasn't sure any would come out. Besides abbot Egbert Weakland, our Primate had arrived and didn't approve of my taking any pictures. Two gave one picture that came out. Should you need additional prints just let me know.

Letter from Fr. Celestine Say to Abbot Flavian Burns
Exhibit 12 (page1)

- 2 -

With the coming of Abbot Primate, others followed, and a Benedictine nun from Korea, the Prioress of a small community, who worked in Korea as a doctor, took charge of the situation. She asked me for a flash light and after looking into Fr. Merton's eye, she pronounced him dead. She replaced the fan as she was requested by a Thai nurse who mentioned that things should be left as they are for the police. Two hours later the doctor and the police came. They took a lot of pictures and took down a few names for further investigation. I was asked by Sister Pia, in charge of the lodgings, to move to another cottage. Two Trappist monks, Abbot Joachim Murphy of New Zealand, and Fr. Angelo Parker, of Tarrawarra abbey, Victoria, Australia, were requested by Abbot Primate to help sister Edeltrud Weist, the Prioress of Korea, to dress up Fr. Merton and lay him on his bed, as the police had taken all the photos they needed. The Thai Manager of the resort, a Thai woman, cut some flowers and made a wreath for Merton. The doctor told us that it could possibly be a heart attack and in reaching out for the fan, Merton grabed it and pulled it towards him. I/M is thought that a better diagnosis than electricution to avoid complications in the police report.

That same evening Abbot Primate was able to contact someone in charge of the U.S. embassy and a lady came over to take notes of the incident and secured the passport of Fr. Merton. The following afternoon I was told that the police wanted to see me to ask more questions. I found Sister Edeltrud, together with Fr. de Gramme in a cottage with the police. The three of us were asked to help fill in as many details as we could remember for the police report. I was asked first, since I lived on the same floor with Merton. Sister Edeltrud and Fr. de Gramme chipped in to complete the details. The police Sargeant had another priest for interpreter. He had a typist bang away at a special typewriter with Thai characters. It took us three hours to get through the report and I was asked to sign to the truth of what I had stated. Thanks! the whole interview over the three of us were about to leave, when the Sargeant said that Sister and Fr. de Gramme had to stay, as that report was just for one witness. Fr. de Gramme, who was so nervous and fidgeting all the time almost blew his top. Sister Edeltrud had enough of the whole thing and requested to postpone the interview for the following day. I had to sign more statements the following day, not knowing what I was signing and hoping that it won't put me into trouble with the authorities. I hope that the police had sent you some of the pictures they took in the room of Merton. They showed us a picture of the base of the fan and mentioned that breakage in the cord at the base of the fan had grounded the whole fan. I remembered that Merton was often bifurca bare footed when in his room, and his fan was on almost 24 hours a day. That added to the intensity of the shock. Up to now we are wondering whether it was electricution or a heart attack. The police wasn't too eager about an autopsy and I heard later that a U.S. army plane flew Merton's body back to States where the autopsy would be performed. Was the immediate cause of death determined prior to his burial?

The day after Merton's death I noticed that the Thais had the cottage scrubbed from top to bottom. They took away the partitions, changed the sagging ceiling, uprooted the plants in front of the windows of the cottage, changed even the soil, and for three nights all lights in the cottage were left on. Our priest interpreter told me later that the Thais are very afraid of ghost. When a person dies in a house, the house is unsaleabl. No Thai in his right mind would dare purchase the house or live in it. The lady-manager of the resort asked our interpreter whether the priests are also afraid of ghosts? When given a negative answer, she asked:" Then why did they leave the cottage ?"

Returning from the Bangkok conference, I narrated the events of Merton's death to the monks of our abbey. One of them, who admired Merton so much claimed that I had practically killed him for not coming to his rescue earlier. I had that same feeling that day I stood in front of Merton's door and realised that I should have been more curious and investigated. I only hope that he would remember all of us, now that he has returned to his reward. Best wishes to your Rev. for a joyous Easter and do keep the undersigned in your prayers.
In Christ,

Fr. Celestine Say, O.S.B.
Prior

San Beda College
P.O. Box 4457 Manila
[illegible]
Mendiola St., Manila, Phil.

June 25, 1969

Mr. John Howard Griffin
3816 West Biddison
Fort Worth, Texas 76109

Dear Mr. Griffin,

Thank you for your letters of June 2 and 4. Please excuse my delay in answering. Tension on campus has kept us quite busy. I shall make up somehow by enclosing you a picture sent me by a Japanese Sister the day after Merton's death. She sent it to me for my collection, but I'll be willing to part with it for the Merton Legacy. As for the negatives you requested, I hope you won't mind, but I'd rather mail them to abbot Flavian as a gift to him and let him decide on their disposal. I feel that I don't have a right over them, although I took them.

A little note on the negatives: I took only two snaps of Merton right after I found him dead. The light condition wasn't too good. So I took a chance by snapping one at 1/8 of a second and another at ¼ of a second. The print you have now came from the second snap. A private laboratory might make a better reproduction, even of the first frame of negative. I was about to take additional pictures, but at that moment, abbot Rembert Weakland, came upon the scene and requested me not to take any more as Father Merton wasn't properly clad. I was afraid that the police might later confiscate my films, but luckily they didn't come to hear about it. The police took a good number of shots of both Merton and the room, and I had to sign that the things were as they were in the pictures, being a witness. Perhaps you might ask to see them in the police files, whould you pass by Bangkok. You print you have with you shows the fan's position before it was moved. The police snaps show the position after they had replaced the fan. Sister Edeltrud, a doctor, removed the fan to examin Merton.

I am afraid that I don't have the address of Fr. Francois de Grunne. You could however inquire from the Secretariat of the A.I.M. by writing Abbot Don Marie de Floris, OSB / 7, rue d' Issy, 92 -VANVES/ FRANCE. Abbot de Floris organized the Bangkok meeting and would have the addresses of all participants.

As for the details of the physical arrangement, here's all that I can remember: On the enclosed photo #1, you can see a bed on the foreground. That was my bed in the exact position as it was. Fr. Merton had one like mine. The floor was not covered by any mattresses then. Its made of some kind of granolitic imitation. My room has two windows facing the front. The mess wire partition seems to be still there. The bed-sheets serving as curtains had been removed. Right after the partition is a small parlor (space of the varnished panels and door). The chairs at the back ground of this picture were in the parlor. Merton's room comes right after this parlor, partitioned by wire mess with bed-sheets as curtains.

Letter from Fr. Celestine Say to John Howard Griffin
Exhibit 13 (page 1)

299

Merton's room had ~~[struck through]~~ There was an adjacent bathroom right under ~~[struck through]~~. I used this adjacent bathroom, as well as Fr. ~~[struck through]~~ that the bathroom on the second floor was clogged. So my room was separated from Merton's by that little palor which had a bathroom, and which (palor) served as a passage to the stairs for the second floor. I believe that the Sister took the pictures right next day after Merton's death. The Thais had already removed the partitions of Merton's room, and even changed the sagging ceiling. They even removed the plants in front of Merton's windows, and changed the soil. Superstition about the ghosts of the departed made them keep the lights of the cottages on for three consecutive nights. No Thai would live in a house where someone had died.

The door of the cottage had only one key for the four occupants, so we agreed to notify each other where to find the key. The maid for the house had a duplicate key and during our conversation one day, Merton mentioned that the maid had entered while we were in the conferences, and had clean up his room, picking up all the things that he had dumped on the floor. This was mentioned in connection with our finding the door unlocked one day when we returned from the conferences(monday). On Tuesday, Merton gave his talk, and during lunch at one p.m. he mentioned that he wanted to catch up on some sleep (siesta). I had the key then, and handed it over to him. It must have been around twenty to 2 p.m. when he left the dinning hall and Fr. Francois accompanied him back to cottage #11. I followed shortly after. I don't remember seeing Merton move around when I entered the cottage. After changing I left my room to use the bathroom of the parlor. While brushing my teeth, I heard the steps of Fr. Francois coming down, and he banged at ~~[struck]~~ the door of the bathroom. When I opened, he was surprised to see me. " I thought you were Merton" he said. "Did you hear any shout"? he asked me. I told him I didn't since I was busy brushing my teeth. Possibly the kids playing near our cottage could have shouted. He left at that. Unfortunately he didn't even bother to look into Merton's room to inquire if anything was wrong. When I left the bathroom, I could see through the parted curtains that Merton's bed was empty. It occurred to me at the moment that he might be sleeping on the floor, either as a penance or because of the excessive heat of Bangkok. I went to my bed and tried to sleep siesta. For an hour or so, Fr. Francois kept pacing the floor in the room above me. He kept opening and shutting his door, and he finally came down and went out. Throughout the siesta I seem to remember hearing some sparkling or crackling sound, and small something burned, but again since the neighboring thais were so near, I didn't bother to investigate. I got up and took a shower, and just as I returned to my room, Fr. Francois returned and went to invite Merton for a swim. Fr. Francois came to my room and told me:" Do you remember a moment ago I thought I heard a should?" "Come and see, something has happened to Fr. Merton. He is on the floor and the fan is on top of him." I rushed to see and we found his door bolted. Fr. Francois told me he would go for help. I kept banging at the door and calling Fr. Merton, hoping that he had just fallen and knocked himself out. Then I noticed that some sparks were emitting from the back of the fan where the switch is, and I realized that it was the sound I heard and the odor of burned flesh. He was clad only with a drawer, without any T-shirt, and bare-footed. His body was not wet, and I thought that perhaps he must have been preparing to go the the bathroom for a shower. While I was standing there, two abbots burst in (abbot odo Haas of Korea, and abbot Donovan of St. Vincent,Pa.). We started pushing the door and abbot Odo happened to push the upper panel and it opened, so he climbed in and unbolted the door. I entered right after him and saw him recoil from a shock as he touched the fan, so I pulled the cord from the outlet. Abbot Donovan took one look and told us not to touch

Letter from Fr. Celestine Say to John Howard Griffin
Exhibit 13 (page2)

anything. He told us that Michael lit a ??? to be said a prayer/s for Fr. Merton. While abbot Donovan went to call for help, abbot Odo suggested to me to take a picture. I'M I'M I'M I didn't.

Abbot Rembert Weakland, upon being notified, came with Sister Edeltrud Weist, OSB, a doctor, and likewise working as a missionary in Korea. She listened to the heart and opened the eyelids and finally pronounced him dead. More people were coming in then so I stepped out for some fresh air, and did not return till late in the afternoon when the doctor of the compound finally arrived. The Thai doctor advanced the theory that Merton may have a heart attack, possibly reached out for the fan and pulled it towards him as he fell backwards. The contusion at the back of his head may have resulted from his fall. The police sergeant took down the names of Fr. Francois, Sister Edeltrud and myself. The following afternoon he questioned us for three hours to fill in the details of his report. He showed us the pictures he had taken. In one of them he mentioned that the cord at the base of the fan was flayed and must have grounded the fan. After looking over the pictures, we had to sign that things were as they are in the pictures. I noticed in one picture that the area around Merton was wet and full of footprints. I was sure that when we found him, his body was dry and the floor dry. Sister Edeltrud told me later that it was urea from the body.

Aside from the burn on the stomach I did not notice any other wounds. In fact it was sister who told me about the contusion on the back of the head. I remember that the feet were bend a bit towards each other, possibly from pain. Of incidents prior to the death I could remember that Merton used the fan a lot. One morning he even left it on when he left the cottage. Likewise he walks barefooted while in his room. I remember hearing his heavy foot steps on the granolitic floor. For one thing, although I noticed the sparks on the switch box of the Hitachi fan, I could not remember if the blades were still turning before I pulled out the cord. I asked abbot Odo whether the shock was strong when he touch the fan, and he said it was not too strong. But then he (abbot Odo) was clothed and with shoes on. I remember that the voltage at the compound was 220 V.

As for Fr. de Grunne, he gave me the creeps. I couldn't understand why he kept pacing up and down during the whole hour and a half of siesta that afternoon when Fr. Merton died, till Mr. John Moffitt, copy editor of "America" told me that Fr. de Grunne was a nervous man and instead of sleeping siesta, would keep pacing up and down. Mr. Moffitt lived with us on the same cottage, but on the second floor, companion to Fr. de Grunne. Even abbot Odo told me that when he encountered de Grunne this afternoon, the first question of Fr de Grunne to them was " Did you have a good swim?" then:" Do you know that an accident has happened to Fr. Merton?" . Throughout the police interview he was extremely nervous and for some moment I was afraid that he might say something foolish and put us in trouble with the Thai sergeant who had to have a translator.

I guess this is all I could remember now. Should there be any other detail that you might like to ask, do not hesitate to do so. I'll try to respond as soon as working hour permit. I am mailing the negatives to abbot Flavian via registered airmail. Unfortunately I had clipped off the role of negative, and the strip composes of three frames only. Let's hope it can be of use still.

Sincerely,
Fr. Celestino Say, OSB
Prior

Letter from Fr. Celestine Say to John Howard Griffin
Exhibit 13 (page 3)

BENEDICTINE ABBEY
(SAN BEDA COLLEGE)
P. O. BOX 4637
MANILA, PHILIPPINES

December 11, 1969

Dear Mr. Moffitt,

Greetings and thanks for your letter of Nov. 28. Before anything else, let me wish you the joys and full blessings of this Christmas. I can hardly believe that a year has passed since our Bangkok meeting and a year to date since the death of Merton. Time certainly doesn't help the memory a bit in recalling the events that surrounded Merton's death. However, I'll try my best to jot down what I can remember.

1. We usually take our lunch at One p.m. and I am not sure if we delay our lunch hour that day? I did remember that Merton was tired and wanted to take his siesta earlier than us, so he asked me for the key to the cottage. It must have taken us about half an hour for lunch, so Merton may have left around one-thirty. I wasn't too long in leaving myself, because I remember seeing Merton and de Grunne ahead of me, walking slowly and chatting. They were quite far ahead of me and I didn't remember seeing them enter the cottage. You were right in saying that we usually walked very slowly because of the heat. When I entered, the door was unlocked and de Grunne had gone upstairs. I didn't notice if Merton was moving around or not at the moment when I entered. I went straight to my room, removed the habit and got my tooth brush and head for the bathroom. I don't remember either whether I notice Merton moving around or not, but went right in and started washing up. Half way through brushing the teeth, I heard the footsteps of de Grunne coming down the stairs and he banged quite loudly on my bathroom door. I opened to see what's the matter and he was surprised to see me. Is everything alright? I thought you were Merton, he told me. Did you hear any shout, he asked me and I said I didn't, so he went back upstairs. I resume brushing my teeth, and returned to my room right after that.

2. What struck me as a string of circumstances that could have fixed the death of Merton more accurately was this:
   a) de Grunne told me later that he was inside the bathroom right above me and he claimed that the shout he heard seemed to have come right where I was. Since he didn't see me enter the cottage, he thought the only person who could have shouted was Merton. Yet when I told him that I didn't hear anything, it didn't occur to him to turn his head to the right, while he was banging at the bathroom and did look into the room of Merton. The curtains covering Merton's partition were very close, and one could see into Merton's room. When assured that I didn't hear anything de Grunne went right back upstairs.
   b) On coming out of the bathroom, it didn't occur to me to look to the left either, into the room of Merton. Nevertheless, I remember seeing Merton's bed empty and at that moment a thought occur to me that Merton must have been sleeping on the floor, as it was either cooler, or that he was doing some form of penance. I remember making a special effort not to follow my curiosity, for the sake of not intruding on the privacy of another, I remember also his remark that the maid had cleared up the mess that he had scattered on the floor and possibly he made us of the cooler floor. Returning to my room I tried unsuccessfully to sleep, as it was too hot, and upstairs, de Grunne was pacing up and down the floor, opening and banging his door. At about three o'clock, he came down and went out. Shortly after he returned and went upstairs. I gave up trying to sleep and went for a shower. Again

Letter from Fr. Celestine Say to John Moffitt
Exhibit 14 (page 1)

-2-

it did not occur to me to look into Merton's room when I passed by to the bathroom. After my shower I returned to my room and was dressing up when I heard do Gruppo coming down. He went to Merton's room first and after a while came to knock at my room. He told me:"Do you remember that I asked you if you heard something while you were in the bathroom? Come and see, something has happened to Merton. He is lying on the floor and the fan is on top of him." I rushed out with him and saw Merton on the floor as he described it. We tried to open the door but found it bolted inside. He told me to wait while he went out to call for help. I started calling Merton's name to see if he had just knock himself out. It was then that I noticed the sparks coming from the switch box of the fan and realized that part of the fan touching the stomach of Merton was turning the skin black. I then remembered the acrid odor of something burned while trying to sleep siesta.

I don't remember seeing the hands of Merton burned at all. I remembered that his body was dry. Later when I looked at the photos taken by the police, I noticed that the floor around him had plenty of footprints, as if the floor was wet. The Benedictine sister told me that it was urea from the corpse. About Odo who was the first one to enter tried to remove the fan and recoiled from a shock. I unplugged the cord. Later I asked him if the shock was strong, he said that it was not very strong. Merton would've gotten a stronger shock because he had no insulation at all, since he was barefooted and only in his shorts. The sister also told me that the only wound she found aside from the burned spot, was the back of the head caused by the fall.

I was under the impression that the electrocution had killed him. Later thinking it over, the verdict of the doctor sound quite plausible. He could have had a heart attack and if grabed the fan and pulled it towards him when he fell. If the current was that strong, his hands would've been stuck to the fan, but his hands were on the floor, yet the sister who examined him told me that the burned parts included the skin covered by the drawers).

In sum, I would say that Merton died before two p.m. Even Dom Bernardo is of this opinion. There is a faint memory nagging at the back of my mind that we were late for lunch one time and I am not certain whether it was that very day that we were late for lunch. Whether he died at 1:35 p.m. or 2:15 p.m. its such a short span of time to be able to say that certainly, for I wasn't aware of the importance of the time and have to judge from the circumstances that I can remember. Definitely, I do not remember seeing any burn in his palms. Definitely, the door was unlocked when I entered. I don't know if Merton found the door unlocked when he entered. Remember a day a two before we found the door unlocked and Merton mentioned that the cleaning woman must have been in, as his room was re-arranged by the maid?

Dom Bernardo's article was published in a magazine locally, but I am not sure which issue it was. If I can find it, I'll send you a Xerox copy. I think I know what you mean by some rumors that you would like to dispel about the death of Merton. One American Journalist dropped in about six months ago and told us that he thinks that Merton was the victim of those who opposed his liberal views. They are trying to tie up his death with that of Kennedy, Martin Luther King, etc. but I think that its rather too far-fetched or streching the imagination a bit too much. I don't see what they could gain by this conjecture? I've sent all negatives that I have of Merton to Mr. Griffin. Here's wishing you the best in your editing of the Bangkok proceedings.

I won't be going to the Korea this coming meeting, but I'll send Dom Bernardo (who'll be ordained this 23rd of Dec.) to represent us with another father. Dom Bernardo can do a better job in the meeting. Should you come over to the Far East do drop in on us. Dom Bernardo should be able to give you some advice regarding the book you intend to write. I am too unprepared to be of any help. If it comes to any Asian spirituality, God bless you and a Blessed Christmas to you.

In Christ,

Celestine, P.S.

Index

Abbey of St. Andre, 52, 102-103
Angleton, James Jesus, 226
Aquinas, St. Thomas, 182-183, 217
Artichoke, Operation, 204
Associated Press, 11, 18, 138, 144-145, 221-222
Augustine, Saint, 90, 272
Baker James, T., 196, 258
Bamberger, Rev. John Eudes, 2-4, 23, 85-86, 89-90, 128.
Barry, Katherine E., 11, 27
Bears, Dean A., 81
Bhansattabutr, Chan, 13, 18, 27
Bonazzi, Roberto, 234-235, 242
Bono, Sonny, 202
Briggs, Kenneth E., 185
Brinkley, Douglas, 28
Brown, Matthew Hay, 204
Brown, Ron, 202
Burkett, Tommy, 178, 259
Burns, Rev. Flavian, 4, 9, 12, 19-23, 25, 29, 36-37, 41, 43-46, 62, 67, 72-77, 84-86, 93, 111-114, 118, 120-121, 124-125, 127-128, 130-131, 143, 148-152, 155-157, 159, 162, 166, 168, 175, 179, 188, 192, 213, 217, 226, 228-227, 235, 240-241, 247, 252, 256, 260-261, 270
Ceasar, Julius, 202
Chagall, Marc, 246
Chaiplab, Tawil, 16-17
Cheongvichit, Boonchob, 17, 27, 71
Christiana, Mother, 262
Clarke, John, iii, iv
Cleaver, Eldridge, 2
Clinton, Bill, ii, 28, 49, 239
Colby, William, 204-205, 211
Craig, Olga, 80
Cronkite, Walter, 214, 271
Cunningham, Lawrence S., 192-193
D'Silva, Sr. Teresita, 8, 88
Davis, Deborah, 212-213
Day, Dorothy, 243
De Grunne, Rev. François, 8-9, 24-25, 31-45, 52, 54-55, 57-58, 62-63, 68, 82-83, 86, 93-103, 112-113, 121, 123-126, 165, 169-171, 181-182, 222, 226-228, 237, 247, 251, 270-271
De la Croix, Sr. Marie, vii, 62, 76, 88, 100, 120, 131, 262

Dietz, Abbot Elias, 256-259, 261
Donovan, Rev. Egbert, 25-26, 41-46, 52-54, 57-58, 81, 84, 86, 95, 97, 113, 142-143, 148, 157, 161, 166-167, 170-171, 181, 189, 205, 248
Donovan, Gen. William, 205
Douglass, James, iv, v, 210, 234-235, 242
Dowling, Kevin, 205
Elie, Paul, 188-189, 191
Enriquez, Rev. Mother Rosemarie, viii
Eudes, Rev. John, (see Bamberger)
Evans-Pritchard, Ambrose, ii, 28, 49, 51
Evans, Insp. Sam, 252
EWTN, 145
Fastiggi, Robert L. 244
Finney, John W., 211
Flavian, Rev. (see Burns)
Florendo, Abraham C., 10, 63, 109, 240
Ford, President Gerald, 204
Forest, Jim, 175-176, 187
Forrestal, James V., 28-29, 50-51, 202, 259,
Fort Marcy, i, ii, 50
Foster, Vincent, i-v, 28, 49-50, 83, 140, 158, 178, 292, 238-239, 260, 270, 279

Francis, Pope, 243-246
Frankel, Max, 211
Geberth, Vernon, 30
Gethsemani Abbey, vi-vii, 4, 11-12, 21-22, 62, 72-73, 75-76, 86, 107, 111, 118, 128, 139, 141, 154, 184, 216-219, 223, 233, 256-257, 260-261, 264, 273,
Goodman, Paul, 214
Goodstein, Laurie, 218
Gordon, Rev. Paul, vii
Graham, Katharine, 212-213
Green, Graham, 2
Griffin, John Howard, 9, 19, 21-25, 33, 35-39, 46, 48, 61, 65-66, 88, 91, 93-94, 98, 100-102, 120-121, 130-131, 134-135, 138, 147-157, 163, 165-168, 172-175, 179, 194-195, 226-237, 240-241, 256-257, 270
Haas, Rev. Odo, 24-26, 41, 43-46, 51-60, 65-66, 95, 112-113, 143, 148, 153, 157, 166-168, 170-177, 181, 188-189, 191-192, 206, 227-228, 248, 263-266, 269
Hagan, John L., 20
Harford, James, 189
Hart, Brother Patrick, 21-22, 24-25, 32, 58, 67, 72-73, 75, 85, 88, 100, 107, 111-112, 117-118, 121-

134, 139-144, 147, 150-151, 153, 156-157, 164-165, 168, 171-172, 176-177, 188, 192-193, 213, 217, 226-229, 247, 256-257, 260, 264-265, 267, 269-270
Henry II, King, 259
Henry, Patrick, 184
Hersh, Seymour, M, 205
Higgins, Michael, 188
Hitachi, v, 64-65, 98, 138, 160, 177-178, 197, 233, 237, 248
Holtzman, Michael, 206
Hoopes, Townsend, 28
Hughes, Rev. John Jay, 178-180, 183
Irvine, Reed, ii, 28
Jadot, Rev. Jean, 10
Jamburе, M.P., 207
John Paul II, Pope, 80
Johnson, Annysa, 218
Jones, Penn, 98, 179, 195, 233-237, 239-242, 267, 270, 272
Jowers, Lloyd, 252
Kelty, Rev. Matthew, 72-73, 216, 273
Kennedy, Ethel, 209
Kennedy, Eugene Cullen, 245
Kennedy John F., i, iv, 50, 145, 179, 194, 202, 209-211, 217, 221, 234, 245, 259, 2678, 270, 272

Kennedy, Robert F., v, 11, 145, 194-195, 209, 234, 241, 259, 267, 270
Kenworth, E.W., 211
Kim, Sister Beda viii
King, Coretta Scott, 252
King, Martin Luther, v, 11, 145, 194-195, 209, 233, 241, 243, 251-252, 259, 267, 270
Kislenko, Arne, 78
Knight, Jim, 194, 216
Knightly, Phillip, 205
Knowlton, Patrick, iii, iv, 28, 50-51, 83
Krishan, Vij, 207
Lax, Robert, 189, 216
Leclercq, Rev. Jean, vii, 101-102, 223
Leo XIII, Pope, 275
Lincoln, Abraham, 243
Long, Huey, 202
Long, John C., 72, 138-143, 203
Mack, Gary, 234, 239-240, 272
Marcoux, Paul J., 218-219
Martin, David, i, ii, iii, 6, 9, 29, 49, 80, 105, 145, 178, 200, 202, 212, 214-215, 238-239, 280
McCoy, Alfred W., 79
McDonald, Joan C., 87, 189-191
McInerney, D.Q., 182-183
Meagher, Sylvia, 50

Merton, Thomas, i, iv, v, vi, vii, 1-5, 8-6, 18-29, 31-47, 52-59, 61-69, 71-78, 80-91, 93-103, 107-115, 117-135, 137-145, 147, 161, 163-185, 187-196, 203, 205-206, 209-217, 219, 221-230, 233-237, 240-251, 253, 255-274
MKUltra, 204, 271
Moffitt, John, 5, 7-8, 10, 22-24, 32-37, 39-43, 48, 52, 54, 57-58, 63-64, 66-67, 82, 88, 94-102, 110-115, 121, 123-126, 128, 131, 143-144, 148, 151-154, 157, 171-174, 179, 194-196, 222, 225-231, 233, 236-237, 241, 247, 265
Mohammed, Abed al Khalid, 80
Mohammed, Khalid Sheikh, 80
Mohammed, Yousef al Khalid, 80
Morey, Brother Lawrence, 128, 261
Mott, Michael, 5, 62, 67, 72, 77, 86-90, 97-98, 125, 132, 143-144, 147, 152, 157, 161, 164-185, 187-191, 193, 209, 213, 216, 247, 264, 268, 270, 273
Murphy, Rev. Joachim, 84

Nakvachara, Dr. Luksana, 13, 15, 16, 47, 61, 71, 83, 85, 148, 191, 247, 249
National Catholic News Service, 137-138, 143-145
Olson, Eric, 205
Olson, Frank, 203-205, 249, 259, 271
Oswald, Lee Harvey, 221, 234, 239, 253
Overman, Stephenie, 144
Parker, Rev. Anselm, 84
Pasternak, Boris, 206
Patrick, Br. (see Hart)
Pearson, Dr. Paul, 5, 172, 206
Perez, Rev. Bernardo, 63, 74, 109, 233, 240-241
Peterson, Dale, 202-203
Phoenix Program, 78, 205, 244, 268
Pia, Mother, (see Valeria)
Pius IX, Pope, 243
Prise, Edward, 28
Ray, James Earl, 251-252
Reynolds, E. Bruce, 205
Rice, Edward, 189, 194
Rodriguez, Miguel, 158
Ruby, Jack, 239, 253
Ruddy, Christopher, 238-240
Rush, Christopher, 30
Sabow, Col. James, 259
Say, Rev. Celestine, vii, 8-9, 25, 31-41, 43-48, 52-56, 58-66, 72, 82-86, 91, 93-

94, 96-101, 106, 109, 112-114, 121, 126, 130-131, 133, 143, 147-163, 165-175, 179, 181, 188-190, 193, 195, 213, 222, 226-228, 230-231, 233, 236-237, 240-242, 248, 250-252, 255-256, 266
Sellner, Edward C., 179-180, 183
Shenker, Israel, 224
Simmons, Ira, 206
Smeyers, Sr. Bernadette M., 878-88, 90
Snyder III, Joseph C., 22
Somerville, Frank P.L., 184
Spellman, Card. Francis Joseph, 234
Starr, Kenneth, iii, iv, 51, 158
Steinman, Kathy J., 80
Stiles, Maynard, 252
Stone, Naomi Burton, 24, 117, 195-196
Sussman, Irving and Cornelia, 133-135, 187
Sweat, Joseph, 137-144, 196
Tandle, R.M., 207
Tholens, Rev. C.P., vii
Thong, Rev. Maxime, vii
Trentadue, Kenneth, 259
Trotsky, Leon, 249
Trump, Donald, 239-240
Tunprasert, Maj. Amnuay, 64

Turley, Hugh, i, ii, iii, iv, 2-4, 10, 16, 50, 72, 74, 76, 84, 86, 88, 128-129, 140, 155-156, 165, 193-194, 206, 235, 238, 256
Umhoefer, Dave, 218
Valeri, Mother Pia, 67, 96-97, 111, 114
Vielmetti, Bruce, 218
Waldron, Robert, 191
Weakland, Abp. Rembert (also Abbot Primate), 10, 14-17, 19, 23, 46-47, 53-54, 60, 71, 74-76, 84, 88, 129, 148, 152-153, 166-167, 172,
Weigel, George, 272-273
Weist, Sr./Dr. Edeltrud, 24, 26-27, 29, 43, 46-47, 54, 57, 59-60, 62, 82, 84, 86-89, 97, 111, 113, 120, 129, 152-153, 159-161, 166-167, 180, 190, 192, 227-228, 248-251, 265
Wheeler, John T., 11, 221-223
Wicker, Tom, 211
Wilford, Hugh, 212
Will, Goerge, 145
Williams, Shirley, 144
Wilson Rose, Nancy, 178
Winchester, Simon, 145
Wisner, Frank, 212
Zimmerman, Carol, 245
Zoll, Rachel, 218

ABOUT THE AUTHORS

Hugh Turley, as a volunteer columnist for the *Hyattsville Life and Times,* is a winner of the National Newspaper Association award for best serious column, small-circulation, non-daily division.

David Martin is twice winner of the Lawrence R. Klein Award for best *Monthly Labor Review* article by an employee of the Bureau of Labor Statistics. Vladimir Kats was his co-writer for the second article.

Printed in Great Britain
by Amazon